ROBERT T. HANDY is Professor of Church History at Union Theological Seminary, New York. He is on the editorial board of the Library of Protestant Thought and on the Commission of Faith and Order of The World Council of Churches. He is the editor of *The Social Gospel in America, 1870-1920* and a co-author of *American Christianity*.

Photography by John H. Popper
Jacket design by Rosalind Lorber

ISBN-0-19-501453-7

A Christian America
Protestant Hopes and Historical Realities

A Christian America

PROTESTANT HOPES AND HISTORICAL REALITIES

❦

ROBERT T. HANDY

New York OXFORD UNIVERSITY PRESS 1971

Library of Congress Catalogue Card Number: 78-161888

Printed in the United States of America

To Sidney E. Mead,
perceptive and creative interpreter of
American religious history

Preface

In studying the religious history of the United States, I have long been impressed with the important role that the idea of civilization has played in the evangelical Protestant denominations that together made up the dominant religious subculture of nineteenth-century America. Researches in the primary sources convinced me that it would be fruitful to seek a fuller understanding of how Protestants related their religious views to their concepts of civilization. It did indeed prove to be illuminating to sample the records of denominational and interdenominational assemblies and meetings of many types, for at such gatherings the underlying assumptions about both religion and civilization often came to the surface as appeals for common action were made. Statements processed and passed by such assemblies have a useful representative character and often disclose in a distinctive way how church people saw themselves in relation to the world about them. I have focused on the English-speaking evangelical denominations which thought of themselves as composing the religious mainstream of the nation and which believed themselves to be especially charged with making America a Christian nation. The largest Protestant bodies of the nineteenth century—Baptist, Methodist, Presbyterian—along with many of the middle-sized and smaller ones, such as the Congregational, Disciples of Christ, and United Brethren churches, clearly identified themselves in this way, and there was a strong evangelical wing in the Protestant Episcopal Church.

From the beginning American Protestants entertained a lively hope that some day the civilization of the country would be fully Christian. The ways in which the hope was expressed and the activities it engendered varied somewhat from generation to generation, but for more than three centuries Protestants drew direction and inspiration from the vision of a Christian America. It provided a common orientation that cut across denominational differences, and furnished goals toward which all could work, each in his own style and manner.

Because foundations laid in the colonial and revolutionary periods affected the nineteenth-century effort to wed religion and civilization, a preliminary chapter summarizes that background. The bulk of the work focuses on the way Protestants envisioned a Christian America and worked toward it in the nineteenth and early twentieth centuries. Some of the most characteristic statements of this guiding hope were made early in this span of years. Such expressions then usually assumed that while the primary concern of true evangelicals would be for religion itself, devotion to the progress of civilization followed closely. Committed to the principle of religious freedom and to the voluntary method, the leaders of the thrust to make America Christian usually failed to sense how coercive their efforts appeared to those who did not share their premises. It was hard for them not to view their opponents as agents of evil, for they were convinced that they were unequivocally on the side of good.

During the course of the century, many Protestants exhibited a tendency, often unnoticed and unintended, to stress more and more heavily the progress of civilization. The continuation of familiar patterns of thought and language prevented them from seeing that they were in effect making the advancement of civilization the greater good, thus subtly reversing the earlier priority.

Many of the struggles and difficulties of organized religion in America can be seen in a fresh light when viewed from this per-the Word preached, Profanation of the Lords Day, disturbing the peaceable Administration and Exercise of the Worship and holy things of God, and the like, are to be restrained and punished by Civil Authority." Furthermore, a company of Christians which departed from the way deemed proper by the others were to be dealt with by civil power. "If any Church one or more, shall grow Schismatical, rending itself from the Communion of other Churches, or shall walk incorrigibly or obstinately in any corrupt way of their own, contrary to the Rule of the Word; in such a case, the Magistrate is to put forth his Coercive Power, as the matter shall require."[25] So the theory was set down, though already the logic of reality was qualifying it in practice.

The history of the Puritan establishments is a long, tortuous tale of struggle, accommodation, and final defeat. But for two centuries they stood as visible evidences of the hold of the idea of establishment on the minds of men. In Massachusetts Bay, where what had been ostensibly drawn as a charter for a commercial company was in effect made into an instrument of government, suffrage was at first restricted to church members. As decades passed, and the children of saints could not always qualify among the elect, theory had to be accommodated to reality. The famous Half-Way Covenant of 1662 was the broadening of the definition of what a church member was, admitting to some but not to all church privileges the children of saints who would "own the covenant" and submit to church discipline.[26] When Massachusetts was merged with Plymouth in 1691, the older restriction of the franchise to church members disappeared. But church establishments were maintained in Massachusetts (which then included Maine), New Hampshire, and Connecticut. In the latter colony, the passage of the Saybrook Articles in 1708 strengthened the establishment by providing for county "consociations" of churches which had more real power than the ministerial associations of Massachusetts.

MINORITIES AGAINST ESTABLISHMENT

In all the colonies there were religious minorities which did not accept the prevailing form of establishment; some because they did not find their church established, others because they were opposed to any establishment. Dissenting groups in colonial times were often treated harshly by the authorities who hoped for religious uniformity. As their numbers increased and they made their weight felt, they won a measure of toleration, and various arrangements whereby their members could have the religious tax applied to their own ministries were worked out.[27] There is no little irony in the fact that members of a Christian church which confidently established itself as the "true church" whenever possible could become articulate spokesmen for religious freedom when they lived under someone else's establishment! So Puritans objected to Anglican establishment in Virginia, and Anglicans in New England demanded their rights as Englishmen. Members of churches which in Europe remained solidly committed to state-church patterns on the American scene could find themselves in minority status, resisting establishment as defined by others. As such groups as Dutch Reformed, Swedish and German Lutherans, Roman Catholics, and Scotch-Irish Presbyterians recognized that on the American scene establishment was not a possibility for them, they looked with varying degrees of enthusiasm to other ways of maintaining themselves and making their particular contributions to the health of Christian civilization. The Catholic proprietor of Maryland, aware that the majority of the settlers in the colony were Protestants, was nevertheless in advance of his time in securing the adoption of an act of toleration by the Maryland legislature in 1649.[28] By granting toleration to all Christians, it was hoped that a religiously diversified colony could survive. But the Church of England later became strong enough in Maryland to secure a church establishment. In the northern and middle colonies where the Anglican forces were not strong enough to do that, the Society for the Propagation of the Gospel operated largely as a voluntary society. Thus England's Established Church came to terms with new situations in the colonies where its establishment was not possible.

Among the dissenters, however, were those who came to North America openly and sometimes militantly rejecting the establishment patterns of European Christendom. At first, their numbers were small, but they gained through further immigration and by winning converts. English Baptists and Quakers, German Mennonites and Sectaries were descendants respectively of the radical wing of Puritanism and the left wing of the Reformation. They believed in voluntary churches and denied the right of magistrates to deal with religious affairs. In colonies in which their influence was strong, and in which pluralistic religious situations early developed, there were no establishments of religion at all—in Rhode Island, New Jersey, Pennsylvania, and Delaware.

The religious freedom of Rhode Island has been often discussed; here the Baptists gathered their first church in America and here they invited others to partake of the freedom they claimed for themselves.[29] From the start, this was a scandal to many, but a beacon of liberty to others and a refuge for those hard-pressed elsewhere. Among the latter were the Quakers, some of whom used the little colony as a base of operations for their attacks on establishments. Members of the Religious Society of Friends first came to the colonies in 1656 as missionaries for Christian faith as they understood it. They asserted that the reality of the "inner light" is offered to every man. They also came as witnesses against the established churches of Christendom and demonstrated boldly against them—four of them paying with their lives on Boston Common for their testimony. Later, Quakers came more as colonizers, but remained devoted to religious freedom. Quaker influence was strong in the areas that later became New Jersey, and of course in William Penn's Pennsylvania (and Delaware, which was separated from Pennsylvania in 1702).[30] Pennsylvania became an important center of Baptist life, and to the colony were drawn numbers of German immigrants, many of them inheritors of sixteenth-century Anabaptist traditions, especially as interpreted by the pacifistic Menno Simons. The Mennonite groups believed in freedom of religion, though they maintained strict discipline within their own congregations, and contributed to the freedom-loving and religiously pluralistic nature of Pennslyvania.

In these four colonies, religious principle and the facts of pluralism combined to bring about societies in Western Christendom which had no established churches—and yet which survived and flourished, not, of course, without considerable inner turmoil. But they lasted—and demonstrated that it was possible to have a viable society without church establishment. Furthermore, the colonies which did have establishments were confronted with ideas and representatives of religious minorities which just would not disappear. Small groups of Baptists and Quakers, for example, soon settled in Massachusetts and finally had to be tolerated. Also numbers of Separates and Baptists from New England, along with Presbyterians, Mennonites, and Quakers from the middle colonies settled in Virginia, challenging the Anglican establishment by their very presence.

THE ENLIGHTENMENT CHALLENGE TO ESTABLISHMENT

The crisis of the colonial church establishments was brought on, not only by the challenge of the dissenters and the perplexities of pluralism, but also from the general rationalistic movements of thought in Western culture which have often been summarized under the term "Enlightenment," and from the tumultuous and divisive religious convulsion in eighteenth-century American life called the Great Awakening.

The emergence of Enlightenment trends in the late seventeenth and early eighteenth centuries was one of those seminal shifts of thought and feeling of which the consequences were widespread and are still influential. Paul Hazard was speaking from the European context, yet in a way that applies also to the New World, when he noted that "even now the force of that movement is far from spent, so far, indeed, that when we deal with our present problems—religious, philosophical, political, social—we are but continuing in a measure the great and unresolved disputes of an earlier day." [31] Impelled by the briliant advances in the science of its time, which seemed to be sweeping mystery from the world, and repelled by the brutality and destructiveness of the terrible religious wars, Enlightenment thinkers proposed to discover the truth about God and the world by utilizing their rational faculties in the examination of Nature. As the complex movement developed along many lines in the eighteenth century, its impact on religion was immense.[32] For some, it led to the espousal of a new faith, Deism. As Crane Brinton has colorfully put it, "there arose in our society what seems to me clearly to be a new religion, certainly related to, descended from, and by many reconciled with, Christianity. I call this religion simply Enlightenment, with a capital E." [33] Some Deists squared their views with Christianity, often by trying to squeeze Christianity into the Deistic framework, while others with greater or less bodness rejected Christianity for the new view. Intense strains were set up within the churches, however, as parties restated traditional theologies with varying degrees of accommodation to the methods and dogmas of the Age of Reason.[34]

The general intellectual and cultural atmosphere was pervaded by currents of thought often indifferent to Christian claims, or openly hostile to them. On the American scene, books of Enlightenment thinkers circulated; such men as Benjamin Franklin, Jonathan Mayhew, Tom Paine, Ethan Allen, and Thomas Jefferson articulated with varying accents and degrees the message of Enlightenment.[35] The impact of these trends of thought upon concepts of religious establishment was not a simple one, however. Some who drank deeply of the new currents remained wedded to the idea that the social order would be more stable and peaceful were the establishments continued. Both in southern Anglicanism where rational religion in its milder forms had wide influence and in New England where Unitarian thought was cutting into Calvinistic orthodoxy, many still defended the state-church patterns.[36] Others who were imbued with Enlightenment ideas were prominent in the drive for disestablishment. Jefferson's role in writing the famous Virginia Bill for Establishing Religious Freedom, passed in 1785, illustrates one way in which Enlightenment atmosphere contributed to the breakup of the established church order. In such a climate, Protestant groups which had long argued for religious freedom on the basis of biblical and theological principle found effective allies and strong leaders in their crusade for liberty.

Though some who were affected by Enlightenment currents did not question the utility of religious establishments, the general impact of the Age of Reason was against revealed orthodoxies and the privileges of establishment. The observable decline of the churches in the last quarter of the eighteenth century was in part a consequence of Enlightenment thought.

THE AWAKENINGS AND THE ESTABLISHMENTS

The patterns of establishment were also being called into question by movements of quite a different kind. First appearing significantly in the 1720's in the middle colonies, the Great Awakenings reached their peak in New England in the early 1740's and then swept southward where they continued in pulsations of religious intensity into the revolutionary period.[37] In the forefront of awakening leadership were men conspicuous in their own day—such figures as George Whitefield, Gilbert Tennent, Jonathan Edwards, and Samuel Davies. The awakenings were intercolonial in scope and had a mighty impact on the religious patterns of the eighteenth century. Methods of mass revivalism with their emotionalism and their stress on intense piety were popularized.

The effects of these outpourings of religious feelings on church establishments were uneven, though the final result was clear. The awakenings did help to strengthen the established Congregational churches of New England—there were important increases in the number of churches and communicants, and Calvinism itself was significantly revitalized in a way that persisted after the excitements had cooled. But the awakenings also stimulated sharp reactions and introduced painful polarizations into church life. Charles Chauncy was the most conspicuous of the liberal Congregational opponents of Edwards and the movement he represented, but there were many who agreed with his opposition to enthusiasm and who played a role in the trends of thought that led to Unitarianism.[38] At the other theological pole were the Separate Congregationalists who left the established congregations because they were too formal, were linked with the state and its taxing powers, and were not responding to new light from the scriptures. Many of these later became Baptists.[39] In the South, it was for the most part the disestablished bodies that profited from the awakening. The Church of England was the one major colonial church that, quite consistently, steadily opposed the awakening; by resisting the tide of the times it inevitably moved closer to minority status and disestablishment.[40] Revivalist religion in all sections had considerable appeal among the lower ranks of society. Negro slaves were beginning to respond in significant numbers to Baptist and Methodist revivalism in the South.[41] One of the major consequences of the Great Awakening was an undermining of the religious establishments.

The new denominations which were emerging, as well as the older ones, found themselves increasingly dependent upon effective methods of winning voluntary support if they were to grow in the competitive situation. The awakening spirit placed the emphasis on the inner religious experience of the individual Christian rather than on the traditional theologies and establishment securities. The defenders of the old way knew well enough what was going on. The Harvard faculty, for example, sharply criticized the most eloquent awakener of them all, Whitefield, saying that the awakening preachers "thrust themselves into Towns and Parishes, to the Destruction of all Peace and Order, whereby they have to the great impoverishment of the Community, taken the People from their Work and Business, to attend their Lectures and Exhortations, always fraught with Enthusiasm, and other pernicious Errors. But, *which is worse, and it is the Natural effect of these Things,* the People have been thence ready to despise their own Ministers, and their usefulness among them, in too many Places, hath been almost destroy'd." [42] The awakening spirit did display itself in many forms, among which there were often sharp disagreements. Yet there was a pervasive sense among the awakeners and those whom they influenced that the future belonged to them and their way. They felt they were witnesses to the coming of the millennium, which God would bring to fulfillment in the not too distant future. Edwards called for a union of Christian people "visibly to unite" in prayer for "that common prosperity and advancement that is so unspeakably great and glorious, which God hath so abundantly promised to fulfill in the latter days." [43] Buoyed up by such expectancies, which were reminiscent of the earliest hopes of seventeenth-century settlers but were now related to the revival, awakeners looked to the future with great anticipation.

As the realities of American life dimmed the earlier hopes for building Christian states in the wilderness furnished with soundly established churches, the awakening vision assured the revived faithful that God would at last bring his millennial kingdom into full visibility. Edwards stated the theory in his careful prose; it was to be reiterated in more earthly idioms in many an exciting revival sermon. Early in the awakening, Edwards said:

> America has received the true religion of the old continent; the church of ancient times had been there, and Christ is from thence: but that there may be an equality, and inasmuch as that continent has crucified Christ, they shall not have the honor of communicating religion in its most glorious state to us, but we to them. . . . When God is about to turn the earth into a Paradise, he does not begin his work where there is some good growth already, but in a wilderness, where nothing grows, and nothing is to be seen but dry sand and barren rocks; that the light may shine out of darkness, and the world be replenished from emptiness.[44]

As time went on, many of the awakened felt that God was doing his work through the revival and the churches that absorbed its spirit much more than through the older forms and established churches. As the patterns of colonial establishment encountered increasing difficulties in the America of growing pluralism and assertive rationalism, new ways of initiating and sustaining Christian faith were at hand—providentially, as the awakened saw it. The goal was much the same—a Christian civilization preparing the way for God's kingdom. It would be realized however, not through the old way of formal establishments, but by God working through those who responded to the outpouring of his spirit.

THE OLD ORDER CHANGES

The older forms did not quickly disappear, of course, but new ways of fulfilling God's will for his church and his world were attracting the faithful. A marked shift away from the theories and practices of establishment under the combined effects of pluralistic realities, Enlightenment reflections, and awakening pieties climaxed during the revolutionary period. Some tried to hold on to the substance of the old by making concessions, by trying to include a number of denominations under the establishment umbrella. This worked for a while in New England. In Virginia, Patrick Henry displayed his oratorical powers in an effort to cling to establishment patterns in modified form, but the combination of Enlightenment leadership and disestablished masses was too great, and Jefferson's Bill for Establishing Religious Freedom was the result. The other Anglican establishments disappeared at about the same time, or soon thereafter.

Though the New England establishments survived the crisis in diluted form, it was clear to almost everyone that a national religious establishment would not be possible in the newly independent nation, and no strong effort to effect one was made when the Constitution was being prepared. The religious question was given considerable attention during the debate over the First Amendment. Madison apparently would have liked to have the remaining establishments in the states eliminated, but the Senate refused to allow this, for those which remained in three New England states had their defenders. Some attempts were made in the course of the Senate debate to have the amendment worded in such a way that establishment or at least public assistance for more than one church might be possible. One proposal suggested that the amendment read: "Congress shall make no law establishing any particular denomination of religion in preference to another," but the attempt failed.[45] The final wording, "Congress shall make no law respecting the establishment of religion, or prohibiting the free exercise thereof," showed that the new nation was breaking with the older forms—with the help and support of many Christians.

Mark DeWolfe Howe has convincingly argued that we should look back at the First Amendment clauses on religion, not only in terms of a Jeffersonian emphasis on separation, but also from the viewpoint of many evangelicals who welcomed "a constitutional proscription of laws relating to religion . . . because of the deep conviction that the realm of spirit lay beyond the reach of government." The First Amendment must be seen in the context of the "evangelical separatism" of Roger Williams and of the many awakeners of the next century as well as in the context of rationalist separatists. "In the age of the sect and the denomination," Howe added, "it was, surely, the rare believer who could discover any advantage in nationalizing religion."[46] Perhaps this overstates it some—such believers were not so rare, especially in certain sections, but they were a declining minority.

Timothy Dwight, Congregational pastor and president of Yale, did not speak for himself alone when he provided a rationale for continued public support of religion. His arguments helped establishments of religion in New Hampshire, Connecticut, and Massachusetts to continue a little while longer. Insisting that legislatures have not only the right but the obligation to pursue measures for the public welfare and morality, he affirmed that:

> to this great purpose Religion in every country is not only useful, but indispensable. But religion cannot exist, and has never existed, for any length of time, without public worship. As every man ought, therefore, willingly to contribute to the support of whatever increases his own prosperity; he is by immovable consequence obliged to support the religion, which by increasing the common prosperity, increases of course his own.

Religion is indispensable to the welfare of a free country, he declared, because

> Morality, as every sober man, who knows anything of the subject discerns with a glance, is merely a branch of Religion; and where there is no religion, there is no morality. Moral obligation has its sole ground in the character and government of God. But, where God is not worshipped, his char-

> acter will soon be disregarded; and the obligation, founded on it, unfelt, and forgotten. No duty, therefore, to individuals, or to the public, will be realized, or performed. Justice, kindness, and truth, the great hinges on which free Society hangs, will be unpracticed, because there will be no motives to the practice, or sufficient forces to resist the passions of men. Oaths of office, and of testimony, alike, without the sanctions of religion are merely solemn farces.[47]

The heavy stress on the inseparability of morals from religion was to remain constant in the evangelical mind of the nineteenth century, though the use of it in support of establishment was to be given up. But that civilization needed religion was to continue to be as axiomatic in the nineteenth-century dream of a Christian society as it had been among colonial Christians. Dwight's hope for continued public support of religion was soon to be defeated, but his emphasis on the importance of the Christian religion for morals and for social health remained an indelible part of the nineteenth-century vision of Christian America.

While a few leaders like Timothy Dwight tried to hold on to the old ways, there was increasing recognition that a new era had come, and that henceforth all religious groups would be dependent on their own efforts. Early in the 1780's William White, a leading Anglican of Philadelphia, declared that "all denominations of christians are on a level, and no church is farther known to the public, than as a voluntary association of individuals, for a lawful and useful purpose." [48] In the changing situation of the revolutionary period, a number of churches seized the occasion to reorganize themselves nationally, both those which had been cut loose from the patterns of establishment (the Church of England became the Protestant Episcopal Church) and others who saw the need for regrouping for the new challenges and opportunities (for example, the Presbyterian Church).[49] Older denominations which had long been autonomous and which had labored for disestablishment (Baptists, for example) were now facing inviting prospects as the old restraints faded, and new churches (such as the Methodist Episcopal, organized as an independent body in 1784) boldly set out to win new converts across the land.

In the new situation, it was possible for churches once sharply divided to recognize each other as partners in many common concerns. The prospect of a broad evangelical consensus had opened invitingly during the Awakening; Heimert sums up many particulars in noting that "it was during the imperial crisis that the evangelical mind glimpsed the bright prospect of uniting the people of America in affectionate union." [50] Bitter tensions between established and non-established churches then blighted such hopes of concord. Yet there was much that both sides had in common. The bitterness between established Congregationalists and disestablished Baptists in New England has been described many times, but as William G. McLoughlin has explained, the Baptists "did not object to the view that Massachusetts should remain a Christian commonwealth" [51] and believed that religion and morality could be maintained only as the institutions of public worship were generally diffused through the communities. They were convinced, however, that this should be done only on a voluntary basis—sharply differing from Timothy Dwight and his kind. The passing of the patterns of colonial establishment did not at all mean that the Christian hope for the triumph of Christian civilization was being given up, but that voluntary ways of working towards it were being extended.

It was a long road from the original intention to continue in the colonies the patterns of church establishment to the triumph of religious freedom in an independent nation. Tensions among the multiplying religious groups, the unsettling contributions of much Enlightenment thought, and the excitements of the Great Awakening all played a role in the crisis and erosion of religious establishments. But the idea of maintaining a Christian society was deeply embedded in the culture, and was by no means given

II

"A Complete Christian Commonwealth" (1800–1860)

> The wilderness shall bud and blossom as the rose before us; and we will not cease, till a christian nation throws up its temples of worship on every hill and plain; till knowledge, virtue and religion, blending their dignity and their healthful power, have filled our great country with a manly and happy race of people, and the bands of a complete christian commonwealth are seen to span the continent.
>
> Horace Bushnell
> *Barbarism the First Danger*

The situation at the close of the eighteenth century did not seem favorable for the future of the churches in America. The Revolution had disrupted many congregations and had been destructive of much church property. The philosophy of the Enlightenment, with its deistic ideas of God and its preference for natural rather than revealed religion, made traditional Christian claims appear antiquated to many, especially among the educated. Probably less than 10 per cent of the population of the United States were church members in 1800, though it must be remembered that church membership had a more serious and disciplined meaning than it usually does now, and that the active constituencies of congregations then were normally considerably larger than actual membership. It has been tempting for Protestant leaders, wanting to put the achievements of the nineteenth century in a strong light, to paint the picture of the churches at the close of the previous century in too somber tones. But without distortion, that picture was not very promising.

The forces of organized religion seemed to be fragmenting at a time when concerted action was needed. The proliferation of religious groups was startling; seventeenth-century church leaders would have been appalled at what the nineteenth century was bringing forth! As we look back at that time from the perspective of the vast spectrum of religious options available in the last part of the twentieth century, the situation does not seem to have been too complicated. According to the best estimates we have, there were only about a dozen denominational groupings of noticeable size. The larger bodies were the Baptist, the Congregational, the Methodist, the Lutheran, the Presbyterian, and the Episcopal. Of these, the Lutherans had a heavy proportion of non-English-speaking supporters and tended to enclave by themselves; the Episcopal churches suffered from their previous connection with the mother country as well as from the ravages of the war, and some feared they would disappear. The smaller groups were the German Reformed, Quaker, Dutch Reformed, Moravian, Mennonite, and Roman Catholic. There were very few Jews, most of whom were of Sephardic (Spanish and Portugese) background.[1] All through the nineteenth century, of course, the number of denominations was to increase spectacularly—by immigration, by division, and by the rise of indigenous bodies. The variety of 1800, however, was sufficient to shut out any realistic hopes of formalized Christendom with established churches in the old style.

THE SECOND GREAT AWAKENING

The story of the rallying of the Protestant forces to overcome the threat of Enlightenment philosophy, to bring the faith into a position of influence in the young nation, and to plant churches in the rapidly opening West has been told many times.[2] Apologists like Timothy Dwight of Yale and Jedidiah Morse of Charleston seized the opportunity provided by the excesses of the French Revolution to declare that they were the inevitable outcome of Enlightenment principles, and to counterattack on behalf of revealed Christianity.[3] The leaders of most denominations adopted the techniques of revivalism both in the settled East and on the raw frontiers of the West in what has often been called the "Second Great Awakening." [4] Revivalism was certainly not a simple phenomenon; educated clergymen of the settled congregations spoke in different tones and had varying objectives and expectancies from some of their western brethren who had less formal schooling but who could thrill frontier audiences which the former would leave cold. Some denominations employed revivalist patterns much more fully than others, and in turn were much more deeply influenced in theology and practice by them—Methodists and Baptists especially. Congregationalists and Presbyterians tried to keep revivalism under tighter ecclesiastical control, while Episcopal and Lutheran churches developed "evangelical" wings not unsympathetic to revivalist emphases, though they themselves retained more classical liturgical and confessional standards. Throughout the nineteenth century, revivalism in its changing phases and many different strands was the most conspicuous, though often highly controversial, source of renewal in Protestant life.[5]

There were also other important movements, some of them directly opposed to revivalism. Unitarianism broke away from Congregationalism in New England, for example, while in the German Reformed Church the Mercersburg theology resisted the "system of the revival" in behalf of the "system of the cathechism." [6] Despite such important exceptions, revivalism in its many forms was the most powerful force in nineteenth-century Protestant life. It provoked schisms and shaped the rise of new denominations. To some degree it permeated most of the American denominations, and contributed much to the common style of Protestant life.

By the opening of the nineteenth century, most churches were already voluntary bodies, dependent on their own resources for survival and growth. As the remaining weakened forms of establishment disappeared (in Connecticut in 1818, in New Hampshire the following year, and in Massachusetts in 1833), all churches had to continue under the conditions of voluntaryism.[7] Denominations which had been deeply immersed in revivalism often adapted most readily to voluntary ways, but all churches of necessity became free churches and had to adapt to the new situation. Though free to go their own ways as autonomous bodies, in fact the Protestant churches shared more in common than was often recognized.

COMPONENTS OF THE NEW CHRISTIAN CIVILIZATION: RELIGION, MORALITY, EDUCATION

The evangelical churches believed firmly in the continuation and extension of Christian civilization throughout their growing nation. Because they had certain differences in theological and liturgical style and because they were in competition with each other in the quest for new members, it has been easy to overlook the important general concern for the advancement of Christian civilization about which they were in essential agreement. With varying degrees of articulation and in slightly varying details, Protestant leaders from many denominations operated on the assumption that American civilization would remain a Christian one, and that its Christian (which for them always meant Protestant) character would become even more pronounced. The Christian character of the nation was to be maintained by voluntary means since the patterns of establishment had proved to be unacceptable and inadequate. Indeed, it was widely asserted that now that civilization in America had been freed of the corruptions of established ecclesiasticism, it could become more Christian than it had ever been. Churches had been disestablished and separated from the state, but the idea of a Christian society certainly had not disappeared. True Christian churches (i.e., evangelical Protestant churches) and Christian civilization with its developing patterns of freedom and democracy would go on from strength to strength together, mutually reinforcing one another. The broad vision of a Christian civilization was widely shared in outline among Protestants who disagreed in many particulars of doctrine and polity. For some, it was making the best of a new situation; for others it was a sign of the coming millennium. But both could stress "religion and civilization" in their preaching and writing.

For the most part, Protestant leaders felt that true religion was the prior and more basic concern, an essential ingredient in a sound civilization. They spent much more time in dealing with religion, where the differences between denominations most sharply appeared, than in talking about civilization, where the agreements were large. They understood that their calling was primarily to the religious vocation; to the work of defining and expressing true religion they devoted their chief energies. Characteristically, Jesse Appleton, president of Bowdoin and spokesman for a Congregationalism in which Puritan doctrine was still the dominant theological force, reminded his generation of the fleetingness of existence:

> Though civil society is a very interesting state of human existence, there is another, which, in point of importance and duration, is infinitely more so. In less than a century, we ourselves, our families, and connexions, together with the present population of our country, and the world, shall, with enlarged capacities for enjoyment or suffering, be transferred to another state. As to the existence and duration of this state, Christianity is the only religion on earth, which gives us authentic and satisfactory instruction.[8]

Another college president, Francis Wayland of Brown, influential Baptist moral theologian, did not need to answer his own rhetorical question: "On what do our hopes for eternity rest, our hopes of pardon and salvation and everlasting life, but on the truths of the Gospel?" [9] In the first half of the nineteenth century, the "great Christian drama of salvation" which had been so vivid in medieval and Reformation times remained the central theme of Anglican, Calvinist, and Lutheran orthodoxies, and was re-emphasized in powerful though often oversimplified terms by the revivalists.

The same religion which held the key to eternity as Protestants saw it, also showed the way to a sound and satisfying civilization. In 1819 the Presbyterian General Assembly, commenting on certain reverses suffered by commercial interests that year, urged all the ministers of the communion "to impress on the minds of their hearers the all-important truth, that the religion of Jesus Christ, in its vital power and practical influence, is the best friend of civil society, as well as essential to the eternal well-being of man." [10] The next year in their annual "Narrative of the State of Religion" the Presbyterians spoke of the exalted place of the central institution of religion, the Church, whose preservation is "the dearest care of Providence," and then insisted that "the presence of this Church is the best safeguard of nations, and its growth and stability the surest pledge of their prosperity and strength." [11] The bishops of the Protestant Episcopal Church also showed how closely the themes of religion and civilization were interwoven in the Protestant mind of the time in their Pastoral Letter of 1826 to the clergy and laity of their communion:

> Blessed religion! which heightens the pleasures and assuages the sorrows of life; which animates to the discharge of present duties, and opens the view the prospect of a happy immortality; and, which is the guardian of civil happiness, in the sanctions brought by it to every branch of social justice and beneficence. . . . You need but look around you to remark how much the disuse of worship of the sanctuary is followed by the deterioration of morals; and how much this tends to the temporal as well as to the spiritual injury of

> many who are prominent in the social system; and to the corruption of the lower classes of society, by example descending to them from the more elevated.[12]

Religious leaders labored both for the advancement of religion and for the improvement of civilization.

Christian hope in the coming glorious kingdom of God was often presented in such a way as to undergird Christian interest in the advance of civilization. Somewhat paradoxically, the intensification of an otherworldly concern provided a basis for this-worldly effort. Many scholars have called attention to the heightening of the millennial hope in the early nineteenth century.[13] The theological details of the millennial vision varied, but a sense of expectancy was widespread. Not only poorly educated itinerant evangelists but also the highest official bodies of the church looked ahead to the millennial dawn. The New York Methodist Conference in a Memorial to the General Conference of the Methodist Episcopal Church in 1808, for example, said: "The fields are white unto harvest before us, and the opening prospect of the great day of glory brightens continually in our view; and we are looking forward with hopeful expectations for the universal spread of Scriptural truth and holiness over the inhabitable globe." [14] Presbyterians in 1815 passed a resolution "that this General Assembly, do approve of concerts of prayer for the advancement of the Redeemer's kingdom, and do recommend it to the friends of Zion in their connexion, as far as may be convenient, to spend the first Monday in every month in special prayer to God, for the coming and glorious reign of Christ on earth." [15] Four years later the Presbyterian "Narrative of the State of Religion" exclaimed:

> We have the happiness to live in a day, Brethren, when the Captain of our Salvation, in a distinguishing manner, is marshalling his *mighty host,* and preparing for the moral conquest of the *world.* The grand contest that has been so

> long conducting, is drawing rapidly towards a termination, that shall be infinitely honourable both to our glorious leader, and to those who have fought under his banner. Not a finger shall be lifted, nor shall a devout aspiration heave the bosom of a single son or daughter of man, to contribute to the advancement, or plead for the glory of the kingdom of the Messiah, that shall not be met with the smiles and crowned with the blessing of God.[16]

Such confident expectations lay behind much of the zeal and energy of the evangelical thrust in nineteenth-century America.

Some interpretations of the millennial hope were clearly literalistic, apocalyptic, and intensely otherworldly in emphasis. They affirmed that only the miraculous second coming of Christ could save the world from despair and inaugurate the glorious reign of God beyond history. But other interpretations—and these came to be more frequently expressed by the leadership of the major evangelical churches—saw the millennium coming as the climax of the Christianization of civilization, fulfilling history.[17] The leader of the Disciples of Christ, to become the largest indigenous evangelical Protestant body in America in the nineteenth century, renamed his journal the *Millennial Harbinger* in 1830, as his flock was rapidly moving in a fully autonomous direction. In the prospectus for the renewed periodical, Alexander Campbell said:

> This work shall be devoted to the destruction of Sectarianism, Infidelity, and Antichristian doctrine and practice. It shall have for its object the development, and introduction of the political and religious order of society called THE MILLENNIUM, which will be the consummation of that ultimate amelioration of society proposed in the Christian Scriptures.[18]

Even those who stressed premillennialist or millenarian views, however, often saw the work of Christianizing society as a preparation for the coming of the Lord.

When in the 1830's a revivalist, William Miller, preached the imminent, literal return of Christ, much of what he said was common to this time. In setting the date of the return for 1843, later revised to 1844, he provoked much turmoil in the churches. Many of the hopeful withdrew from their congregations. Disillusionment then spread among many of them when the consummation did not occur. From the faithful remnants the Adventist churches were formed.[19] For the most part, evangelical leaders avoided precise date setting; President Appleton had stated the usual conviction: "When the millennium will commence, or what in particular will be the state of things, during that happy period, I know not." [20] The Episcopal bishops had put the promised consummation very far off indeed:

> The advancement of our holy religion will probably continue, as it has been heretofore, gradual, but sure. Ages may roll away, and empires may rise and fall, before there shall come the promised era, when "all the kingdoms of this world shall be the kingdoms of the Lord and of his Christ." But, as we rest our expectations of that event on the rock of his never failing promise, we have reason to rejoice in whatever promotes the accomplishment of it, by extending the profession of Christianity over the immeasureable wilds of this immense continent.[21]

But however and whenever the kingdom was to come, for many Protestants the millennial expectancy provided a goal for civilization as well as for religion; it provided a religious coloration to their thought about civil society. For them, the religious quest and the civil process, though clearly distinct, moved toward the same happy climax.[22]

Though the millennial hope glowed brighter at some periods than at others, and among some groups more than others, there was virtually universal and consistent emphasis among Protestants on a basic and familiar theme—morality as the all-important link between religion and civilization. There were many who continued the familiar arguments which Timothy Dwight had employed, that without religiously based moral standards civilized society would collapse. President Appleton believed he had demonstrated beyond doubt that "as the knowledge and spirit of Christianity are diffused, the temper and practices of men become more pacific, reason is more regarded, and the passions of the human heart, if not subdued, are chastened and restrained." Hence the answer to the following questions he asked seemed obvious enough to him and to his readers:

> Do you believe, that any State, community, or nation can be powerful, tranquil, and permanently happy, if their morals are extensively depraved? Would not the most alarming depravation of morals result from a general disbelief in the Christian religion? Would the happiness of families, would property or life be secure in a nation of deists? If Christianity is the most powerful guardian of morals, are you not, as civilians, bound to give it your support and patronage? [23]

In the first half of the nineteenth century, the moral arguments that had been used on behalf of the colonial religious establishments were now employed to support the Christianization of society by voluntary means. The Episcopal bishops in 1808 observed that "there are many evidences before our eyes, how little there is in the world adorned by the attribute of moral virtue, in any other association than as embodied with and growing out of the high and leading sense of revelation." [24] The assertions of Protestant leaders were generally accepted in the larger society, in theory if not consistently in practice! Francis J. Grund, Austrian-born observer and journalist, put the matter this way in 1837:

> The religious habits of the Americans form not only the basis of their private and public morals, but have become so thoroughly interwoven with their whole course of legislation, that it would be impossible to change them, without affecting the very essence of their government. . . .

> The deference which the Americans pay to morality is scarcely inferior to their regard for religion, and is, in part, based upon the latter. The least solecism in the moral conduct of man is attributed to his want of religion, and is visited upon him as such. It is not the offence itself, but the outrage on society, which is punished. They see in a breach of morals a direct violation of religion; and in this, an attempt to subvert the political institutions of the country. These sentiments are all-powerful in checking the appearance of vice, even if they are not always sufficient to prevent its existence.
>
> With Argus-eyes does public opinion watch over the words and actions of individuals, and, whatever may be their private sins, enforces at least a tribute to morality in public.[25]

Protestants generally accepted the separation of church and state, but stoutly resisted any sense of the separation of religion and morals from public well-being.

In much of the religious writing of the time, the word "morals" was used as a euphemism for civilization itself. The Presbyterian "Narrative of the State of Religion" in 1815, for example, had the statement: "From reports submitted by the several Presbyteries, it appears, although causes of deep humiliation undoubtedly exist, true religion and sound morals are, on the whole, making a very gratifying progress. Infidelity has become insignificant, both in the numbers and talents, of those who affect it." [26] As "infidelity" was for them a generic term representing all that was wrong in a naturalistic, Enlightenment civilization that had come to grief in the Reign of Terror during the French Revolution, so the term "morals" was used in a generic way for the civilization in which Christian morality was in principle respected. An emphasis which had been an important part of colonial Christianity—the necessity of maintaining a sound moral order if the peace and safety of civilization were to be secure—was now directly continued by the voluntary churches. An important part of the definition of a Christian civilization was a stress on the moral code of Protestantism. Thus when hard times fell upon the nations, the Presbyterians believed that the only hope would be in their return to God and in the whole nation's return to Christian morality:

> The Assembly therefore are firmly persuaded, that the effectual remedy for these evils, under God, is to be found only in a recurrence to those principles and duties of our holy religion, which are not less conducive to the temporal welfare of men, than to their eternal happiness; and that they have no hope, that general prosperity can be restored to our country, until there is a return to those habits of industry, temperance, moderation, economy and general virtue which our common christianity inculcates.[27]

"Morality" was considered to be an indispensable accompaniment of true religion and both to be essential to the progress of the best civilization. Protestants felt broadly responsible for the state of civilization in their land, and felt that their contribution of a religiously based morality was especially important to the whole.

In the field of public education the Protestant concern for the advancing of morality and civilization demonstrated itself clearly. A literate populace was understood to be essential so that all could read the scriptures and be informed about the advances of civilization. A scholar of public education, David Tyack, has written:

> Evangelical ministers fought each other in their churches with malicious abandon, competing in that scarce commodity, church-goers. But in supporting public schools, they generally declared a truce. Tocqueville noted that the sects differed in modes of worship but they preached "the same moral law in the name of God," and this moral law could be taught in the common school.[28]

On the basis of his detailed researches into the Oregon school system, Tyack found broad agreement among ministers and schoolmen that there was a middle ground between secularism and sectarianism, a Protestant common denominator. He added: "It is difficult today to recapture the tone of thought and feeling of those who saw the common school as an integral part of their crusade to create the Kingdom of God across the land." [29] It is difficult because that Protestant common denominator—the idea of a Christian civilization rooted in a Protestant morality—has largely disappeared from the general culture, though remnants of that position are still to be found. But for both churchmen and schoolmen of that period, there was little difficulty, for they assumed that religion and civilization were partners. In a study of public education in New York, where the city finally took over the formerly Protestant Public School Society in 1842, Timothy L. Smith has explained that

> it was not secularism but nondenominational Protestantism which won the day. An evangelical consensus of faith and ethics had come so to dominate the national culture that a majority of Protestants were now willing to entrust the state with the task of educating children, confident that education would be "religious" still. The sects identified their common beliefs with those of the nation, their mission with America's mission.[30]

Probably the last sentence should be qualified with an "in part"; the churches did maintain their own particular religious identity and put their spiritual work first, but in the movement for a morally sound civilization they identified with the common national effort. In his study of the Disciples of Christ in this period, David E. Harrell found that "Alexander Campbell often equated 'Protestantism,' 'Universal education,' and 'free republican institutions'—he believed that they must all stand and fall together." [31]

William Bean Kennedy has explained why Protestants in the first half of the nineteenth century favored public education so strongly:

> Protestants supported public schools because they saw them as a means for moral and spiritual instruction. They were conscious of the values of literacy and citizenship training, but for them the key was moral education. They expected basically a continuation of what they knew to have been the case for centuries: the schools in Western Christendom taught Christianity because it was a fundamental part of the society to which they belonged.

Noting that the Protestant churches were thus committing to public hands educational tasks that historically had been theirs, Kennedy observed that "the Erastian implications of that commitment were not clear even to those whose traditions were most un-Erastian." [32] Or to put it another way, the overtones of religious establishment implicit in much of what they did then was not clear to them, because as they developed new ways they did not realize how much of the old patterns they carried over the wall of the separation between church and state into their new vision of Christian civilization.

A continuing debate that ran through the century was on the question of whether civilization must precede Christianization or vice versa. The Committee on Missions of the Methodist Episcopal Church put the matter one way in declaring to their General Conference in 1840 that "the entire history of our missionary operations has demonstrated that the heathen must be brought under the influence of Christian principles in order to be prepared for civilized life." [33] But the other view was often stated, especially by those entrusted with responsibility for missions to the Indians. In 1787 a Society for Propagating the Gospel among the Indians and Others in North America had been formed; it was financed both by private and Massachusetts state funds. A brief history of the society summarized its philosophy succinctly: "Believing that to civilize these people is one great and necessary step towards christianizing them, the Society have supplied the Indian inhabitants of New-Stockbridge with many implements of husbandry, such as ploughs, chains, and hoes." [34] Robert F. Berkhofer, Jr. has found that "the debate over whether first to civilize or to Christianize the savage raged throughout the pre-Civil War period." He observed, however, that "in the actual operations of the various societies, civilization and Christianity were inextricably combined." The problem, he concluded, was really one of semantics rather than of actual difference.[35]

The discussion was continued with some vigor within the communions, however. The theological tensions between the "millenarians" and the "millennialists" often intensified the debate. Those inclined toward millenarianism more often stressed Christianization first, while the others often put civilization first. The continuing divergence was one of the reasons that the evangelicals had trouble stating their concept of Christian civilization clearly: they could find agreement in generalities but not in particulars. Harrell's comment on the Disciples is revealing:

> The most significant symptom of the diverging emphasis within the Disciples mind was the emergence of differing attitudes on the proper method of prosecuting moral reforms. The sectarian segment of the group contended that the church ought to be the sole regulator and arbiter of Christian morality. As far as the world is concerned, it could be made moral only by first making it Christian. On the other hand, the liberal element in the movement believed that the Christian was obligated to lend his influence to the great moral crusades which recurrently swept the nation. These men were convinced that if the world could be made moral it could then be made Christian—indeed, making the world moral was part of making it Christian. Prior to 1865, however, most Disciples did not consistently act on either of these principles.[36]

This deep inner tension which expressed itself in many ways did not stop Protestants from working towards the triumph of Christian civilization, but it did tend to keep them from being too specific as they described and pursued their vision of a Christian America.

Sidney E. Mead has argued perceptively that after disestablishment, pietistic Protestant groups which had once allied themselves with the rationalists to secure religious freedom soon formed a united front with the major main line denominations, including those formerly established. "This alignment of traditionalism and sectarian-pietism against rationalism gained a tremendous victory for Christianity in the popular arena," he wrote, "placing its marks and peculiar strengths and weaknesses upon all subsequent American Protestantism." The united front of Protestants of various heritages and theological positions led to considerable imprecision in thought and expression; in Mead's words, "its weaknesses effectively scuttled much of the intellectual structure of Protestantism." [37] What it lacked in precision of thought, however, it characteristically sought to overcome by zeal and moral fervor.

THE VOLUNTARY WAY TO CHRISTIAN CIVILIZATION

Evangelical Protestants hoped to prepare the way for the triumph of Christian civilization both by building up their own churches as aggressively as they could, and by extending their influence in the nation through voluntary societies designed to achieve specific ends. In one sense, of course, the churches themselves were voluntary societies, made up of those who, externally at least, were free to join or not to join, to support or not to support a given church. But each denomination was committed to certain distinctive tenets of faith, and was limited in the way it could press for its particular claims in a free and pluralistic society. A way of engaging in common Protestant action without compromising the particularity of each group was needed. So beyond the churches were formed voluntary societies of individuals drawn from many denominations. These voluntary agencies, Protestant but nondenominational, could press for certain general objectives in the larger society on the basis of the common vision of civilization.

In employing the techniques of voluntaryism, the churches were very much in tune with their times. In the 1830's, the Unitarian leader, William Ellery Channing, rather humorously discussed the voluntary society movement:

> In truth, one of the most remarkable circumstances or features of our age, is the energy with which the principle of combination, or of action by joint forces, by associated numbers, is manifesting itself. It may be said, without much exaggeration, that every thing is done now by societies. Men have learned what wonders can be accomplished in certain cases by union, and seem to think that union is competent to every thing. You can scarcely name an object for which some institution has not been formed. Would men spread one set of opinions, or crush another? They make a society. Would they improve the penal code, or relieve poor debtors? They make societies. Would they encourage agriculture, or manufactures, or science? They make societies. Would one class encourage horse-racing, and another discourage travelling on Sunday? They make societies. We have immense institutions spreading over the country, combining hosts for particular objects.[38]

The churches made extensive use of the voluntary society approach, finding it a useful bridge across the gap between church and civilization which had been widened by religious freedom, church-state separation, and pluralism.

The common concerns of denominations which had sharp differences on certain theological and ecclesiastical issues could be articulated and acted out in societies made up of Christian individuals from many churches. While the churches had certain limits in working toward moral goals for the society at large under the conditions of freedom and separation, the societies were free as "secular" agencies to go as far as they could. James F. Maclear has demonstrated how New England churches quickly saw the advantages of the voluntary society way. He has written that

> coincident with the fall of the New England Establishments, an expansion of interdenominational voluntary societies was undertaken. The Connecticut Moral Society of 1813 was the beginning of many such foundations, spreading from New England to New York and the Middle West. These moral societies were seconded by organizations for allied purposes —tract societies, Bible societies, temperance societies, missionary societies, Sabbath School societies—all striving to extend "that influence which the law could no longer apply." [39]

Voluntary societies were often formed first at the local or state level, and then gathered into national societies to accomplish some specific mission or reform task. Millions of words were written in the heyday of the societies, and millions have been written since about them, so that we have a growing body of knowledge about them and their able secretaries, their interlocking directorates, their methods, their cooperation in a "benevolent empire" in the 1830's, and their successes and failures.[40]

The potentialities of the societies for religious advance early attracted the attention of evangelical leaders. The indefatigable Lyman Beecher, long a conspicuous leader in Congregational and Presbyterian churches, saw the values of the voluntary agencies before disestablishment in New England, and even more so thereafter. In 1812 he preached a famous sermon, "A Reformation of Morals Practicable and Indispensable." In order to secure "the execution of the laws against immorality in a time of prevailing moral declension," he argued that a strong influence, distinct from the government, independent of popular suffrage, and superior in potency to individual efforts, was needed "to enlist and preserve the public opinion on the side of law and order."

This "most desirable influence" he found in "local voluntary associations of the wise and the good." These associations could awaken public attention, form public opinion, render the violation of the law disgraceful as well as dangerous, and teach the virtuous part of the community their strength. In short, Beecher saw the voluntary societies as "a sort of disciplined moral militia, prepared to act upon every emergency, and repel every encroachment upon the liberties and morals of the State." [41]

Others soon became equally enthusiastic, often with a broader vision. Though many Presbyterians were later to be troubled by the fact that the voluntary societies were not under the control of their judicatories—one of the causes of the Presbyterian schism of 1837–1838—in 1815 the General Assembly was excited about the potentiality of Bible societies:

> Words are wanting to express the inestimable value of these societies; which, by putting the book of life into the hands of the needy, enrich them with heavenly treasures; and which, embodying, so to speak, the zeal of all Christian denominations, and knitting to each other persons, who however they may differ on many points of greater, or of minor importance, agree in affirming the word of God to be the only infallible rule of faith and practice; neutralize the asperity of the bigot and the sectarian, and reconcile the contending members of the same great brotherhood. The tendency of Bible societies to produce this auspicious result is not now a matter of experiment: facts have ascertained it.[42]

Two years later a pastoral letter emanating from the assembly extended the enthusiasm to the whole burgeoning movement:

> Such mighty plans of benevolence; such wonderful combinations; such a general movement of mankind, in promoting the great cause of human happiness were, surely, never before witnessed! The days of darkness, we fondly hope, are passing away; and the period drawing nigh when the angel bearing the trumpet of the everlasting Gospel, shall carry

> his holy, life-giving message to every kindred, and people, and nation and tongue.[43]

The millennial overtones were not infrequently sounded in support of this new and voluntary way to the kingdom of God.

Methodists officially in the early 1830's were quite cautious in their endorsement of the general voluntary societies, favoring those under their own direction. A General Conference resolution in 1832 stated "that we regard the establishment of Bible, Sunday-school and Tract societies under our control, separate and distinct from similar associations denominated national or American, as highly expedient, necessary, and salutary, and demanding the united support and hearty cooperation of all our preachers, travelling and local, as well as all the members and friends of our Church." [44] Hence the dissolution of their own Bible society in 1836 in favor of Methodist support for the American Bible Society was all the more significant, and emphasized the common basis on which evangelicals of all types stood—the Bible. "This step, it is believed," it was observed at the quadrennial General Conference in 1840, "was dictated alike by a regard for the best interests of the Methodist Episcopal Church, and the cause of our common Christianity in general; and it was hailed as a new and interesting period in the history of the American Bible Society." [45] This shift did point to a more positive Methodist attitude toward the voluntary societies by the later 1830's.

When a Baptist voice, that of Francis Wayland, spoke of the voluntary societies in 1838, he could assume wide acquaintance and acceptance of them on the part of his readers:

> It is not necessary, in commencing a discussion of this subject, to repeat the eulogiums which have been so frequently lavished upon voluntary associations. They have been denominated the peculiar glory of the present age, so emphatically the age of valuable inventions. They are fre-

> quently supposed to be the great moral means, by which the regeneration of the world is to be effected.[46]

So the denominations generally were able to urge their members to support the societies, for despite continuing differences in theology and polity they recognized that they were in partnership for the Christianization of an America in which their freedom to be different would be respected.

It was hoped, however, that some form of Christian union might arise out of the experiences of men of different persuasions working together in the societies. The Presbyterian Pastoral Letter for 1817 was encouraging:

> Endeavour to maintain A SPIRIT OF HARMONY WITH ALL DENOMINATIONS OF CHRISTIANS. While you *contend earnestly for the faith once delivered to the saints,* and bear a faithful testimony to the Apostolic doctrine and order, which we profess to receive; let no bigotry, or prejudice, no party rancour or offensive crimination, pollute your testimony. Remember that the period is approaching, when all real christians shall see eye to eye; when they shall be united in opinion as well as in affection.[47]

The main body of Methodists, though not finding themselves ready to unite with other Methodist groups of German background in 1844, did agree that "the spirit of the age seems to demand a friendly co-operation of all evangelical denominations in reforming the world." [48] At times this spirit of cooperation expressed itself in practical terms at the local level. In San Francisco in 1849, the various congregations joined together to appoint a "city chaplain." "Joining in the common effort," Louis Wright has explained, "were Methodists, Baptists, Presbyterians, Congregationalists, Episcopalians, and Mormons." [49]

Though there was a real sense of cooperation and partnership among the denominations at certain levels, it is also true that the barriers between them generally remained high, and that bitter theological debates raged.[50] For the churches as churches, the religious issues were of the greatest importance, as they involved the eternal destinies of men, and in conducting their own households of faith, they put such matters first.[51] The concern for civilization was an important but a secondary one; having protected their citadels of faith, they were free to join forces in appropriate, and usually indirect, ways with brother evangelicals to preserve the common Christian civilization. Thus they were protecting the ground on which they all stood, and together were preparing the way among the people for the particular appeals each would make for his own group.

The evangelical vision of Christian civilization was of a free, literate, industrious, honest, law-abiding, religious population. Though the rhetoric might vary some among the different denominations, there was a general agreement on such goals as an effective educational system, a sound legal order, and a widespread network of religious institutions. Through these agencies it was believed that standards of personal and public morality would be maintained and improved. In this effort, several particular issues emerged as especially important, for they served as indices of progress toward the desired Christian civilization. The intensity of the nineteenth-century drive to maintain the observance of a strict Christian Sabbath, for example, comes as a surprise to many twentieth-century Americans, but it was then seen as an important sign of evangelical advance. Protestant America was agitated in 1810 when Congress passed a law that post offices should be open and mail carried every day of the week—including Sunday. This touched off a steady stream of protests and petitions, and various societies were formed to crusade for the maintenance of Sunday observance.[52] The evangelical denominations joined in the struggle with a will. The Presbyterian General Assembly in 1815 petitioned Congress to close the mails on Sunday, arguing that public policy, pure morality, and undefiled religion combined in favor of a due observance of the Sabbath. In the evangelical mind, public recognition of Sunday as a holy day provided a clear sign of a Christian civilization, one which allocated protected time for the work of the churches. "Were this grand pillar of the Christian fabric removed," the Presbyterians argued, "the whole building would fall to the ground."[53]

The effort to stop Sunday mails failed at that time, however; Congressman Richard M. Johnson, chairman of the House Committee on Post Offices and Post Roads, resisted in a forceful statement that argued that "it is the duty of this Government to afford to *all*, to Jew or Gentile, Pagan or Christian, the protection and the advantages of our benignant institutions on *Sunday*, as well as every day of the week."[54] But Protestants hammered away at the problem, throwing their weight behind the local and state laws which set Sunday apart. Methodists in 1844 were to divide on the slavery issue, but they were united on the Sabbath issue:

> Resolved, That it be the duty of all our preachers to enforce frequently from the pulpit the divine obligation which all are under to keep the Sabbath day holy; being fully convinced, that were this precept blotted from the decalogue, and men left without the restraints which it imposes, religion (and of course morality) would cease to exert their saving and hallowed influences.[55]

Protestant leaders in their personal lives often sought rigorously to follow the Sabbath principle. Bela Bates Edwards, later seminary professor and editor of leading religious periodicals, showed the influence of his Puritan forefathers in his New Year's resolutions of 1830:

> Do every thing on Saturday, in the way of preparation, which I can. Begin the Sabbath at sunset on Saturday. Do not visit nor engage in any secular business on Sabbath evening.

> Spend a principal part of the Lord's day in prayer, in meditation, in reading the Scriptures. Strive to do what God has commanded in order to secure his smiles. Never introduce topics of worldly conversation, or criticisms on sermons. Avoid spending the Sabbath away from home, or from my room, if possible.[56]

Such men argued that the spirit of Old Testament Sabbath regulation was applied under the Christian dispensation to the first day of the week, the Lord's day of resurrection, and resisted the polemics of the seventh-day sects which maintained a Christian Sabbath on Saturday.

Those who demanded strict Sunday observance insisted that the principle of a day's rest in seven was planted in the very order of nature and in the original constitution of man. Both man and society need a regular break in activity, they argued, insisting that Sunday observance is a good civil as well as a good religious practice. "The Lord's Day, viewed in a political light entirely," affirmed the Presbyterians in 1818, "affords so many benefits calculated for the promotion of present enjoyment in all the relations of life, as to claim for it, the veneration and homage of sound statesmen."[57] Conscious that many were opposed to their effort to maintain a heritage from the religious past, especially in its New England and Calvinist forms, they battled back, protesting each new sign of change.

Samuel Miller of Princeton was typical of many who were distressed by the increase in Sunday travel. Touching on the wonderful advances in means of transportation available to the citizen in the 1830's, Miller continued:

> But, if the patriot be an intelligent *Christian*, he will perceive in this extended scene *one feature* which will fill him with anguish and deep apprehension. I refer to that deplorable profanation of the Lord's-day which is so conspicuous on *all* of the lines of our steamboats, Canals, and Rail-Roads, and on *some* of them so obtrusively and shamefully con-

> spicuous, as if the object were to insult as well as to rob God; and to render public feeling as speedily and as thoroughly as possible callous to the outrage on all religious decorum, by giving to it all possible familiarity and publicity. Is it not a fact, that, in a community nominally Christian, and in the midst of the richest Gospel privileges, our public conveyances are studiously made so attractive, by cheapness of fare, by crowds, and by every species of public allurement, in their Sabbatical excursions, that their gains are far greater on that day, than on any other day of the week? [58]

On the Sabbath issue, Protestants whose background had been in state churches readily teamed up with those who had opposed all religious establishments. McLoughlin has said that at the dawn of the nineteenth century "the Baptists, while denying the need for religious taxes, nevertheless insisted as much as the Trinitarian or evangelical 'theocrats' like Jedidiah Morse, Timothy Dwight, and later Lyman Beecher, upon the necessity for strict enforcement of the Puritan blue laws and Sabbatarian restrictions." [59] Protestant forces across a wide sweep of denominational and theological opinion persistently struggled for the Sabbath as a day apart—a day that would characterize American civilization as Christian. For them, this was a distinctive symbol of the kind of Protestant culture they were laboring to maintain and extend —hence their concern for what in retrospect may seem to be a petty and legalistic matter.

Another crusade, to make the country a temperate if not a prohibitionist society, played a somewhat fluctuating but generally expanding role in the evangelical Protestantism of the nineteenth century. Quite different from the struggle to *retain* Sabbath observance as a legacy from the past, the temperance issue was largely new. Though of course excesses in drinking had been condemned in colonial Protestantism, especially among Methodists, the adding of temperance to the definition of Christian civilization was for the most part an innovation of the nineteenth century. Drinking had been generally accepted in church functions in the colonial period and into the early nineteenth century. The drinking habit appeared to be on the increase in those years; according to one estimate, "the consumption of spirits in 1792 was two and a half gallons per person; in 1810, four and a half gallons." [60] For the evangelical mind, a drunken man was a poor example of citizenship in a Christian commonwealth. After the separation of church and state, the continuing Protestant effort to secure a Christian civilization had to proceed chiefly by influencing personal behavior. (One of the main reasons for emphasizing Sabbath observance was to provide opportunity and sanction for exercising such influence.) Intemperance was a readily visible sign of poor personal behavior, of a lack of self-control if not of dissoluteness. The increase in the consumption of alcohol in the new century suggested a decline in personal morality and was seen as a threat to Christian civilization. A determined campaign against intemperance was launched.

Lyman Beecher led the way again. In 1808 he preached a series of sermons on intemperance which were published in a number of editions. Soon the evangelical forces were adding temperance to their profile of Christian America. The Presbyterians, in their Pastoral Letter of 1818, characteristically showed the determination of well-intentioned religious leaders to save all Americans from what they understood to be a vice. Describing the plight of the man who has become a drunkard, they said:

> The certain and acknowledged prospect of the wreck of his family, his fortune, and his character; and even of the ruin of his immortal soul, is not sufficient to arrest his course: and yet perhaps the same man may formerly have been in such a state of equilibrium or indecision upon this subject, that the smallest motives might have prevented the formation of a habit, which in its maturity has become so irresistible.—This consideration is certainly sufficient to justify an effort for saving our fellow man from the domination of so destructive a vice. For this purpose we earnestly recom-

> mend to the officers and members of our Church to abstain even from the common use of ardent spirits. Such a voluntary privation as this, with its motives publicly avowed, will not be without its effect in cautioning our fellow christians and fellow citizens, against the encroachment of intoxication; and we have the more confidence in recommending this course as it has already been tried with success in several sections of our Church.[61]

Ten years later the Methodists rejoiced "in all the laudable and proper efforts now making to promote this just object, so important to the interest both of the Church and nation," and resolved "that we neither drink ourselves, (except medicinally,) nor give it to visiters [sic] or workmen." [62]

Even in churches which did not espouse the temperance cause as avidly as did Methodists, Presbyterians, and Baptists, considerable temperance conviction spread. The Episcopal bishop of Ohio, Charles P. McIlvaine, a member of the evangelical wing of his church, was a forceful advocate of temperance. In one of his tracts, he summed up his case in these words:

> Here, then are three important points which we may safely assume as entirely unquestionable:—that *our country is horribly scourged by Intemperance;* that *the time has come when a great effort is demanded for the expulsion of this evil;* and that *no effort can be effectual without being universal.* Hence is deduced, undeniably, the conclusion that it is the duty and the solemn duty of the people in every part of this country, to rise up at once, and act vigorously and unitedly in the furtherance of whatever measures are best calculated to promote reformation.[63]

MacIlvaine made it clear that "the measures best calculated to promote reformation" meant total abstinence, for the first drink leads to the second, and so on, so that the line between moderation and excess is quickly obscured—therefore, he argued, do not touch a drop. The movement went through several shifts of emphasis in this period,[64] but by the 1850's was manifesting itself in state prohibition legislation. A total of sixteen states and territories had taken some kind of action in restricting liquor traffic before the Civil War. The new, voluntary form of Christendom was to be a temperate one, if evangelicals could make it so.

THE LIMITS OF PERSUASION

The goal of a fully Christian civilization was to be realized by the methods of persuasion only—so most Protestant leaders sincerely believed. They were heartily in favor of religious freedom. One would expect a Baptist like Francis Wayland to insist that as valuable as the truth of the Gospel is because the hope of eternity rests on it, still "we have no right to *force it* upon another." [65] It is perhaps more surprising to find an Episcopal bishop of high-church views, John Henry Hobart, singing the praises of religious freedom:

> It is the *religious freedom* of my country that constitutes, in my view, one of her proudest boasts. Protected as religion is by the state, which finds in her precepts and spirit and sanctions the best security for social happiness and order, she is left free to exert her legitimate powers, uninfluenced and unrestrained by any worldly authority whatsoever. And the happy effect is seen in the zeal with which her institutions are supported, as far as the ability of an infant country, and a spreading, and in many cases scattered and humble population, will admit.[66]

In the wide spectrum of Protestant opinion between such churchmen, there was enthusiastic acceptance of freedom, and insistence that the institutions of religion and those of government be kept free and apart. Confident that they were on the side of truth, Protestants generally believed that in the end they would prevail and that good men would be persuaded of the truth of their claims.

Sidney Mead has explained that the establishment of religion had rested upon two basic assumptions: "that the existence and well-being of any society depends upon a body of commonly shared religious beliefs—the nature of man, his place in the cosmos, his destiny, and his conduct toward his fellow men—and that the only guarantee that these necessary beliefs will be sufficiently inculcated is to put the coercive power of the state behind the institution responsible for their definition, articulation, and inculcation." [67] Religious freedom did not mean for Protestant leadership the giving up of the necessity for a body of commonly shared religious beliefs, but it did mean the rejection of legal sanctions in favor of persuasion. Perry Miller stated the matter in somewhat different terms:

> Calling upon all the people to submit to a uniform moral law, they [leaders of the revival after the Revolution] at the same time had to concede that American Christianity must and should accept a diversity of churches. . . . Thus accepting the liberal consequences of the Revolution in the form of republican governments, and so abandoning the dream of theocracy, and equally surrendering (except for rhetorical flourish) the idea of a people in a national covenant with their Maker, these insurgents proposed to salvage the Protestant solidarity by the main force of spiritual persuasion.[68]

But what when persuasion fails? Can a nation retain both full religious freedom and a particular religious character?

Many efforts were made by Protestant spokesmen to explain how a nation could be both distinctively Christian and yet fully free religiously. The Episcopal bishops in 1832 devoted much attention to this question. They noted that the courts required "an appeal to the Rewarder of the good, and the Punisher of the wicked" in the administration of justice and in securing the obedience of all orders of men to the laws, yet insisted that such could not be construed to be "a restraint on the religious freedom which is so happily possessed by the citizens of the United States." For civil rule must sustain the fundamental truths of religion, without which there would be no social tie, "or any obligation of law extending to the conscience." So, the bishops affirmed:

> On various occasions, and in various ways, our national legislature has manifested its sense of the obligation of those provisions contained in the several constitutions of the individual states, which presume the Christian religion to be a part of the law of the land. But this establishment is of such a liberal cast, as secures freedom of profession and of worship to every denomination of Christians, living in obedience to the laws.[69]

According to this point of view, widespread among Protestants of the time, there is always the freedom to do good, from the perspective of the Christian moral tradition, but those who do wrong according to that perspective will find themselves justly curbed by the law. Bela Bates Edwards put it more bluntly still:

> Perfect religious liberty does not imply that government of the country is not a Christian government. The Christian Sabbath is here recognized by the civil authorities in a great variety of forms. Most, if not all, of our constitutions of government proceed on the basis of the truth of the Christian religion. Christianity has been affirmed to be part and parcel of the law of the land. The Bible is practically, however much opposition there may be theoretically, *read* daily, in one form or another, in a large proportion of the common schools supported by the State. There is convincing evidence to show that this real, though indirect, connection between the State and Christianity is every year acquiring additional strength, is attended with less and less of exception and remonstrance.[70]

The means were to be voluntary and persuasive, but the goal of a Christian society was as clear as it had been in the days of legal establishment, even clearer.

The evangelicals were so sure of the truth of their position that they assumed that good men would be persuaded of it, or at least would accept it enough to go along. Those who did not could properly be pushed into line by the power of public opinion and the weight of the law. In a widely quoted sermon, Ezra Stiles Ely, a Presbyterian pastor, boldly called all Christians to unite to elect to public office only those friendly to Christianity and who believed in divine Revelation. Such combined Christian influence, he insisted, was surely no infringement on liberty! "It deprives no man of his right for me to prefer a Christian to an Infidel," he declared. "We are a Christian nation: we have a right to demand that all our rulers in their conduct shall conform to Christian morality; and if they do not, it is the duty and privilege of Christian freemen to make a new and a better election." [71] Most Protestant spokesmen were more indirect in their approach.

The coercive side of the effort to make America a Christian nation showed also in some of the particular reform crusades. When Charles G. Finney, the most prominent revivalist of this period, recognized that there were those who would not go along with the "glorious reform" of temperance, his prescription of what to do was clear enough:

> And multitudes will never yield, until the friends of God and man can form a public sentiment so strong as to crush the character of every man who will not give it up. You will find many doctors of divinity and pillars of the church, who are able to drink their wine, that will stand their ground, and no command of God, no requirement of benevolence, no desire to save souls, no pity for bleeding humanity, will move such persons, until you can form a public sentiment so powerful as to force them to it, on penalty of loss of reputation.[72]

Clearly, as the evangelicals saw it, when persuasion failed, the "wise and good" might resort to pressure through public opinion and the law. Gardiner Spring once put concisely what many were saying: "Liberty without godliness, is but another name for anarchy or despotism." [73] When the leaders of the Protestant crusade confronted those who resisted what seem to them obviously to be the true and right way, they were ready to use social pressure and moral coercion. It is interesting to observe that when they were focusing on their central spiritual and theological tasks, the Protestants' commitment to religious freedom was most genuinely displayed. They sincerely wanted to win as many as they could to the faith which meant so much to them. But as they worked with other evangelicals on the basis of common ideas about a Christian civilization, they were more ready to limit freedom of the opposition. Believing that by the separation of church and state they had separated religious from secular concerns, they seem to have been largely unaware of how much specifically Protestant content they had in fact invested in their understanding of state and society. Groups which did not share their basic premises could become only too painfully aware of it.

For those who stood outside the general Protestant perspective, the earnest professions of concern for freedom made by the evangelicals could sound rather hollow. Immigrants and Roman Catholics (and there was a large overlap between the two groups) were often treated with scorn and occasionally with violence. The number of Catholics had increased from about 30,000 in 1790 to some 600,000 forty years later. This steadily enlarging minority seemed to threaten Protestant hopes for the future of America. There was little general understanding of the realities of Catholic life in Protestant America, for the polarizations of the Reformation and Puritan periods persisted in Protestant consciousness. The ugly trails of anti-Catholicism and nativism wind together through nineteenth-century history.[74] While most Protestant leaders were opposed to mob action, in their effort to keep under control those who were not persuaded by the vision of a Christian America they did help to create an atmosphere in which unpleasant and unjust things happened. The vehement anti-Catholic propaganda by such leaders as Lyman Beecher and Horace Bushnell[75] were at least indirectly contributory to some destructive mob actions in the 1830's and 1840's. The influx of Irish immigrants in the 1840's further alarmed many natives. In reaction to the Catholic "threat," an interdenominational American Protestant Association was formed in 1842. Its aim was to coordinate the activities of the various anti-Catholic groups. "By the middle of the 1840's the American churches were able to present a virtually united front against Catholicism," wrote Billington. "Swept away by the pleas of organized nativists, they had accepted the challenge to make America the scene of a new Reformation in which Popery would be driven from the land and the work of Luther and Calvin brought to a successful end."[76] Many of the Protestant voluntary societies participated in the anti-Catholic agitation. The great devotion to religious freedom showed its limitations when the hope for a Protestant America seemed in jeopardy.

The Jews, much fewer in number, were generally regarded by Protestants as an acceptable minority which had been able to find asylum in free America, and which offered opportunities for missionary concern. Quite typical was the very brief chapter Robert Baird put into the 1844 edition of his pioneering work, *Religion in America*, repeated verbatim in later editions. Noting that the Jews now find "full enjoyment" of civil rights in the land, he reckoned that at the time he wrote there were about fifty thousand of them, with some fifty synagogues. He reported that "A few instances of conversion to Christianity have taken place, but only a few, the attention of Christians, we may truly say, not having been sufficiently turned to that subject."[77] He thought that their small number led them to be overlooked, and was pleased to note the development of evangelical interest in working among them. By that date the Ashkenazic Jews from middle and northern Europe vastly outnumbered those of Sephardic background.

The Protestant forces displayed their most serious inner weaknesses in confronting the fact of slavery in America. Over the slavery issue, the evangelical crusade for a Christian America sharply divided. Evangelicals who shared much of the same Christian vision for their country encountered an obstacle that split them apart, and on the fundamental moral issue of human freedom.

In the early part of the century there was considerable antislavery sentiment of a moderate, gradualist type, South as well as North, among evangelicals and among those whose primary motivation was humanitarian. Many such antislavery moderates believed in colonization—in sending emancipated blacks to colonies in Africa. Colonization was usually predicated on the view that Negroes were inferior to whites; hence few blacks responded with much enthusiasm to such a program, and its actual achievements were not very impressive.[78] Within the nation, the treatment of the freed slaves was usually prejudicial in church as in secular life; the segregated pew was the symbol of the acceptance by many Christians, North and South, of beliefs in the inferior status of the Negro.[79]

Even before the important shifts in thought and feeling that took place in the 1830's—the spread of militant abolitionism in the North, and the deepening attachment of the South to slavery—the gulf over the slavery question was widening within evangelical circles. In 1804, Methodists printed two *Disciplines;* the section on slavery was left out of the edition for the southernmost states.[80] The antislavery spirit continued to be strong among many Methodists, however, and the General Conference passed several rather firm resolutions. In the face of the deepening determination of many Southerners to maintain slavery—a determination in which many Christians shared—the General Conference in 1816 voted concurrence with a committee report which glimpsed the unpleasant truth and admitted defeat.

> The committee to whom was referred the business of slavery beg leave to report, that they have taken the subject into serious consideration, and, after mature deliberation, they are of opinion that, under the present existing circumstances in relation to slavery, little can be done to abolish a practice so contrary to the principles of moral justice. They are sorry to say that the evil appears to be past remedy; and they are led to deplore the destructive consequences which have already accrued, and are likely to result therefrom.

The extent of the "destructive consequences" in their century and ours were tragically to outrun anything they imagined. They assigned responsibility for the hopeless situation primarily to governmental authorities, though admitting Christian involvement: "Your committee find that in the South and West the civil authorities render emancipation impracticable, and, notwithstanding they are led to fear that some of our members are too easily contented with laws unfriendly to freedom, yet, nevertheless, they are constrained to admit that to bring about such a change in the civil code as would favour the cause of liberty is not in the power of the General Conference." [81] Here was the admission early in the century that a basic moral issue was dividing religious men even as they were claiming a special responsibility for the morality of the civilization of which they were a part.

A similar capitulation occurred in Presbyterian history. One of the firmest antislavery statements passed by a major church body was that of the General Assembly in 1818, which unequivocally said: "We consider the voluntary enslaving of one part of the human race by another, as a gross violation of the most precious and sacred rights of human nature; as utterly inconsistent with the law of God, which requires us to love our neighbour as ourselves; and as totally irreconcilable with the spirit and principles of the Gospel of Christ, which enjoin that 'all things whatsoever ye would that man should do to you, do ye even so to them.'" [82] Though this was passed unanimously, there was considerable resistance to it beneath the surface. Open opposition soon appeared. Some who accepted the resolution of 1818 did so only on colonizationist grounds. For the very next year after that striking declaration, the assembly adopted an overture favorable to the colonization society, observing that "In the distinctive and indelible marks of their colour, and the prejudices of the people, an insuperable obstacle has been placed to the execution of any plan for elevating their character, and placing them on a footing with their brethren of the same common family." Somewhat piously, they added: "In restoring them to the land of their fathers, the Assembly hope that they may be opened, not only for the accomplishment of that object, but for introducing civilization and the Gospel to the benighted nations of Africa." [83] Many who did seriously oppose slavery rationalized church acceptance of it on the grounds that the New Testament did not condemn slaveholding and that the church should not meddle in temporal affairs. So John Holt Rice, prominent Presbyterian minister of the South, wrote: "I am most fully convinced that slavery is the greatest evil in our country, except whiskey; and it is my most ardent prayer that we may be delivered from it. . . . The reason why I am so strenuously opposed to any movement by the church or ministers of religion on the subject is simply this. I am convinced that any thing we can do will injure religion, and retard the march of public feeling in relation to slavery." [84]

"The march of public feeling in relation to slavery" was to go in quite other directions than that which Rice wished, both in the South and in the North. The fear of slave revolts, inflamed by the Nat Turner insurrection of 1831, and the militant abolitionism of the immediatist type, symbolized by William Lloyd Garrison and the *Liberator*, contributed to the hardening of proslavery thought in the South. At the same time, abolitionism was being disseminated among northern evangelicals by such leaders as Theodore Dwight Weld and the agents of the American Anti-Slavery Society. The disruptions of the denominations soon followed. The impact of the slavery controversy played some role in the Presbyterian schism of 1837–38, though formally the issues were theological and jurisdictional.[85] The two largest Protestant bodies, Methodists and Baptists, did split over slavery in 1844 and 1845.[86] Both parts of already divided Presbyterianism were finally to redivide over the slavery issue explicitly in 1857 and 1861. Other denominations which did not formally split suffered intense inner tensions.[87]

In these divisions, both sides clung to the hope of the triumph of Christian civilization, but one side saw it increasingly as one without slavery while the other saw that institution as supported by Christian teaching and well-suited to the alleged inferiority and low level of civilization of the blacks. Shadows which were not to be dispelled were beclouding the vision of Christian America. Those who shared the same basic evangelical viewpoint and who spoke so insistently about morality and its role in civilization had divided over a moral issue. The ideal of a Protestant nation was not strong enough to overcome the differences of opinion and practice concerning slavery. The inability of the Christian forces to resolve the issue properly and peacefully has had tragic consequences for the nation, for the churches, and for the blacks. In view of the economic, political, and social situation of the sections and the voluntary character of the religious organizations, perhaps there were no viable alternatives before the churches. Convinced that theirs was a Christian civilization, some Protestants justified the slave system in religious terms, while others employed the same concepts in support of radical abolitionism. Fateful limitations in the search for a Christian America were painfully disclosed.

As we look back now, the limitations in the way the Protestant majority handled immigrants, Catholics, and the slavery issue are clear, and we see what many of the consequences have been. Although there were those, both within that majority and outside it, who called attention to those limitations at the time, Protestantism then believed itself to be securely rooted in its culture and was confident it could solve the problems and overcome the difficulties. By mid-century, its impact on American life was impressive, and it had every expectation of fully reshaping the civilization in its image. Winthrop S. Hudson has even suggested that by the time of Lincoln, "the ideals, the convictions, the language, the customs, the institutions of society were so shot through with Christian presuppositions that the culture itself nurtured and nourished the Christian faith." [88] I have argued elsewhere that "in many ways, the middle third of the nineteenth century was more of a 'Protestant Age' than was the colonial period with its established churches." [89] Protestants had come a long way since the dark days of "infidelity" at the close of the eighteenth century, and they saw no reason that with God's help they should not go on to complete victory. Horace Bushnell stated the hope in glowing terms as the century drew near midpoint: "The wilderness shall bud and blossom as the rose before us; and we will not cease, till a christian nation throws up its temples of worship on every hill and plain; till knowledge, virtue and religion, blending their dignity and their healthful power, have filled our great country with a manly and happy race of people, and the bands of a complete christian commonwealth are seen to span the continent." [90]

Religion and civilization fit together freely but closely in this evangelical vision of a Christian America. Evangelicals were convinced that the vision could be fulfilled with God's help by voluntary means, by good men working together for true religion and enlightened civilization, opposing together alien influences that ran counter to their goals.

III

Defending Protestant America (1860–1890)

In the thirty years following the outbreak of the Civil War, some uncomfortable realities stood in the way of evangelical hopes for the early triumph of Christian civilization in America. Serious inner divisions and tensions plagued the Protestant forces. The facts of industrialization, urbanization, immigration, and intellectual revolution posed serious challenges to the evangelical expectancies which had been nurtured in the predominantly rural atmosphere of the early nineteenth century. Nevertheless, the Protestant forces rallied confidently to battle for the Christianization of American life along familiar lines. Evangelicals reaffirmed their faith in the full transformation of American life into a Christian society, and they labored for that end.

The conviction that they were fighting for the triumph of Christian civilization inspired many on both sides during the grim, bitter years of civil strife, 1861–1865. That war, like all wars, was a terrible simplifier which carried men of diverse backgrounds and of many shades of opinion into one side or the other and set them against each other. On both sides, the Protestant spirit was religiously dominant, and both sides found much assurance from their religious leaders that they were the true defenders of Christian America. "For those Southerners who believed they were God's chosen people and that the Confederacy was a part of God's plan," wrote James W. Silver, "it was a matter of simple semantics to identify religion with politics and patriotism." Many *did* believe they were the chosen, for "the church was the most powerful organization influencing the lives of men and women in the South in the days before and during the Confederacy." Clergymen were "quite successful in helping the people to identify God, the right, and the destiny of history with slavery, the Confederacy, and the war." [1] Southern Presbyterians, for example, recorded in 1864 that "we hesitate not to affirm that it is the peculiar mission of the Southern Church to conserve the institution of slavery, and to make it a blessing both to master and slave." [2]

Most northern clergymen were just as sure that God willed Union victory. Outspoken among them was the Methodist bishop, Gilbert Haven, who now identified the old theme of America's destiny with northern success. "To save this land to universal liberty and universal brotherhood, supported by universal law and sanctified by universal piety, is to save all lands," he preached in 1863. "It may take all our sons, all our treasure, all our generation to destroy the enemy that is seeking to prevent this consummation." But with faithfulness to God, the bishop declared, will come victory over the rebellious host without and the rebellious spirit within; "then shall other nations behold the image of the transfigured Christ shining in our uplifted face, that will glow, like that of Moses, with the radiance of his divine countenance." [3] Morale on both sides through the years of struggle was often sustained by the conviction that theirs was a holy cause, while the victory of the opponent would extinguish the torch of a truly Christian civilization. Of course there were some among the faithful on both sides who did not view the struggle in such unambiguous terms, but the most popular voices of the day did not dwell on the qualifications. At war's end, evangelical hopes for a Christian America had been brightened for the North, and soon were revived again in the South.

Following the war, southern Christians perforce accepted the arbitrament of arms, and once again began to relate their vision of a Christian civilization to the reunited nation. They remained ideologically undefeated, clinging to the end of the century to the convictions that had led them to support the Confederacy. Rufus B. Spain has explained how the Southern Baptists "refused to admit that secession and slavery were wrong in any way, constitutionally or morally, and denied any responsibility for causing the war. Because God had overridden their views through the instrumentality of war, they would accept His will, but they would change none of their views." [4] Though they continued to believe what the Confederacy had stood for, they affirmed that God had his reasons for what had happened. Since God required obedience to political authority, they gave it—though obviously seeking to regain control over local political arrangements as soon as they could. Not only did they return to the Union, they began to interpret it once again as God's agent for the spread of Christian civilization. A report on the state of home missions to the Southern Baptist Convention as early as 1866 resumed a familiar theme:

> God has given to our country a great and growing influence, and the propagation of the Christian religion here must exert a vast reflex influence upon the destinies of mankind. America is the radiating center whence high and ennobling influences beam upon the world; and we are enlightening mankind in brightening the radiance of our own piety.[5]

Within the nation, Baptists, with other southern Christians, felt a particular call to see that pure, evangelical Christianity at its best was maintained.

The stance of that other giant among southern denominations, the Methodist Episcopal Church, South, was similar. "The great majority of the Southern people had emerged from the War with their dislike of Yankees increased and their devotion to Southern principles intensified," wrote Hunter D. Farish many years ago in his study of Southern Methodism. "They were unwilling to recognize any but the unmistakable accomplishments of the War, the emancipation of the slaves and the restoration of the Union." [6] In their General Conference the year after the end of hostilities, the Southern Methodists adopted the following resolution:

> That two or more of our Bishops be requested to wait upon the President of the United States and tender him appropriate expressions of gratitude for the restoration of our Church property, and to further assure him that we, as a body of ministers of Christ, enjoin on our congregations submission to "the powers that be;" and that, while we stand aloof from all party politics and deprecate any intermeddling of churches or ministers, *as such,* with political affairs, we yet feel it to be our duty cheerfully to comply with the apostolic injunction to make "supplications, prayers, intercessions, and thanksgivings for all men—for all in authority, that we may lead quiet and peaceable lives in all godliness and honesty." [7]

Formally, at least, the leading Protestant bodies were once again attempting to fulfill their mission of religion and civilization in a reunited nation.

EVANGELICAL DIVISIONS: SECTIONAL, RACIAL, THEOLOGICAL

The schisms which had disrupted the leading evangelical churches before the war proved to be long lasting. The reunion of the nation did not lead to the reuniting of the sectional divisions of the denominational families. Christians on both sides adhered to the views for which they had fought. Tension remained high during the Reconstruction period, with its military occupation until 1877. In those years, many northern Christians regarded the South as open to ecclesiastical occupation, too, while southerners, resisting, saw northerners as having diluted the Gospel with political concerns. The Southern Methodist bishops in 1866, for example, reported their apprehension that "a large proportion, if not a majority of Northern Methodists have become incurably radical. They teach for doctrine the commandments of men. They preach another Gospel. They have incorporated social dogmas and political tests into their Church creeds." [8] The three major evangelical bodies which had sizable southern memberships remained divided.[9]

Well before the Civil War, the tendency of southern Protestantism toward a tight evangelical orthodoxy had been apparent. Afterwards, in the sting of defeat, religion became a refuge. As Samuel S. Hill, Jr. has summed it up, "the prologue and aftermath of the Civil War sealed the South's tendency toward introversion . . . Although not everyone's name appeared on church rolls, scarcely anyone dissented from the old-time religion which reigned supreme everywhere." [10] The patterns of faith and church life which had been shaped in the early part of the century thus largely became religiously normative in the South. They were slower to change there, too, as sociological factors combined with psychological and religious ones to resist alterations and to conserve the old. "The rural homogeneity of the South," declared Kenneth K. Bailey, "was little disturbed by immigration, industrialization, new intellectual currents, and all those other forces which were elsewhere transforming society." [11] So evangelicals who had much in common religiously continued to be divided sectionally.

The Protestant hopes for a Christian America were beclouded by this continuing division in the evangelical world. Protestants who shared the same basic faith felt the need of a deeper sense of common identity and mutual understanding if their drive for a Christian civilization were to succeed. By exchanging fraternal delegates at national gatherings, and by participating in such nondenominational meetings as those sponsored by the Evangelical Alliance and other agencies, northern and southern evangelicals cautiously groped toward some feeling of oneness. Their common devotion to Anglo-Saxon civilization assisted in this tentative and uneven development.[12] Meanwhile, the split in evangelical ranks remained very real.

There was another major division in the world of evangelical Protestantism which took on vastly greater dimensions after the Civil War. The movement of Negroes in large numbers into their own denominations could be interpreted on all sides as consistent with the long-accepted patterns of freedom and voluntaryism. The story of the separation of the growing body of black Christians into the Negro denominations is a highly complex one, but the leading historical treatments agree on several main points.[13] With all too few exceptions, whites South and North believed in Negro inferiority, and resisted any ideas of social equality. Though there were variations in viewpoint, there was widely pervasive resistance to accepting the blacks as equals among Christians. The Southern Methodist "Bishops' Address" for 1886, for example, declared their unwillingness to be "hurried forward by sentimental extravagance in the direction of the discolored current of social equality, through the agency of the schoolroom, the congregation, or the Conference; for there is no conceivable result that would compensate for the crime against nature which this theory deliberately contemplates."[14] The separate Negro churches had been originally founded because of the unwillingness of whites to accept Negro worshipers as equals. After the war, continued white unwillingness was one of the main reasons for the withdrawal of the great majority of black Christians from the major denominations into their own. "Well before the end of the sixties," declared Rufus Spain, "Baptists had come to accept the separation of their Negro members as both inevitable and desirable."[15] Many black Methodists were drawn into the African Methodist Episcopal and the African Methodist Episcopal Zion Churches, while the Colored Methodist Episcopal Church of America was organized around former

Southern Methodist Negro congregations with the willing co-operation of the parent church.

It was also true that "the church was the first community or public organization that the Negro actually owned and completely controlled."[16] Here was a world of his own, one in which he could be free, and in which he would not be mixed with those who considered him inferior, and in which there was opportunity for aspiring leaders. Though the society denied him freedom in various ways, in his own church the Negro joyfully found genuine freedom.

In many respects, the Negro denominations were patterned religiously very much after the evangelical denominations of which many Negroes had been a part. Styles of worship, religious life, polity, missionary concern, and revivalistic fervor were recognizable as those of the parent bodies from which they now became largely isolated, though with distinctive contributions out of the black experience. As Bishop J. W. Hood of the African Methodist Episcopal Zion Church put it in a letter to the General Conference of the Southern Methodist Church:

> Circumstances over which we have no control have drawn a line between the two races, in all their social relations, as marked and distinct as the nose upon a man's face. It is not a line of hate, or dread of contact, but a line sanctioned by custom till it has all the force of law. This social line has made the African Church a necessity. Possibly we have more branches of the Church than we need, but, until we can see our way clear to unite in one, we shall have to continue to imitate our white brethren, each branch using our best efforts to spread the Redeemer's kingdom.[17]

For a long time, many Negro churches used the literature produced by the white denominations. The greatest help to the burgeoning black churches from old-line Protestantism came in the educational field, as churches, especially northern ones, founded many schools and colleges for the freed slaves.[18]

Though there were devoted missionaries from white denominations carrying out significant educational ministries among blacks, the two evangelical worlds, much alike in many respects, largely went their own ways. The white denominations treated the black churches with patronizing politeness; this racial division in the evangelical world did not trouble them as the sectional one did. In the crusade for Christian America as the white leaders customarily saw it, the role of the Negro churches was to be a humble one.

The Protestant world of the postwar period was shaken by another division, one which produced sharp internal tensions rather than new denominations. Though the rise of liberal theology caused repercussions almost everywhere in Protestantism, the North especially felt its impact. As liberal parties became prominent in many denominations, the intellectual revolutions of the nineteenth century influenced the thinking of increasing numbers of Protestant clergy and laity. Traditional views of biblical authority, chronology, and interpretation were upset for many as the theory of evolution was popularized and as the techniques of historical criticism were applied to sacred documents.[19] Evangelical denominations which had raised high barriers against the earlier liberal heritage from the Enlightenment as represented in Unitarianism and Universalism now found themselves harboring increasingly self-conscious liberal parties. In most cases leaders of such groups sincerely affirmed their evangelical intentions and their devotion to revealed, historic faith, but at the same time they expressed their determination to use the tested conclusions that emerged from scientific and scholarly findings. As Henry Ward Beecher, eloquent and controversial pastor of Plymouth Church in Brooklyn, interpreted the theory of evolution, he did not fear it but welcomed it.

> That great truth—through patient accumulation of fact, and marvelous intuitions of reason, and luminous expositions of philosophic relation, by men trained in observation, in think-

> ing, and in expression—has now become accepted throughout the scientific world. . . . And that it will furnish—nay, is already bringing—to the aid of religious truth as set forth in the life and teachings of Jesus a new and powerful aid, fully in line with other marked developments of God's providence in this His world, I fervently believe.[20]

To those schooled in the tradition of the Bible as the basic authority for all life, the new movement was highly disturbing, for it seemed to threaten the very heart of faith. Hence considerable anxiety and turmoil accompanied the growth of the liberal groups in the churches, highlighted by certain sharp crises when a conspicuous liberal was tried for heresy, or when a seminary went over to the new theology.[21] Those who clung to the older views were often inclined to see in the rise of liberal elements a capitulation to materialistic and naturalistic enemies which had to be overcome if America were to become a truly Christian nation. The dream had long been of an America *won* to the Christian way—but now there appeared to be a growing difference as to what that way really was. From the conservative viewpoint the liberals, with their positive evaluation of a scientifically oriented culture, seemed to be wavering on first principles. The very forces that felt themselves called to lead in the Christianization of America were plagued by this theological tension in their ranks.

THREATS TO PROTESTANT HOPES

Handicapped by divisions and tensions, the evangelical Protestants faced some complex and formidable problems which became widely identified as seriously threatening the future of Protestantism. Immigration had stirred the anxieties of the evangelicals before, as when the Irish and Germans had poured into the country in great numbers in the 1840's. Immigration after the Civil War reached new peaks, especially in the 1800's. Increasingly many of the newcomers were from southern and eastern Europe; among them were large percentages of non-Protestants: Roman Catholics, Jews, Eastern Orthodox, and the secularly oriented. In his widely read work, *Our Country*, Josiah Strong, secretary of the Evangelical Alliance, listed immigration as the first of the "seven perils" confronting the nation; the others were Romanism, Mormonism, intemperance, socialism, wealth, and the city. With customary vehemence, he declared that "during the last four years we have suffered a peaceful invasion by an army, more than twice as vast as the estimated number of Goths and Vandals that swept over Southern Europe and overwhelmed Rome."[22] Among them, Strong explained, were many of the pauper and criminal classes, many illiterates, many drinkers, many Roman Catholics, and many Mormon converts—most of the perils were somehow related to immigration. Of the well over thirteen million immigrants who came into the country from the end of the Civil War to the beginning of the twentieth century, it was the Catholic element that especially troubled the Protestants. Particularly as the tide swept increasingly from southern and eastern Europe after 1880, bringing in some two and a half million Catholics in two decades, did the threat to the Protestant character of America stimulate sharp anxieties in many evangelical leaders. The increase in Jewish population was also very great. It jumped from about a quarter of a million in 1880 to three times that number by 1900; well over half of the newcomers were Yiddish-speaking refugees from East Europe. Though this influx did play a role in the increase of anti-Semitism in American life, it was largely concentrated in relatively few places and did not present the problem to Protestantism that Catholicism did.

The maintenance of a Protestant cultural pre-eminence required a broad popular base, and evangelical leaders were greatly disturbed because trends in immigration were affecting that base. Leaders of Catholics and Jews were also troubled by the changing patterns of immigration, but for somewhat different reasons. The trouble the Americanized Catholics of longer standing had with the strange new immigrants is an important part of their history in this period.[23] Likewise, the rather well-educated, largely middle-class Ashkenazic Jews of German background were overwhelmed by the flood of uncultured, poverty-stricken Yiddish refugees from Poland and Russia. Both groups took heroic measures to deal with the human tide, but inasmuch as they were not the dominant groups in the culture, they were not threatened in the same way that the Protestants felt themselves to be. To a vast gathering of church leaders on "National Perils and Opportunities" called by the Evangelical Alliance in 1887, H. H. Boyesen of Columbia, in a frank plea for immigration restriction, revealed his negative views on recent immigrants from Naples and Sicily: "I have, during the past year, again and again seen the Battery Park black with these creatures (in fact, preternaturally black), and the odors which surrounded them turned the milk of human kindness within me, and made me marvel at the heedless hospitality of the American nation, which was willing to mingle this coarse and brutal strain in their own fresh and vigorous blood."[24] It was not only immigration from Europe that was upsetting. The General Assembly of the Presbyterian Church in the United States of America also feared the influx of the Chinese, especially on the Pacific Coast, and asked that "mission work among them be prosecuted with unceasing vigor, so that their coming among us may not occasion harm to American society, morals, and civil institutions, and that their conversion, by the blessing of God, to the Christian faith may be followed by their consecration to the work of evangelizing their native land."[25] To make newcomers both Christians and good citizens seemed to be but the two sides of the same coin to the evangelical mind of the time. But the increasing difficulty of accomplishing this in view of the trends in the size and source of immigration was arousing Protestant anxieties anew in the later decades of the century.

The vast increase in population played some part in the deepening undercurrents of unrest with the philosophy of individualism which was then so dominant in Protestant thought, especially in social and economic matters. Historians of social Christianity have described the hold of laissez-faire teaching on the nineteenth-century Protestant mind. Henry F. May has described the period of 1865–1876 as "the summit of complacency" during which Protestants generally found the prevailing individualistic social and economic philosophy entirely satisfactory.[26] There were many whose economic philosophy was primarily a gospel of grab, but those influenced by religious teaching were more inclined to state a gospel of wealth in which they added a doctrine of stewardship to the defense of private property and its acquisition by industry and thrift. Andrew Carnegie gave classic expression to the individualistic philosophy which millions of Americans accepted axiomatically in his famous 1889 essay, "Wealth."[27] How pervasive such views were is rather neatly illustrated by the views of a black boy growing up in the 1870's in western Massachusetts who later observed: "My general attitude toward property and income was that all who were willing to work could easily earn a living; that those who had property had earned it and deserved it and could use it as they wished; that poverty was the shadow of crime and connoted lack of thrift and shiftlessness. These were the current patterns of economic thought of the town of my boyhood."[28] W. E. B. Du Bois was later to change his mind, but that he held such views then is one illustration of how widespread they were. Yet the growth of vast concentrations of wealth, especially when they were flaunted in irresponsible ways in the face of poverty, troubled Christians in whom a sense of economy, thrift, and stewardship had been deeply ingrained.

Undercurrents of challenge to the popular gospel of wealth were already flowing among industrial workers, and among some intellectuals who believed that prevailing views were inadequate. The trend of labor to organize to fight for a larger share of the profits was, however, a disturbing reality for many Protestants. American Protestantism was predominantly rural and small-town in orientation and viewpoint; evangelicals usually thought of themselves as falling into that vague but vast grouping styled "the middle class." As James McCosh, president of Princeton, told the Evangelical Alliance in 1887: "This [class] supplies the great body of members of the American churches. Upon this class, or rather classes, the church depends for its sustenance, and the means of extending its usefulness at home and abroad. They constitute the bone and sinew of our churches, as they do of our country."[29] Middle-class and Protestant complacency was threatened by both the unrest of the laboring and poor, by the vast increase of wealth, especially when displayed conspicuously. Such developments posed disturbing challenges to the reigning philosophy of individualism. The road to a Christian America was seemingly becoming more difficult because of developments such as these.

Protestantism in prewar days had advanced significantly in an America predominantly rural and small-town, an America in which natives of British background were usually in control. But after the war the evangelical forces were faced with the spectacular growth of cities and the unprecedented expansion of industry which made them possible. The burgeoning of cities before the war had already presented Protestants with problems enough, but now they swelled to formidable proportions.[30] Of course, many Protestants raised on the farm were doing well in the cities; their rural virtues often stood them in good stead as they made their way. But they also found the cities increasingly dangerous; here gathered aliens, immigrants, and Roman Catholics who followed ways of life which often contrasted sharply with the Protestant style. In much Protestant preaching and writing, the cities were symbolized as places where all the elements that threatened Christian civilization were concentrated. Typical was a remark of a fraternal delegate to the General Conference of the Methodist Episcopal Church in 1884: "Chicago, Cincinnati, New Orleans, and New York, and I know not how many more cities, give too sad and mournful examples of wide-spread infidelity and immorality of many kinds." [31] Josiah Strong named the city as his seventh peril, the sum of the others, and emphatically "a serious menace to our civilization." [32]

As they reflected on Protestantism's internal divisions and tensions, and on the complex and threatening problems in thought and society, occasionally some Protestant leaders revealed their uneasiness and spoke of the possibility of decline. An Episcopal clergyman, William Reed Huntington, who has been especially remembered for his work for Christian unity, recognized (and deplored) that the trend of the time was against the continuation of a Protestant nation by voluntary means. He was not impressed with the frequent argument that America remained a Christian nation because of such things as Thanksgiving proclamations, chaplains in legislatures and the military, and pious mottoes on coins:

> These vestiges of Christianity, as we may call them, are printed on the sand. The tide has only to crawl up a few inches further to wash them clean away. There is nothing in the theory of the Republic that makes such usages an essential part of the national life. They rest for the most part upon the precarious tradition of colonial days; or if on statute law, what is statute law but the creation of temporary majorities? The moment popular opinion sets against them, all these relics of an established religion must go by the board. They are not the natural fruit of our system; they are but reminders of an old order of things that has passed away; fossils embedded in the rock on which the existing structure

> now stands. One by one they will probably be chipped out and set aside as curiosities.[33]

This was not only perceptive, it has proven to be prophetic. At the time, however, evangelical leaders seemed confident that popular opinion could be maintained in their favor; at times their very stridency suggests an underlying uncertainty. Indeed, a sense of a certain erosion of spiritual depth and direction creeps into official deliberations. Typical of many similar comments is the observation of the Southern Presbyterian "Narrative of the State of Religion" for 1875: "Nearly all the Presbyteries speak despondingly on the subject of family worship. This seems to be a general cause of sorrow in all parts of our Church."[34] An Episcopal bishop, reflecting on the state of the ministry in a book published in 1884, remarked: "Nothing relating to the Christian Religion is more characteristic of these closing years of the century than the allegation, pressed every day with increasing emphasis, that the influence of the Christian Priesthood on the thought and life of the time has not only changed in its form and direction, but that it has declined in bulk and force."[35] The bishop did not agree with the allegation, yet he had to admit that in the fields of education, charity, and the press the ministry was less influential than it once had been.

CRUSADING FOR CHRISTIAN CIVILIZATION

In spite of difficulties, however, the churches were triumphantly expanding numerically and were steadily gaining in the percentage of the population in their memberships. One estimate of the size of nine major Protestant denominational families found that the increase in church membership went from about four and a half million in 1860 to about twelve and a half million in 1890.[36] Church extension in the West was being carried out on an impressive scale. The Protestant forces were confident that they could resolve the inner tensions and deal with the challenges before them. They maintained as an important goal of their work the full Christianization of America. They believed that God would continue to lead his chosen people to fulfill their mission in the nation of destiny. In the difficult months of the first year of the war, Matthew Simpson, well-known Methodist bishop, promised a group of seminary students in Chicago that:

> Some of you may live to see the day when every land shall be Christian. . . . Some of you will live until there shall be missionary centers in every land; some of you may live till the brightness of millennial glory shall sweep over this earth and make it but the threshold of the greater glory on high.

America would have a special role in this consummation; as Simpson told a British audience in 1870: "God is making our land a kind of central spot for the whole earth. The eyes of the world are upon us." Simpson's colleague, Edward Thompson, painted a picture of a time not far distant when America would have a population of one hundred million, "without an adulterer, or a swearer, or a Sabbath-breaker, or an ingrate, or an apostate, or a backslider, or a slanderer; hundreds of thousands of homes without a prodigal, a quarrel, or a heart-burn, or a bitter tear." [37] Guided by visions such as these, evangelicals confidently carried their Bible-centered, revivalist, and missionary-minded interpretation of Christian faith as shaped in earlier periods into the postwar era. Though liberals and conservatives might disagree on the nature and dating of some of the biblical materials, they could agree on such a statement as the following, adopted by the Methodists in endorsing the American Bible Society (as most of the denominations did): "We receive the Holy Scriptures as the word of God given to be a lamp unto the feet, and a light unto the path of all men; the rule of faith and practice; its principles interpenetrating the best form of civil government, and molding the highest type of civilization." [38] Here was stated a central thesis in the Protestant crusade as it was then widely conceived; the interpenetration of biblical principles with the best form of civil government to mold the highest type of Christian civilization.

The revivalistic techniques which had been systematized earlier were continued throughout the Civil War, and in both sections of the reunited nation thereafter. "During the Civil War soldiers on both sides experienced well-known revivals of religious fervor," declared William A. Clebsch, "which issued in moral improvements such as observing the Sabbath, praying, Bible reading, eschewing profanity and strong drink and loose women, and keeping company with fellow Christians." [39] The great exponents of revivalism in the latter part of the century were Dwight L. Moody in the North and Samuel Porter Jones in the South. The story of Moody has been often told by both admirers and critics.[40] Whether one views Moody primarily as a great winner of converts to the faith or more of an energetic lay leader who rallied Protestant enthusiasm in a changing time, Winthrop S. Hudson's assessment fits: "A towering figure in the American religious scene during the last half of the nineteenth century, Moody more than any other single individual determined the religious climate of the country in the immediate post-war decade and he stood near the center of almost every agency devised by the churches to implement their task." [41] One of Moody's most insightful interpreters concluded that he "was effective because he appealed to the traditional and familiar in the religious realm." [42] When so much was changing, he called for the continuation of the familiar evangelical virtues and values for which many Americans had considerable nostalgia.

In the South, Sam Jones, reformed alcoholic turned Methodist evangelist, rose to fame in the 1880's. He rallied his converts to join with established Christian forces in a crusade against sin in society. He sought "to encourage paternalistic charity on the one hand, and on the other to impose the moral code of rural

Georgia upon every individual in the country whether he wanted it or not." [43] Both Moody and Jones were but the most conspicuous among hundreds of revivalists. It was not only the professional evangelists, however, who perpetuated revivalism. Hundreds of pastors and hosts of laymen were thoroughly revivalistic in their approach. Though changes in the revivalistic pattern can be discerned in this period, essentially it was not greatly different from the system worked out in the days of Finney, with a characteristically oversimplified, moralistic interpretation of Christian faith. As Perry Miller summed it up:

> After 1860, American Protestantism was called upon to confront the forces of a new age—of industrialism, urbanization, economic conflict. To begin with, it had only the armory of weapons with which it had been equipped by the Great Revival—concepts of sublimity, of the heart, of benevolence, of the millennium. But above all it was committed to the absolute conviction that, amid a multitude of forms, revivalistic piety was the primary force in maintaining "the grand unity of national strength." [44]

To that list of concepts, I would add missions; when the denominations gathered in assembly, the missionary purpose and concern for the spread of Christianity everywhere was articulated constantly in many ways. For example, in the words of a Southern Baptist report, "contemplating the salvation of the millions of China, it presents to us the *true* idea of the sublime." [45] The missionary zeal of those years sent workers into hundreds of locations in the swiftly opening West at the same time that work in foreign places was being expanded. In such efforts, evangelical bodies North and South, white and black, great and small felt themselves engaged in a mighty thrust. Just prior to the Civil War, Henry Highland Garnet, Presbyterian minister and black abolitionist, had founded the African Civilization Society, the avowed purpose of which was to bring about "the civilization and christianization" of Africa.[46] The delegates of the Seventeenth General Conference of the United Brethren were told in 1877 that "as a branch of the great family of evangelical workers, we must perform our part." [47] Eight years later, fraternal greetings were brought to the brethren by a representative of the Evangelical Association, S. P. Streng. The recorder inserted audience reactions:

> Your church and ours are both missionary churches, I had almost said, or we are nothing. [Yes, yes.] Missionary enterprise is our very life. [Truth.] We might as well die if we do not do missionary work.[48]

More attention was given in the records of the national conventions of the evangelical denominations to missions than to any other single topic.

An important part of the missionary resources of the time were devoted to Indian work. Here the intimate interrelationship between the religious and the civilizing aspects of Protestant work showed with particular clarity. Discussing Indian missions in the 1860–1900 period, R. Pierce Beaver states:

> The missionary work of this period was carried out on the same basic assumption which had been held every since the days of the Mayhews and John Eliot in the 17th century, namely, that "evangelization" and "civilization" were the two primary goals and that they must be effected simultaneously. The inevitable products of evangelization was believed to be civilization, the Gospel bringing the desire for and persistent effort toward the Anglo-American culture which was the very flowering of the Gospel. Progress in civilization, on the other hand, was expected to lead the Indian to the acceptance of Christianity.[49]

Overwhelmingly, mission work was done by voluntary means, primarily through denominational channels. Evangelical forces rejoiced in religious freedom, and wanted to make the most of the opportunities it provided to win the nation and the world to Protestant Christianity.

One interesting exception to this general pattern took place in these years, when President Grant, troubled by corruption and incompetence on the part of Indian agencies, decided to give all agencies to religious denominations to be carried out as missionary work. This "peace policy" was opposed by the "Indian Ring" (a political group believed by many to dominate the federal Indian Service), who were given only about a tenth of the agencies. Many Protestants also objected to the way an allocation for a particular area was given exclusively to a certain denomination, forcing others who had been at work there for years to withdraw. The heated issue of the public financing of the sectarian schools which were conducted under this policy finally led to its defeat, and the last appropriations were made in 1899.[50] Thereupon all missions were conducted along voluntary lines, consistently with the principles of the separation of church and state.

As Protestants reaffirmed their revivalistic, missionary thrust in the effort to win converts and to Christianize American life amid the changing realities of the latter nineteenth century, they were forced to use approaches and methods unknown to their predecessors. Seeking to affirm a continuity with them, and stilling fears of those who felt they were being swept along too fast, they continued to talk about the importance of the Christian Sabbath. For them, the continuation of Sunday observance was a sign that the Christian civilization which meant so much to them was still publicly recognized. The first session of the newly created National Council of the Congregational Churches passed a strong resolution which opened with these words: "Amidst the multiplied activities and enlarging enterprises which engross the mind and conserve the strength of our citizens, the rest of the Sabbath is indispensable to the continuance of health, virtue, and Christian principle in this nation."[51] So it went in church after church; for example, the Committee on the State of the Church declared to the satisfaction of Northern Methodists in 1884 that "a proper recognition of the sanctity of the holy Sabbath is one of the chief cornerstones in the foundation of the Church and of our Christian civilization." [52]

It was increasingly difficult, however, to secure what evangelicals deemed to be the proper recognition of the Sabbath in those years. The war itself contributed to the decline, as was recognized during the struggle itself. "The *desecration of the holy Sabbath* is another crying sin of our land, which we fear abounds in our army," mourned a pastoral letter of the Presbyterian Church in the Confederate States.[53] Later analyses of the problem added other factors in accounting for the decline. A report to the Congregationalists in 1877 summarized the situation in a long sentence: "Owing to the demoralization consequent on the late civil war, and the laxity of all moral restraints growing inevitably from such social disturbances; owing to the introduction and acceptance of trans-atlantic theories and practices; owing to the mixed character of our great population, representing too many divergent types of thought, to say nothing of the deep-seated, subtle, and pervasive opposition of our fallen nature to such claims as emphasize the authority and sovereign ownership of God,—Sabbath desecration has assumed alarming proportions, and summons the churches of Christ to a new and vigorous campaign for its repression." [54]

Neglect of Sabbath observance was most frequently blamed on immigrants. "Nearly all the Presbyterial Narratives speak of the frightful prevalence of Sabbath desecration," declared the first "Annual Narrative of the State of Religion" to be produced by the reunited Presbyterian Church in the United States of America, the predominantly northern body that was formed as Old School and New School united in 1869–1870. "This vice grows with the growth of immigration from the nations of Europe." [55] There were many diatribes against the "continental

Sabbath" with its relaxed ways, its music, feasting, and drinking.

Paradoxically, one of the ablest statements on Sabbath observance was made by an "immigrant," Swiss-born, German-educated Philip Schaff, prominent theologian and church historian. Speaking before the National Sabbath Convention in 1863, he dealt with the critical dilemma of Protestants who wanted the general observance of the Sabbath without violating their principles of religious freedom and the separation of church and state. He explained that:

> The Anglo-American theory makes more account of the distinction between the *religious* and the *civil* Sabbath than the Continental, and lays greater stress on the necessity of the latter. It regards the civil Sabbath as essential for public morals and the self-preservation of the state.

On the basis of this distinction he argued that the Sabbath laws do not militate against religious freedom any more than the laws upholding monogamy. On the contrary, they actually are a support to civil and religious freedom, he argued, for freedom without law is licentiousness and ruin to any people. He maintained that:

> Our separation of church and state rests on mutual respect and friendship, and is by no means a separation of the nation from Christianity. The religious Sabbath cannot and ought not to be enforced by law; for all worship and true religion must be the free and voluntary homage of the heart. But the civil Sabbath can and ought to be maintained and protected by legislation; and a Christian community has a natural right to look to their government for the protection of their Sabbath as well as for the protection of their persons and property.

Schaff was too good an historian not to know that the Sabbath tradition that had developed in Britain was more rigorous than most other historic Sabbatarian positions, but nevertheless he insisted that:

> it is none the less true and scriptural in all its essential features. It is one of the noblest contributions which Great Britain has made to the cause of evangelical truth and piety. Far from being a relapse, it is a real progress in the cause of Christianity and civilization; . . . It is an essential part of American Christianity and morality, and one of the strongest common bonds which united the different Protestant denominations.[56]

His was perhaps the clearest articulation of the position which most evangelicals accepted.

Many defenses of Sunday observance in this period emphasized the secular value of the day of rest, though obviously were concerned also to protect spiritual values. George W. Bacon, for example, Congregational pastor in New Jersey, preached a series of sermons on the Sabbath, arguing that its observance was being accepted by many Christian nations and will triumph with the kingdom. Leonard W. Bacon, also a Congregational minister, later republished his brother's sermons together with some addresses of his own, occasioned chiefly by the sailing of an excursion steamer on Sunday at Norwich, Connecticut. The Christian sees the laws for Sunday observance in religious terms, he argued, but every citizen should see it as a good civil law. When the Christian as citizen seeks to uphold the civil law, he is not enforcing religion but merely what the law provides—a weekly civil holiday. "And it is not your duty as a citizen to enforce God's law upon your neighbors, but to sustain human law, which God requires men to obey, and citizens to sustain, and magistrates to execute."[57]

Though many of the devout continued to observe the Sabbath rigorously, and in some areas rather strict laws were maintained or passed, on the whole there was a decline in Sunday observance, especially in the North.[58] From within the citadels of evangelical leadership, however, the decline was resisted, and the very vehemence of the counterattack shows how difficult it was becoming to maintain the Puritan Sabbath even among those who were supposedly its supporters. M. C. Briggs, for example, strongly indicted the decay of Sunday practices within many churches:

> The indifferences of multitudes of the professed friends of the Sabbath; the ignorance of other multitudes of its grounds and claims; the puerile pretenses for secularizing the day; the facility of guilty compromises; the pompous formality; the pride of display; the sensationalism miscalled "preaching"; the needless and thoughtless Sunday travel, the self-accommodating ministerial exchanges; the Sunday pleasure seeking; the feeble excuses offered for voluntary absence from the house of God; the social visiting; the open profanation of the Lord's day by excursion-trains to camp-meetings, and advertised preaching in places of irreligious resort; the putting forth of the doctrine of expediency, or precedent, or temporal benefits, or apostolic example, or patristic usage, as the only "authority" for Sabbath-keeping—these are counts in an indictment of many church members, and some ministers, whose example is a thousand times more damaging to the Church's influence and the Sabbath's proper sanctification than Saturday-Sabbathism and open-mouthed infidelity in all their shapes and names and moods and tenses.[59]

Though Sunday practices were changing, the Sabbath dogmas were maintained by the churches as part of their understanding of what Christian civilization was. Their stance was important in maintaining Sunday legally as a day apart, though defenses increasingly shifted to considerations of general health and well-being.

While the Sunday observance struggle was cast largely in defensive terms, the temperance crusade in the years after the Civil War took on a new militancy. The prewar temperance movement had sought to win the evangelical faithful to total abstinence, and also to secure laws for the restriction or prohibition of the sale of alcohol wherever possible. In more than a dozen states, there was some kind of temperance legislation before 1860. The war interrupted this reform movement as it had others, so that in some states legislation was withdrawn, and liquor traffic increased.

The renewal of the temperance crusade was marked by the organization of the Prohibition party in 1869 and the Woman's Christian Temperance Union (W.C.T.U.) in 1874. The churches soon began to stress temperance with new vigor. The northern Presbyterians found in 1875 that there was "unusual" interest in the cause throughout their church. "This subject is evidently looming up to one of great importance in the Church," the annual narrative on religion declared, "as there is scarcely a Presbytery that does not allude to it." [60] Two years later they found the continuing excitement a cause for rejoicing and unanimously adopted a resolution which characteristically interpreted "temperance" to mean total abstinence: "With profound gratitude and joy to God, we record the increased interest and activity everywhere apparent in the cause of Temperance; we hail the revival of interest in this subject as only another manifestation of the quickened concern in all things, religious and moral, with which God is baptizing our land. Already hundreds of thousands have taken the pledge of total abstinence." [61]

The Congregationalists found the cause especially appropriate, for "the churches of the living God are themselves the direct and divinely appointed agencies for all such work," and acting in their own appropriate ways should "be found in the front rank in this particular and vital contest for righteousness." [62] As is well known, Methodists both northern and southern were especially concerned about this cause. Northern Methodists insisted that "complete legal prohibition of the traffic in alcoholic drinks is the duty of civil government," for such traffic is "the most gigantic evil of the age in which we live, and its overthrow should be sought by all good citizens, without regard to denomination, party, or nationality."[63] Southern Baptists were somewhat slower to join the temperance bandwagon, for the movement did run counter to some well-established southern customs. But once they became convinced that drunkenness was the cardinal sin of the land, they threw their growing weight into the movement; "by the mid-1880's total prohibition was *the* Baptist position."[64]

When evangelicals gathered to discuss common problems, temperance was often stressed. At the 1887 gathering called by the Evangelical Alliance, Robert S. MacArthur, pastor of the Calvary Baptist Church of New York, delivered a powerful attack on the saloon. "It does not hesitate at murder as one of its instruments," he exclaimed. "It stalks abroad through the land, destroying all that is noblest in our civilization and holiest in our religion."[65] On the same day, J. F. Hurst, Methodist bishop of Buffalo, showed something of the evangelical proneness to exaggeration and overly simple solutions in his remarks:

> Let the saloon once take its departure from the American soil, and there will be such a destruction of the separating forces of our polyglot population, such a clearing up of the misty atmosphere which leads the employer and the wage-earner to believe that each is the other's foe, such an appreciation by the unevangelized of the beauty and force of Christianity, such a flowing of the multitude into the Christian churches, that the treasury of every church in the land will be over-strained, to provide even temporary places of worship for the millions who are controlled and absorbed by a new affection.[66]

The tendency of crusaders to see their particular opponent as the last enemy to be defeated before the glorious triumph of the right is almost classically illustrated in this characteristic comment. There was a high degree of evangelical consensus on temperance.

Joseph R. Gusfield has advanced and richly illustrated the

thesis that rurally oriented, predominantly native, and Protestant elements in the nation were committed to a culture in which self-control, industriousness, and impulse renunciation were accepted and praised. In the latter nineteenth century this way of life was being challenged, and the status of those who adhered to this way was being threatened. The temperance drive, Gusfield affirms, was an effort of the challenged groups to show that their way was still the dominant, publicly recognized one, to win as many as possible to that way—and to force the issue on those who would not see the light. In a summation, he says:

> Several factors of nineteenth-century religious and economic change produced problems of deep interest to a segment of middle-class Americans for whom abstinence was an accepted and honored part of their culture. Temperance activities were part of the ways in which they reacted to the development of a large number of underprivileged, low-status persons in the society. Within this context total abstinence was a doctrine of change and assimilation of the nonconformer into middle-class life, an expression of the terms by which social and economic success had been gained by the Temperance adherent and could be gained by the reformed drinker. In this fashion the total abstainer bolstered his feeling that his culture dominated the ideals of his society—through Temperance, he tried to incorporate alien cultures and deviant actions into his framework of values.[67]

Much of Gusfield's work is based on a study of the W.C.T.U. He shows that after the election of Frances Willard, noted feminist and reformer, to the presidency of that organization in 1879, the union was sympathetic to many of the more advanced reform movements of the time. "The progressivism of the movement lay in part in its concern for the industrial and urban human refuse, the poor and underprivileged whose very presence clashed with its view of a moral society." [68] The prohibitionists *were* concerned about the urban poor; characteristically they hoped to "raise" them into self-sufficiency and respectability.

The temperance cause was a very important aspect of the struggle to maintain the patterns of Christian civilization in America, and was seen by the churches as a promising religious renewal movement. "The late temperance revival has been a revival of religion," [69] declared the Congregationalists, while the Presbyterians found that "the religious quickenings of communities prepared the way for the Temperance reform on Christian principles." [70] Temperance was an increasingly important part of the strategy of Christianization in this period; the eagerness to enact its program into law reveals again something of the onesidedness of the evangelical understanding of freedom. To them, of course, a purified, reformed, Christian America must be a dry America; those who could not or would not see that were regarded as trapped by the evil forces to be overcome if the country were to fulfill her destiny as a Christian nation.

The crusade for women's rights has been interpreted in an able study as primarily a secular movement in which women were seeking their full rights of political citizenship.[71] Though religious leaders were enlisted on both sides of the struggle, the work of Alan P. Grimes has made it clear that there was an affinity between the evangelical and suffrage movements in the late nineteenth century, especially because of the concern of many women with temperance. Seeking to explain why the first woman suffrage laws emerged in the West (in Wyoming and Utah territories in 1869), Grimes explains that "there was a marked tendency, especially in the West, for supporters of prohibition to support woman suffrage as an effective means of achieving their goal." He quotes Susan B. Anthony, who reported that the supporters of woman suffrage in an unsuccessful campaign in Colorado in 1877 "were native-born white men, temperance men, cultivated, broad, generous, just men, men who think." The opponents, she felt sure, were foreigners of many backgrounds, "educated under monarchical principles." [72] Though the feminist movement seems not to have been a significant part of the quest for a Christian America, there were those who did include it, particularly because of their interest in temperance. In the South however, the feminist movement was generally resisted.[73]

The campaigns for Sabbath observance and temperance were conspicuous and controversial at the time because they emphasized distinctive and publicly visible aspects of the drive for a Christian civilization against practices deemed alien to that goal. They conjoined the characteristic evangelical emphasis on personal morality with concern for certain specific laws. The churches were also concerned with many other moral issues, such as dishonesty, profanity, gambling, dancing, smoking, the weakening of marriage ties, and the frequency of divorce. These concerns were often stressed in preaching and in popular evangelical literature. In evangelical teaching such issues were customarily treated as matters of personal morality, as part of the churches' regular work of helping to mold a law-abiding citizenry. Moral standards as an inseparable part of the Christian life were stressed in the work of local congregations, in the curricula of Sunday schools, in the pages of religious publications, in the ministries of itinerant evangelists, and in the work of missionaries in the West and overseas.[74] It was all part of the work of Christianizing a civilization, though it was less spectacular and less controversial than the crusades for the Sabbath and for temperance. In these, Protestants believed that they were defending a Protestant civilization against the forces that would destroy it, forces growing in strength through the new immigration coming from southern and eastern Europe in unprecedented waves.

Through its many branches, activities, and crusades, Protestantism deeply influenced the culture of its time. Herbert G. Gutman has put it well: "Protestantism in Gilded Age America permeated the social structure and the value system of the nation more deeply and in different ways than heretofore emphasized by that era's historians." [75] But as the churches sought to Christianize American civilization in this difficult and changing period, they themselves were undergoing some significant shifts of emphasis.

IV

"The Religion of Civilization" (1860–1890)

> Christianity must show itself the religion of civilization, competent by its vital force in a savage community to quicken progress to civilization, competent in civilization to stimulate, purify, guide and ennoble it.
>
> Samuel Harris
>
> *The Kingdom of Christ on Earth*

The divisions of Protestantism in the years following the Civil War have already been mentioned, but there was also a new interest in unity among Christians in those years. Before the war Protestants had worked together primarily as individuals in the various voluntary societies, many of which had a distinctly evangelical character. Though some societies declined and new ones were born, in general they continued to provide important channels for common Protestant cooperation and action. The vast expansion of nondenominational Sunday school work, in which lay leadership was especially prominent, was one of the most significant developments in evangelical voluntaryism in this period.[1]

There was also a growing concern for closer relationships among the churches themselves. The exchange of fraternal messengers between churches was on the increase; frequently such visitors gave public expression to the longing for some kind of larger unity among the denominations. "Indeed, 'union' is fast becoming the watchword of Christendom," declared James K.

Nichols of the Methodist Protestant Church to the General Conference of the Southern Methodist Church in 1870.[2] Characteristically, each church usually revealed its own distinctive stance in speaking of unity. The Episcopal Bishops' Pastoral Letter for 1883, for example, disclosed their concern for the historic episcopate when they declared:

> Thinking and studying men who are also believers are everywhere looking for grounds of Christian unity. It is a glorious hope of our time. We hold that the vantage ground is with us, because experience, Christ's words and right reason affirm together that unity must appear if at all by growth from a historic root, not by a construction or welding of platforms.[3]

Some thought wholly in terms of larger spiritual unity while others were interested in organizational interrelations and mergers, but generally there was increasing interest in "Christian union."

Interdenominational agencies which would be under the control of church bodies and in which churches would participate regularly and officially were to come later, but the need for such agencies was clearly manifesting itself. The Presbyterian Church in the United States circulated letters to various communions in 1882, seeking some kind of concerted effort on behalf of Sunday observance. There was recognition that the combined influences of the churches would be necessary in order to make significant public impact: "The Assembly would not recommend any overture, either as citizens or as ecclesiastics, to the Congress of the United States, until the cooperation of the great bulk of the Evangelical Churches of the whole country may be obtained."[4] How to obtain the effective cooperation of churches for stated tasks was to take decades to work out, but the discussion of the need for greater unity was intensified in this period.

Those who expressed the longing for fuller expressions of unity often based their positions on theological grounds: the followers of the one God made known in Jesus Christ should make their unity more visible in practice. It was also clear that the external pressure of the times was a factor in the new interest. As Roswell D. Hitchcock, professor at Union Theological Seminary in New York, put it before the gathering of the Evangelical Alliance in 1873: "Infidel bugles are sounding in front of us, Papal bugles are sounding behind us. And evangelical Protestants are not standing shoulder to shoulder. It would be idle to say that we are not alarmed." He expressed the hope of many evangelicals in saying: "We assert the unity of Protestantism, in spite of its manifold diversities and divisions." He noted that not only was Protestantism menaced but Christianity itself. He was somewhat in advance of the Protestant opinion of his day in hoping for "spiritual recovery" in Roman Catholicism, and in affirming that "we set forth Christian unity as the goal toward which not merely all Protestants, but all Christians, are tending."[5] In general, however, evangelical resistance to Catholicism was only a little diminished, and Catholics were not usually included in the visions of Christian union.[6] Unity in Protestant terms seemed challenging and difficult enough.

That much of the growing interest in unity was closely related to the determination to maintain and extend Christian civilization was often stated. Richard S. Storrs, well-known Congregational pastor of Brooklyn, summed it up in a paper prepared for a large gathering of churchmen in Washington called by the American branch of the Evangelical Alliance in 1887: "But if all who love the truth and the Master, who value righteousness, who feel in themselves the impulsions of charity, and who are determined to make our Christian civilization secure and permanent, and to perfect its beauty, shall combine—as they may—to dissipate error, to conquer vice, to subdue the forces of misrule, to extend the range of pure religion, and to further that magnificent welfare which education, virtue and religion subserve, then the energy of their cooperative purpose will infallibly be recognized, its power will be felt, and evil influences will widely cower and shrink before it."[7] Such a phrase as "the energy of their cooperative purpose" aptly caught the mood of Protestants who sincerely believed in maintaining the separation between religion and politics, between church and state, and yet who sought and expected to have their views prevail in the culture of their time.

THE KINGDOM OF GOD AND CHRISTIAN CIVILIZATION

Restatements of the doctrine of the kingdom of God provided theological grounding for the increased interest in Christian unity, especially in relation to the church's role in civilization. For example, an influential, full-scale treatment of the kingdom motif was provided by Samuel Harris, Dwight Professor of Systematic Theology in Yale College, who lectured on the theme of "The Kingdom of Christ on Earth" to the students at Andover Seminary in 1870. Most of the lectures were published in *Bibliotheca Sacra*, then a widely circulated theological journal. In 1874 they appeared in book form. Harris was a solid, comprehensive interpreter of the Protestant tradition; he had been influenced to some extent by Horace Bushnell, whose theological work was to be appropriated especially by the liberals. Harris related his own thought about the kingdom of God to the millennial hope which had been so important in American Protestant life. "The idea of his kingdom on earth, and the expectation of its progress and triumph in fulfillment of the prophecy and promise of the gospel, have become familiar elements of human thought and determinant forces in human action," he affirmed. "The sublime idea of the conversion of the world to Christ has become so common as to cease to awaken wonder. Its realization is the object throughout Christendom of systematic, persistent, and energetic action, and elicits every year heroic consecration and self-sacrifice." [8]

The coming of the kingdom of God on earth would be a complete solution of the problem of man's history and destiny, insisted Harris. Like most of those who were articulating similar views, he never identified the kingdom with any particular organizations. The kingdom is organizing rather than organized; it is an organizing principle which produces organizations. It is "the life which creates the organization, penetrates and purifies also the family and the state, renovates individuals, and blooms and fructifies in Christian civilizations; and these also are its historical manifestations. . . . In the variously organized churches of history, without doubt, the life has been revealed and organized. But no one has been the only and complete outgrowth and manifestation of the life." [9] The coming of the kingdom will mean progress in civilization and in Christian unity. But there must be no confusion between the organizations of government and of religion; they must remain separate. This does not mean, however, that "in making, adjudicating, and executing laws, government is exempt from obeying the law of God. Government has no right to shut out the light of Christianity, and go back and take up heathen morality." [10] Future progress toward the kingdom comes as individual members of society become freely conformed to the spirit and law of Christ. Christianity itself is perfect and cannot be transcended, Harris taught, though he admitted that men too often fail to apprehend it fully and that its organizational expressions in the past have been deficient.

Harris spoke with great confidence of the triumph of the kingdom and the full Christianization of civilization. He specifically criticized the literalistic premillennialism that had been characteristic of the Millerite movement and which was then being advocated among adventist and some other conservative Protestant groups. He associated himself with the postmillennialist view that the second advent will come after, not before, the triumph of the kingdom of God on earth. There was fairly wide consensus in the evangelical denominations on that point at that time.[11] Timothy Smith concluded that "the most significant millenarian doctrines of the mid-nineteenth century were not those of William Miller, but those which grew out of evangelical Protestantism's crusade to Christianize the land." Indeed, Smith found that the chief result of the Millerite excitement in the denominations was to hasten by reaction the acceptance of postmillennial views by Baptists and Presbyterians. Though other views had some following, which were to find resurgence later, "by and large . . . the peace of 1865 found leaders of the revivalistic sects consecrated to the task of building a Christian commonwealth in America." [12]

The majority of evangelicals were quite prepared to rely fully on voluntary means in working toward the Christian commonwealth, though a few, especially among the more conservative, sought guarantees of the nation's Christian character by constitutional amendment. In 1864 a convention of evangelicals in Cincinnati launched the National Reform Association, the purpose of which was "to maintain existing Christian features in the American government, and to secure such an amendment to the Constitution of the United States as will indicate that this is a Christian nation, and will place all the Christian laws, institutions and usages of our government on an undeniable legal basis in the fundamental law of the land." [13] When a small, conservative denomination, the United Brethren in Christ, endorsed this program, they quite naturally justified it by reference to the doctrine of the kingdom of God. They pledged their sympathy, their prayers, and their "active cooperation in this effort to Christianize our political life, and look forward with faith to the time 'when the kingdoms of this world will become the kingdom of our Lord and of his Christ.' " [14] Significantly, evangelicals of many shades of theological opinion found the doctrine of the kingdom of God on earth highly appealing.

The doctrine was much emphasized by the liberal elements which were then emerging within evangelicalism. Early evangelical liberals were influenced by the currents of Ritschlian thought then so conspicuous in Germany, where some of them had studied. They found congenial the Ritschlian tendency to link religion and civilization as bearers of ideals and values which overcome the downward pull in man, thus advancing the kingdom. Liberals were to put a progressively interpreted concept of the kingdom of God central in their theology, but characteristically the doctrine was stated in terms broad enough to include those of various theological positions. Such men as Harris and others like him were not crusading for liberalism but were trying to state views that represented an evangelical consensus. Similarly, Henry Boynton Smith, prominent Presbyterian theologian and president of Union Theological Seminary, saw the course of history as "the record of the progress of the kingdom of God, intermingling with and acting upon all the other interests of the human race, and shaping its destiny. . . . In the whole history of man we can trace the course of one shaping, o'ermastering, and progressive power, before which all others have bowed, and that is the spiritual kingdom of God, having for its object the redemption of the man from the ruins of the apostasy."[15] The kingdom idea was in many respects a spiritualized and idealized restatement of the search for a specifically Christian society in an age of freedom and progress. Protestants with somewhat different theological perspectives concerning the kingdom of God could nevertheless find sufficient in common to work together for its coming.

PROTESTANTISM AND THE PUBLIC SCHOOLS

Perhaps at no point did the evangelical consensus which bridged denominational and theological gulfs show itself more clearly in action than in the common effort to maintain the public schools as part of the strategy for a Christian America.

Protestants were generally agreed that the elementary schools need not be under the control of particular denominations, for their role was to prepare young Americans for participation in the broadly Christian civilization toward which all evangelicals were working. David Tyack has reported that educational leaders in Oregon said in 1884 that "there *must* be a *religious* basis to our educational system; an acknowledgement of our religious obligations, and the natural and common presentation of incentives to piety, must have their place in the common school, or it utterly fails of its mission, and will soon go to way of all effete institutions. . . . This *does not* involve either cant or sectarianism." [16]

Mark Sullivan once examined the seeming contradiction between the inclusion of rigorous provisions for the separation of church and state in various state constitutions with the actual religious tone in the schools in the later nineteenth and early twentieth centuries. "What happened was that the States carried on a system of education in which practically all the traditions and most of the influences were religious," he declared. "The spirit of the schools was religious and continued so. So deeply embedded was the spirit of religion in the common schools of America that nothing short of a revolution, or a trend immensely long, could have uprooted it." [17] He illustrated the generalization by quoting from textbooks in use in the period. Warren's *Common School Geography*, for example, included these words: "Christian nations are more powerful, and much more advanced in knowledge than any others. Their power also is continually increasing. . . . There is little doubt that in the course of a few generations the Christian religion will be spread over the greater part of the earth." Sullivan concluded: "To the child of the '70's and '80's, the spirit of religion in the schools gave a sense of definite relation to the universe, of eternity of personality; caused his mind to dwell frequently on things of the spirit, and gave him a personal sense of spirituality; caused him to have reverence. Most important of all, it provided him with comfort-bringing definiteness of rules in the otherwise difficult area of right and wrong—in short, supplied him with standards." [18] Evangelical leaders saw no reason why the schools should not continue to be the bearers of Christian civilization, unofficially, of course, but effectively.

In the field of education the conflicts between Protestants and Catholics came more quickly to the surface than in many other areas. Though some of the old accusations and charges against the Roman Catholic Church were regularly repeated in Protestant circles, on the whole there seems to have been some abatement of the intense hatreds of the 1840's, especially after 1876. Yet Protestants did not recognize the Roman Catholic Church as an evangelical church, and maintained a steady polemic against "Romanism." They especially distrusted the alleged subservience of Catholics to their priests, and the predominance of the Irish influence in the hierarchy.[19] Many shared the view expressed by Daniel Dorchester before the Washington meeting of the Evangelical Alliance: "We believe that the Roman Catholic Church is inimical to the best progress of society, and in direct antagonism to the historic religion of the nation—the religion of the Holy Scriptures." [20] The Catholic population was steadily rising, of course, and Catholic parents in ever greater numbers were discomforted by the Protestant tone of many school systems. Catholic criticisms of such systems and their determination, expressed at the Third Plenary Council at Baltimore in 1884, to build a parochial school system that would include every parish touched Protestant anxieties. The Congregationalists adopted a report which exclaimed: "We cannot abandon our public-school system on account of the difficulties with infidels or with Roman Catholics." [21] The Bible must be read in the schools, they insisted —let the Douay version be used for the Catholic pupils. The Methodist bishops saw it this way:

> The combined and persistent efforts making [sic] by the Bishops and priests of the Romish Church to destroy our

> system of common schools, attract much public attention. The general diffusion of virtue and intelligence among the people furnish the only sure basis on which civil and religious liberty can rest. It becomes us, therefore, cordially to unite with all intelligent Christians and all true patriots to cherish the free institutions bequeathed to us by our Protestant forefathers, in giving an intelligent, firm, and earnest support to the civil authorities in maintaining, extending and rendering more perfect and efficient our system of primary education, until all the people throughout the land shall share in its benefits and participate in its blessings.[22]

Criticism of the public schools seemed to most Protestants to eat away at the foundations of the Christian America they envisioned.

The anti-Catholic spirit manifested itself at other points, of course. On the mission fields, domestic and foreign, Catholics and Protestants faced each other, and deeper feelings surfaced. "We have set up the missionary standard in Hayti," declared B. F. Lee, president of Wilberforce University, and fraternal delegate of the African Methodist Episcopal Church to the Methodist General Conference in 1880, "to assist in rescuing that gem of the ocean from the hand of Romanism." [23] Oftentimes it was papalism, or ultramontanism, or "jesuitism" that was singled out for attack—if only such forces as these could be defeated, the argument ran, then millions of Roman Catholics would no longer be so misled. So Frederick A. Noble asked for the support of the National Council of Congregational Churches in a new effort for the spiritual conquest of the West. He described the enemy in these words: "Selfish, subtle, determined, unscrupulous, this Jesuitical form of Romanism which holds New Mexico and large parts of adjacent regions in its grasp is the same foe to learning and liberty and progress, and to all the rational and moral forces which go to the making up of an advanced civilization, that it was when Pascal stripped away its pretensions and uncovered its hideousness, and smote it till it reeled with his withering scorn." [24] Noble was seeking aid for building "Christian Schools for the New West." Here evangelicals could find common cause in spite of sectional, theological, and denominational differences.

A CONCEPT AND ITS CONSEQUENCES: ANGLO-SAXONISM

As immigration brought in increasing numbers of persons from Central and Southern Europe, there was a strong tendency for American Protestants of the major denominations to stress their identity with the English-speaking, Anglo-Saxon world. When Samuel Harris discussed the role of human agency in the advance of the kingdom of God, he insisted that some are especially commissioned for the glorious work. "God has always acted by chosen peoples," he declared. "To the English-speaking people more than to any other the world is now indebted for the propagation of Christian ideas and Christian civilization." [25] Americans drew from many current English writings on Anglo-Saxon destinies, often characteristically adding that the highest expression of Anglo-Saxon civilization would be in the United States.[26]

Another Samuel Harris, the Episcopal Bishop of Michigan, expressed the theme of the identity of American Protestantism with Anglo-Saxonism to the applause of the Evangelical Alliance's Washington meeting of 1887. The reporter noted the enthusiasm of the audience as Bishop Harris proclaimed that:

> the consistency of the divine purpose in establishing our evangelical civilization here is signally illustrated in the fact that it was primarily confided to the keeping of the Anglo-Saxon race. By reason of its peculiar characteristics and its training in history, that race was singularly fitted for its task: endowed with a certain race conservatism and a certain persistency of race type, it has sturdily maintained itself, even to the present time. Refusing to depart from its own type, it

> has compelled other peoples to conform to that type and constrained them to accept its institutions, to speak its language, to obey its laws.

Therefore, Harris argued, in spite of the "enormous immigration," American civilization has mainly continued to be an Anglo-Saxon civilization, preserving old Anglo-Saxon ideas of home and school. "And so," he concluded, "it has come to pass that, although our nation is composite, it continues to be homogenous, obeying the laws of Alfred and speaking the language of Shakespeare and Milton." [27]

James M. King, Methodist minister from New York, set the same theme in world perspective: "Christianized Anglo-Saxon blood, with its love of liberty, its thrift, its intense and persistent energy and personal independence, is the regnant force in this country; and that is a most pregnant fact, because the concededly most important lesson in the history of modern civilization is, that God is using the Anglo-Saxon to conquer the world for Christ by dispossessing feeble races, and assimilating and molding others." [28]

Protestant leaders felt quite confident of their ability to assimilate non-Anglo-Saxon immigrants. An "Americanized" Philip Schaff argued that "foreign immigration from the different nationalities and churches of *Europe* may for a while retard, but cannot arrest, and will ultimately benefit, our civilization and Christianity by widening it and infusing into it the best elements of the Old World and of past ages." [29] While some were concerned about restricting immigration, others were confident that Anglo-Saxon leadership, the produce of centuries of development, had nothing to fear in a cosmopolitan civilization.

The stress on the leadership role of white, native, Anglo-Saxons within Protestantism helped to bring southern and northern evangelicals into closer harmony. Southern Baptists in 1890 were expressing views widely prevalent throughout the nation in saying "that the religious destiny of the world is lodged in the hands of the English-speaking people. To the Anglo-Saxon race God seems to have committed the enterprise of the world's salvation." [30] The southern white Christians had long since come to the conclusion that the races must be kept strictly apart; the influential Jeremiah B. Jeter, for example, in the *Religious Herald* of Richmond in 1869 had said that to admit Negroes into churches on an equal basis would lead to "the mongrelization of our noble Anglo-Saxon race." [31] The passage of the years did not modify these attitudes. The paternalistic and haughty attitudes of white Christians toward blacks often found expression; the role of the Anglo-Saxon was magnified as that of the Negro was minimized or denied. David Reimers has supplied much documentation; in 1889 a writer in the *Southern Presbyterian* said that the Negro "needs most emphatically the *influence of pure gospel truth;* its regulating, restraining, purifying, elevating power. . . . He has natural defects, and perhaps some physical disadvantages, as well as intellectual; but his chief disability is moral. He needs higher, purer, and stronger principle." A Southern Baptist Committee on Missions to the Colored People put it even more bluntly: "Their ignorance, superstitions, and immoralities tell upon us. . . . We must Christianize and educate them in self-defense, and all the higher motives of religion should impel us to cultivate this home field." [32]

In the North, some voices called for recognition of the Negro as an equal. Gilbert Haven, a Methodist bishop who had labored for the abolition of slavery, predicted that the "complexion at which we now profess to revolt we shall look upon with pleasure," and ornately prophesied intermarriage: "And the hour is not far off when the white-hued husband shall boast of the dusky beauty of his wife, and the Caucasian wife shall admire the sun-kissed countenance of her husband, as deeply, and as unconscious of the present ruling abhorrence as is his admiration of her lighter tint." [33] Such voices as Haven's were less often lifted as time went on; the trend increasingly was for northern opinion to accommodate to southern views. "During Reconstruction and the remainder of the nineteenth century," Reimers concluded, "northern and southern Protestants often disagreed over the status of the Negro in American society. But they were moving closer together in both practice and preaching." Finally, "northern Protestants submitted to segregation, though they generally did not declare it was ordained by God or dictated by the law of nature." [34] The growing harmony between northern and southern white evangelicals in the interests of Christian civilization was at the expense of black evangelicals. Many well-intentioned white Christian leaders accepted the situation without serious probing or reflection because they believed that much had been done for the Negro with the ending of slavery, and that now he should be grateful for what had been done for him and should patiently educate himself to fit into the world's best civilization.

When Negro fraternal delegates spoke to white denominational conferences, they could seem to be identifying themselves with the concept of American Christian civilization. So B. F. Lee as a representative of the African Methodist Episcopal Church said to Northern Methodists in 1880: "We stand with you in the strong band of Christian love, in the strong band of the cross of Christ and of a common country, in the interests of humanity, in the interests of pure home and pure hearts, pure politics, pure government, and a purer, higher, grander, and more noble conception of the grand object and aim of man." [35] The Negro church literature of the period, however, reflects bitter realization of the trends in race relations. When J. B. Stansberry spoke on "The State of the Country" to the Philadelphia Annual Conference of the African Methodist Episcopal Church, the leading Negro magazine at the time, *The A.M.E. Church Review*, reprinted the address. Although he gladly acknowledged some exceptions, Stansberry found that a great majority of the whites are "as bitter against him [the Negro], in their prejudices, as wormwood, as gall. This is demonstrated, in the southern section of the country, in its most perfect form. The assassinations, the shooting down of innocent and defenseless Negroes are evidences of their intense and hellish hatred." [36] He felt that the prejudice was as great in the North, but that it expressed itself in other ways, in exclusion from hotels, restaurants, places of business and entertainment.

The confident assurance of white Protestants that theirs was the highest religion and that they stood in the vanguard of a perfect civilization was exasperating to Negro leaders. As T. Thomas Fortune, leading Negro journalist and founder of the Afro-American League, stated in an article in the same journal: "That he [the Negro] has been treated as a brute instead of a human being—robbed of his liberty and of his honest wage, scourged and harassed as was the blind Samson—is an ineffacable blot upon the humanity and the religion of the white man, and no reflection whatever on him." [37] An editorial, reflecting on the matter, declared that:

> we have already sufficient data to show that a race upon the level of a brute can be lifted to the very height of civilized life. Then this question of civilization is by no means settled. We are firmly of the opinion that the best expression of Christian civilization is yet to be seen, and who knows but that some of the very characteristics of the Negro that are discounted by the present civilization, are the very things needed for that higher and better which is to come.[38]

Few whites would have understood that prophetic statement then, for they were convinced that centuries of preparation had equipped the Anglo-Saxon Protestants to lead in the world victory of Christian civilization. August Meier has observed that "in the years after the compromise of 1877 the swelling sense of national unity between North and South was accomplished at the expense of the Negroes, their subordination in the American social order being the price paid for this compromise." [39] The growing harmony between northern and southern Protestants was an important part of the swelling sense of national unity, and its price was also the subordination of the Negro in church life. The vision of a Christian America had at best only a secondary place for blacks.

THE NATION AS UNIFYING AGENT OF THE GOSPEL

The overarching vision of a Protestant America to be won by voluntary means subtly changed in a significant way during the course of the nineteenth century. In many ways the image of a Christian America in the Gilded Age was much like that held widely among evangelicals in the first half of the century, but one very important shift in overall perspective was taking place. The change was not everywhere evident, and there were those who resisted it, but it was pervasive and in restrospect can be clearly discerned.

In the earlier period, the priority of the religious vision was strongly and widely maintained; it was Christianity *and* civilization, Christianity as the best part of civilization, and its hope. In the latter part of the century, however, in most cases unconsciously, much of the real focus had shifted to the civilization itself, with Christianity and the churches finding their significance in relation to it. Civilization itself was given increasingly positive assessment, chiefly because it was understood to have absorbed much of the spirit of Christianity. When Professor Samuel Harris lectured at Andover he explained that "modern civilization is characterized by ideas derived from the gospel of the kingdom; the brotherhood of man and the fatherhood of God; philanthropy; the promise of human progress; the rights of man; the removal of oppression; the reign of justice and love displacing the reign of force."[40] Charles Loring Brace, Congregational layman and philanthropist, expressed in a comprehensive way a view widely held in his well-known *Gesta Christi.* "There are," he wrote, "certain practices, principles and ideals—now the richest inheritance of the race—that have been either implanted or stimulated or supported by Christianity." Brace listed a number of them: "regard for the personality of the weakest and poorest; respect for woman; the absolute duty of each member of the fortunate classes to raise up the unfortunate; humanity to the child, the prisoner, the stranger, the needy, and even the brute; unceasing opposition to all forms of cruelty, oppression and slavery; the duty of personal purity and the sacredness of marriage; the necessity of temperance; the obligation of a more equitable division of the profits of labour, and of greater co-operation between employers and employed," and so on. "Ideals, principles and practices such as these are among the best achievements of Christianity," he found.[41] With many others, Brace implied that henceforth such achievements were to be carried primarily by civilization.

In the centennial year of 1876 the Methodist bishops praised their nation highly, saying that "here the human spirit of Christianity has been signally exemplified in generous hospitality to aliens, in the mitigation of penal laws, in protection and opportunity given to woman, in care for the rights and interests of labor, in the overthrow of slavery, in war waged against intemperance, and in successful effort for international arbitration. Here have been added to the visible agencies by which the world shall be subjugated to Christ a free, great, and enlightened nation, and a Church vital with the missionary spirit of its Lord."[42] Here the nation itself as bearer of civilization was elevated as an agency of the subjugation of the world to Christ! The mission of Christian faith was virtually being identified with national destiny, with the progress of civilization. Professor Samuel Harris had not hesitated to dramatize the corollary of such doctrine: "Christianity must show itself the religion of civilization, competent by its vital force in a savage community to quicken progress to civilization, competent in civilization to stimulate, purify, guide, and ennoble it."[43] And a few years later, his namesake Bishop Samuel Harris found that "The civilization which is established here has its peculiar character, and we believe that it is the outcome of centuries of our Christian development, and that essentially, and in its ideal form, it is the very flower and consummation of that development. Any essential change, therefore, in our civilization we would esteem to be a grievous loss, and any departure from its type would be a degeneration, whether radical or reactionary."[44] Perhaps orthodox southern evangelicals might suspect a liberal influence in statements of that type, but in practice southern Protestantism also sanctified the dominant trends of its civilization.

By stressing the Christian character of civilization, Protestants could identify a form of unity above their many divisions. The churches continued to be divided denominationally, sectionally, and racially. The longing for wholeness, partially disclosed in the interest in some kind of Christian union, found more concrete satisfactions in the advance of Christian civilization in the nation. Here was the real bond of Protestant unity. Protestants did not deny that American civilization had problems and shortcomings, but the leading spokesmen felt it was on its way to fuller, even ultimate, perfection. One of the most effective interpreters of this point of view was an Episcopal rector, Elisha Mulford. In *The Nation*, an important book first published in 1870 and later reprinted, Mulford acknowledged his debt to such thinkers as Hegel, Stahl, and Maurice. He declared that "the nation" was an organic unity with a moral personality, and served as "the power and the minister of God in history." Though it has blemishes, the nation is holy, has a divine unity in Christ, is lifted above divisions and distinctions, and "is ordained of God to do his service."[45] Though few could draw on idealist thought as readily as Mulford, or write so fully, there were many who were attracted to this general viewpoint. John E. Smylie has suggested in a probing historical article that "the unity which Christian theology localizes in Christ and the church was actually realized, insofar as it was realized at all in American experience, in the nation." [46]

Guided by a strong sense of the God-given mission and destiny of the Christianized nation and of their own role in it, Protestants generally had difficulty in seeing a number of the basic changes in American life for what they really were, especially those related to the influx of immigrants, the growth of cities, and the revolutions of thought. They also failed to see how their attachment to an idealized America was having a reverse impact upon them. Their religion was becoming more and more patterned after the culture. In Smylie's words, "instead of Christianizing the nation, the churches have been nationalized." [47] The evangelicals of that period did not see—perhaps they could not see—what seems obvious to us, looking back, that they were often expressing quite understandable class and economic interests in their speeches and actions, but always interpreting their aims and deeds almost wholly in a religious frame of reference. They found a sense of unity in a concept of civilization which had socio-economic and racial aspects, yet they interpreted their position in simple evangelical terms.

From the vantage point of the late twentieth century, the larger picture with its complex components can be more fully seen. Alan Grimes has outlined one relevant frame of reference for studying them in the context of their time:

> At issue was a conflict over styles of life or modes of existence. On one side was the older, conservative, rural, essentially Protestant and Puritan way of life which the native-born liked to think of as typically American; on the other side was the new or "faster" style of life that accompanied late nineteenth-century urbanization, and was ostentatious, crude but sophisticated, and enthusiastically "wet." The former drew its nourishment from farms, small towns, and

> a traditional way of life; the latter style was fed by mining, factories, immigrant labor, and the new modes of wealth made possible by burgeoning capitalism.[48]

The churches were not only to some extent nationalized, but in considerable measure were also accommodated to particular socio-economic and ethnic groupings in the nation.

Within the evangelical world of that time, as represented, for example, by a congregation at worship in the Sabbath, or when gathered in some national denominational or nondenominational assembly, it did not seem that way at all, of course! It seemed as though one were in a God-inspired, divinely led, righteous movement struggling against misguided if not evil persons and institutions which stood in the way of the fuller expression of Christian civilization, and which were hindering the triumph of the promised kingdom of God on earth. Such evil forces, it seemed to the evangelicals, must not be allowed to grow; the final triumph was sure, of course, but meanwhile it was given to them to fight evil in the hopes that full deliverance would soon come. Within the evangelical world, it seemed as though one were standing with the saints and martyrs of the past, aligning oneself with those Christian forebears who labored for a Christian America. If only one worked harder, witnessed more, gave more, loved more—and hated evil more—then perhaps victory would soon come, and the voluntary way to a fully Christian nation would accomplish what all the establishments in history had failed to do. Confirmation of this general stance sometimes came from the outside; Methodists heard a welcome word at their General Conference of 1884. "If there be a Christian nation in the world you are one. Nowhere else do we find the power of the Gospel so active in manifold directions as in this Republic; nowhere so widely diffused in all directions; nowhere else does it touch society at so many points for good," cried Samuel S.

Nelles, president of Victoria College in Canada, giving an evangelical opinion on American civilization.[49]

Another observer from outside the country, Lord Bryce, offered his famous judgment in 1888:

> The matter may be summed up by saying that Christianity in fact understood to be, though not the legally established religion, yet the national religion. So far from thinking their commonwealth godless, the Americans conceive that the religious character of a government consists in nothing but the religious belief of the individual citizens, and the conformity of their conduct to that belief. They deem the general acceptance of Christianity to be one of the main sources of their national prosperity, and their nation a special object of the Divine favour.[50]

Most Protestants in the America of 1890 saw themselves as belonging to the national religion, a religion of civilization. More than they knew, evangelicals were convinced that theirs was a Christian civilization on the way to victory and perfection. What had been secondary to the evangelical mind of the early century had pushed itself toward the center; Protestants invested more and more of their hopes in the progress of civilization and in the advance of the Christian nation. The divided churches found a sense of larger unity in working toward those ends.

The shift in Protestant emphasis that has been described here was real enough, but it was by no means a total shift. Many persons remained unsatisfied with the quality of the religious life of the time, and many sought more tangible expressions of Christian unity, paving the way for later developments. Yet Protestant confidence that the Christianization of America would soon be more fully realized generally remained high; because they assumed that religious freedom and the separation of church and state had eliminated the possibility of too close ties between religion and culture, they were often largely oblivious as to how far they had moved toward a religion of culture. Relating primarily to the dominant middle-class, Anglo-Saxon parts of the culture, main line Protestants often failed to take seriously the fundamental changes going on about them.

V

The Christian Conquest of the World (1890–1920)

American Protestantism approached and entered the twentieth century in a mood of great confidence. To be sure, the years from 1890 to 1920 were troubled by several periods of economic difficulty, by growing awareness of acute social problems and by participation in two wars, but the assurance of the churches that this was to be the "Christian century" was not seriously shaken. The churches themselves entered the period in a vigorous and growing condition; membership was continuing to increase proportionately faster than a rapidly expanding population. In the 1895 edition of his massive work, *Christianity in the United States*, Daniel Dorchester, a Methodist pastor, enthusiastically summarized the advances of evangelical Christianity during the nineteenth century. He said:

> Christ, reigning over a territory hitherto unrivaled in extent; great benevolences, awakened and sustained by a deeper religious devotion; rapidly multiplying home, city, and foreign mission stations, the outcome of intelligent consecration; magnificent departments of Christian labor, many of them heretofore unknown, and none of them ever before so numerous, so vast, or so restlessly active; the great heart of the Church pulsating with an unequaled velocity; the fires of evangelism burning with unwonted brightness on multiplied altars; and a religious literature such as has characterized no

> other age, eminently practical, intensely fervid and richly evangelical, emanating from her presses; all conspire to show that more than ever before God has a living Church within the churches, towering amid them all in its mightiness—the strength, the support, the central life of all; and that an increasing number of true believers are "walking with him in white," a grand constellation of light and purity—a bright Milky Way from earth to heaven.[1]

Dorchester sought to dramatize the strength of "evangelical" churches in a series of colorful charts, one of which showed that of all the church organizations in the country, 151,172 were "evangelical," 10,231 were Roman Catholic, while "all others" accounted for 3894.[2] Evangelicals believed they would continue to dominate the religious scene.

Protestant confidence was sustained, not only by such optimistic observations, but also by the pervasive assumption that America was still a Christian nation. No less an authority than the Supreme Court in one of its famous cases gathered evidence to show how religious the nation was. Noting that the state constitutions provided "organic utterances" which speak for the voice of the entire people that the Christian religion was part of the common law, the court went on to say:

> If we pass beyond these matters to a view of American life as expressed by its laws, its business, its customs and its society, we find everywhere a clear recognition of the same truth. Among other matters note the following: The form of oath universally prevailing, concluding with an appeal to the Almighty; the custom of opening sessions of all deliberative bodies and most conventions with prayers; the prefatory words of all wills, "In the name of God, amen"; the laws respecting the observance of the Sabbath; with the general cessation of all secular business, and the closing of courts, Legislatures, and other similar public assemblies on that day; the churches and church organizations which abound in every city, town, and hamlet; the multitude of charitable organi-

> zations existing everywhere under Christian auspices; the gigantic missionary associations, with general support, and aiming to establish Christian missions in every quarter of the globe. These, and many other matters which might be noticed, add a volume of unofficial declarations to the mass of organic utterances that this is a Christian nation.[3]

The future seemed secure for the continued advance of the churches in such a nation.

The self-assurance of Protestants was based not only on religious belief but was also rooted in the relative stability and order of the life-style of nineteenth-century middle-class white Americans. Henry Seidel Canby once declared that "confidence is a habit which must be acquired young and from an environment that is constant and rhythmically continuous."[4] the pace of life had been steadily quickening, especially in the cities, as the generation which was to lead the main line Protestant forces so confidently into the new century was growing up. But many evangelical leaders were products of the open country or small towns; as late as 1900 about two-thirds of the population of some seventy-five million was considered rural. More significantly, whether raised in country or city, most Protestants were schooled in an atmosphere in which the universe was felt to be friendly. The order and regularity of the natural order were pictured as a reflection of God's law. In such a universe, the eye of faith could see all things working together for good to them that loved God.

Evangelicals were certain that the universe was friendly both to the progress of Christianity and to the moral and spiritual advances in civilization for which the churches stood. In his Ely Lectures at Union Theological Seminary in New York in 1890, Lewis French Stearns, liberal theologian at the Congregational seminary at Bangor, Maine, employed the familiar argument that much of civilization's progress was due to Christian influences. He claimed that such things as the recognition of the rights of individuals and groups, the establishment of democratic government, the abolition of slavery, and the growth of charity were primarily the result of the Christian leaven. "In a word," he declared, "our many-sided modern civilization, with its immense superiority over that of the heathen and ancient times, is the effect of Christianity." [5] Evangelical spokesmen were also sure that such a civilization would go on advancing, for divine influences were at work within it. Protestant confidence was sustained by the conviction that both natural and cultural environments were favorable to evangelical goals and hopes, for the power of God was working in both. Small wonder their optimism was so great! Regular services of worship, in which "God's great book" was constantly cited, provided them keys for understanding the plan of the ages as it was being worked out in nature and history to a glorious climax. Thus the buoyant faith that the great certainties remained untouched and were progressing to victory despite the vicissitudes of time were bolstered week by week. Evangelical confidence was deep-rooted in spiritual soil; that there were indeed those who could not or did not share in the brimming sense of self-assurance should not obscure for us how general and powerful that sense was.[6]

Protestants believed that they were in the very vanguard of true progress, and that Christianity as they understood it "is the highest and purest form of religion in the world, and contains the highest and purest conception of man and society." [7] Those words of a Baptist leader, Samuel Zane Batten, were axiomatic among his fellow evangelicals. Another Baptist, William Newton Clarke, the first prominent systematic theologian of evangelical liberalism, expressed the thought in a slightly different way: "Something has made Christianity the boldest of the religions that lay claim to universality; and that something is an inward sense of its own divine excellence, surpassing all other faiths." He admitted that there might be some truth and goodness in other religions, but "the sense of pursuing the unparalleled good is characteristic of Christianity, wherever Christianity is at its best." [8]

It would unnecessarily belabor the obvious to show in detail how the sense of Christian confidence about the future of civilization and the church's place in it was operative in the life of the denominations. William E. Dodge, a noted lay leader and a conspicuous figure in the calling of the famous Ecumenical Missionary Conference in New York in 1900, expressed the prevailing view in saying: "We are going into a century more full of hope, and promise, and opportunity than any period in the world's history." [9] Though of course in these years there were certain changes in mood as economic, social, and military crises came and went, in general a pervasive sense of confidence prevailed among Protestants and in the culture of which they were a part. Progress in science and technology, in democratic reforms, and in the expansion of industry and philanthropy was interpreted by religious leaders largely as a product of the advance of Christian civilization and as a sign of the coming of the kingdom.

PROTESTANT HOPE FOR WORLD CIVILIZATION

From its earliest days, Christianity in America had a world vision, a dream of a world won to Christ. In the missionary thrust of the eighteenth and nineteenth centuries it sought to turn the dream into reality. As the nineteenth century drew to a close, the belief that Christian civilization would soon dominate the world primarily through the agency of Anglo-Saxon achievement seemed very near to fulfillment for great numbers of American Protestants. In 1890 Lewis French Stearns proclaimed:

> Today Christianity is the power which is moulding the destinies of the world. The Christian nations are in the ascendant. Just in proportion to the purity of Christianity as it exists in the various nations of Christendom is the influence

> they are exerting upon the world's destiny. The future of the world seems to be in the hands of the three great Protestant powers—England, Germany, and the United States. The old promise is being fulfilled; the followers of the true God are inheriting the world.[10]

The forthcoming Christian conquest would be a peaceful one, as they saw it—a victory by the sheer weight of numbers and enthusiasm, of commitment and confidence. Stearns continued:

> Looking at the matter in the large, we can have no question that Christianity has been from the first certain of its universal conquest. No other religion can vie with it. There is no likelihood that any religion will ever appear to enter into rivalry with it . . . The facts are manifest. The unbeliever sees them as fully as the Christian. Deny them he cannot. To explain them in any other way than upon the assumption that Christianity is divine, is, to say the least, a difficult matter, with regard to which unbelievers are at cross-purposes among themselves.[11]

Josiah Strong had been influential in spreading such views through his writings and his leadership in the Evangelical Alliance. His expectancies increased toward the end of the century. "We have seen that the world is evidently about to enter on a new era, that in this new era mankind is to come more and more under Anglo-Saxon influence," he declared in 1893, "and that Anglo-Saxon civilization is more favorable than any other to the spread of those principles whose universal triumph is necessary to that perfection of the race to which it is destined; the entire realization of which will be the kingdom of heaven fully come on earth." He believed that the perils to which he had called attention so dramatically a few years before would be overcome: "We have seen that the Anglo-Saxon is accumulating irresistible power with which to press the die of his civilization upon the world." [12]

Similar attitudes were often expressed by foreign mission

leaders, by those who had served the missionary cause in distant lands. For example, Sidney L. Gulick, missionary of the American Board of Commissioners for Foreign Missions, declared in 1897: "Christianity is the religion of the dominant nations of the earth. Nor is it rash to prophesy that in due time it will be the only religion in the world." He was convinced that the non-Christian religions would become Christian—such was the divine plan.

> By the intellectual, moral, commercial, and political blessings—in a word, by the civilisation which God has given and is still giving to those nations which have adopted Christianity—he has indicated His approval; it is evident that He intends that these Christian nations shall have the predominant and moulding influence in the world at this state of its development. The real reason why Christian nations are predominant is because they, more than others, have discovered and loved and lived the truth, the eternal principles on which God created this world.[13]

Gulick was not hesitant to put this in general political terms, though he expected the conquest to be moral and peaceful:

> It is Protestant Germany and especially Puritan England that have grown in influence and power. No peoples have been so controlled by the religion of Jesus Christ as the Anglo-American. No peoples have absorbed it so fully into their national life, and have so embodied it in their language and literature and government. No peoples, as a natural consequence, have so succeeded in establishing prosperous, self-governing colonies and nations . . . God means that the type of religion and civilisation attained by the Anglo-Saxon race shall have, for the present at least, the predominating influence in moulding the civilisation of the world. And everything points to the growing predominance of the Christian religion and Christian civilisation.[14]

Such comments as Gulick's— there were many like it—point to the lack of a self-critical sense among the Protestant leaders of the time. But to them it seemed evident that Christianity would win the pagan world and that the future of the "Christian" nations was especially secure.

The spread of such attitudes influenced many Protestant interpretations of the Spanish-American War and its outcomes. The exciting events of the late 1890's which led up to the war of 1898 and to the acquisition of new territories (chiefly the Hawaiian Islands, Puerto Rico, and the Philippine Islands) greatly stimulated the anticipation of the world victory of Christian civilization. Yet there were important differences of opinion; not all were enthusiastic about the positions summarized above.

American Protestants were divided in their attitude toward the short, decisive war of 1898, though majority opinion finally settled in its favor about the time war was declared.[15] At first there had been considerable restraint. Many Protestant leaders at the time of the sinking of the battleship *Maine* in Cuba in February 1898 urged suspension of judgment until the facts could be ascertained. They applauded President McKinley's resistance to congressional militants. But the flood of reports of the inhuman treatment of the Cuban rebels by the Spanish authorities allowed militant crusaders among Protestants to gain a wide hearing in the churches. By late March, jingoist statements like this one by a Methodist minister of Brooklyn could be featured in the press:

> The cannon has generally torn holes in the walls of barbarism and heathenism, through which the Gospel of Christ has had the most effective entrance. One reason why the Anglo-Saxon has carried the cross of Christ so high has been because the edge of his sword has been so keen. Much blood has already been shed in behalf of the freedom of Cuba; it may be that Providence will require a little more, and that of our soldiers and sailors to make the purchase complete.[16]

By April voices from many pulpits were calling for intervention in Cuba as a moral duty; more and more American clergymen "felt that the ends of history required American intervention in Cuba itself in order to further liberty and civilization."[17]

The struggle was often interpreted as a battle between incompatible civilizations. As W. H. P. Faunce, influential Baptist minister who later became president of Brown University, loftily stated it: "Spanish and American civilization could not exist side by side, separated only by a narrow strip of Southern sea, without sooner or later coming into opposition, any more than fire and water could touch without generating steam. . . . She [Spain] stands convicted of incompetence, of oppression, of cruelty, of such incompetence as permits the slow death of one-tenth of Cuba's population and the swift destruction of a ship of a friendly power bound on a peaceful mission."[18] Religious spokesmen had little doubt who would win in the clash of civilizations. As they saw it, the expected victory would again demonstrate God's guidance over his chosen forces. The editor of the *Methodist Review* said: "We shall be much disappointed if the final outcome of the war does not show that it was one of God's most efficient agencies for the advancement of true Christian civilization and the ushering in of brighter times for the human race."[19] There was some exploitation of the anti-Romanist theme in all this; the hold of Rome over Spanish culture was seen by some as holding her back from full participation in the modern world.

The "splendid little war" was so short and so "successful" that the crusading spirit seemed fully justified. Many Protestant interpreters, sure of the guidance of God over human affairs, viewed the war's outcome as evidence of the divine blessing on America. Even those who had opposed the war and the addition of the territories—especially the Philippines—could nevertheless accept with the majority the responsibilities of "Christian expansionism" once the new situation had in fact provided the opportunities. During the war and after, there were some convinced anti-imperialists in Protestant ranks; they were sharply opposed to the taking and holding of overseas possessions.[20] But most of them came to accept a distinction between imperialism and expansionism and were willing to support missionary work wherever it was possible, including the new territories.

Christians who did accept imperialism presented their cause in such a way as to appeal as widely as possible to a broad constituency. "American imperialism, in its essence," one spokesman declared, "is American valor, American manhood, American sense of justice and right, American conscience, American character at its best, listening to the voice of God, and His command nobly assuming this republic's rightful place in the grand forward movement for the civilizing and Christianizing of all continents and all races." [21] Josiah Strong hastened to show that even the role of armies was shifting in the new era:

> But as the world is gradually being civilized and civilization is gradually being Christianized, armies are finding new occupations. As *The Outlook* says: "The army among Anglo-Saxon peoples is no longer a mere instrument of destruction. It is a great reconstructive organization. It is promoting law, order, civilization, and is fighting famine and pestilence in India. It is lightening taxes, building railroads, laying the foundations of justice and liberty, in Egypt." [22]

Lyman Abbott, the editor of the influential journal cited by Strong, was a defender of Christian imperialism who proclaimed that "it is the function of the Anglo-Saxon race to confer these gifts of civilization, through law, commerce, and education, on the uncivilized people of the world." He met a criticism posed by anti-imperialists with these words:

> It is said that we have no right to go to a land occupied by a barbaric people and interfere with their life. It is said that if they prefer barbarism they have a right to remain barbarians. I deny the right of a barbaric people to retain possession of any quarter of the globe. What I have already said I re-

> affirm: barbarism has no rights which civilization is bound to respect. Barbarians have rights which civilized people are bound to respect, but they have no right to their barbarism.[23]

In the debates about the war, imperialism, and expansionism, the various Protestant parties may have disagreed about many details, but they rarely disagreed about the importance of missionary expansion everywhere in the world.

In the denominational presses and at religious assemblies confident expectation that Christianity was on the way to world conquest was frequently expressed. The Quadrennial Address of the Bishops of the United Brethren Church in 1901 was characteristic:

> In a political sense Christendom is today the world. If we take the map of the globe and mark off the possessions and spheres of influence of the Christian powers, there will be little or nothing left to the independent control of non-Christian governments. The islands of the sea are all appropriated; the Western Continent is wholly under Christian rule; the partition of Africa among the Christian nations of Europe is well-nigh complete; Asia is slowly coming under the control of Christian nations.[24]

England and America were considered to be in the very forefront of Christianity's world conquest. A representative of the British Wesleyan Conference, Thomas Allen, brought greetings from English Methodism to the General Conference of the Methodist Episcopal Church in 1900. "I believe in the election of nations to work out definite purposes of the divine mind," he said. "And England's mission seems to be to serve the purposes of colonization and Christianity. . . . We are a ruling race, and no doubt we have got the defects as well as the excellencies of our qualities." Then he linked Christians on both sides of the Atlantic in a common enterprise: "We are allied in blood, our principles of self-government are the same, our interests are identical in various parts of the world; and there are strong reasons why we should be friends, and why we should cooperate for the advancement of civilization and for the triumph of Christianity throughout the earth." The next morning an enthusiastic delegate moved that inasmuch as the "cooperation of America and Great Britain makes for peace on earth, Christian civilization, and the holding of the open door for the propagation of the Gospel," the British colors should fly beside the American flag. The motion was tabled—after all, it was only at that very conference that it had been decided permanently to display the *American* flag on the platform—but the sentiment was widely shared.[25] A Southern Baptist paper, the *Christian Index* of Atlanta, had the year before rejoiced in the new *rapprochement* of England and America, exclaiming: "Oh, let the stars and stripes, intertwined with the flag of old England, wave o'er the continents and islands of earth, and through the instrumentality of the Anglo-Saxon race, the kingdoms of this world shall become the kingdoms of our Lord and His Christ!" [26] Protestant spokesmen often expressed the hope that American evangelicals, in cooperation with those of other lands, especially England, would lead the way in the Christian conquest of the world.

NEW THRUSTS IN WORLD MISSIONS

The expectation of peaceful world conquest by Christian civilization, an expectation that seemed to come dramatically nearer with the exciting events around the turn of the century, gave a new intensity to the already pronounced missionary concerns of evangelical Protestantism. "Missionary fervor reached a high water mark during the imperial years after 1890 and the first two decades of the twentieth century," declared Paul H. Varg in his study of American Protestant missions in China.[27] The missionary advances of those years caught the interest of almost all groups of Protestants, for it was widely believed that this was the way the world was being made Christian and was being prepared for the coming of the kingdom of God. Foreign missions provided the means for pressing toward world Christian civilization. Though various theological tensions were felt within and between the communions, a unifying partnership was found in facing the challenge of missions. The Protestant Episcopal Church, for example, had its share of internal tensions, but the Pastoral Letter for 1901 sought to gather all the faithful for a great missionary crusade: "And lastly, beloved in the Lord, we bid you carry away from our great synod as the watchword of our battle for the time to come—missions, missions, missions." [28] Home missions were included, but the greater excitement centered on foreign missions.

The backbone of the Protestant missionary thrust was the denominational missionary society, assisted by a member of non-denominational and interdenominational agencies. In the last third of the nineteenth century, the missionary force was rapidly increasing. By 1900 there were over fifty mission boards in the United States and eight closely associated agencies in Canada which were directly involved in sending missionaries abroad. There were nearly fifty auxiliary societies. The total North American missionary staff overseas was about five thousand.[29]

A powerful movement that added great numbers and resources to Protestant missions and exerted effective unifying tendencies emerged in the late nineteenth century. The story of the Student Volunteer Movement for Foreign Missions with its various related movements and the impact they made on the whole Protestant missionary enterprise under the leadership of Robert P. Wilder, John R. Mott, Robert E. Speer, Sherwood Eddy, and others has been told many times.[30] At an international student conference at Mt. Hermon, Massachusetts, in 1886 under the leadership of the famous revivalist, Dwight L. Moody, a group of some two hundred and fifty college men found their attention arrested by an enthusiastic minority of missionary-minded students. A Baptist missionary who had come uninvited, Dr. William Ashmore, was asked to speak. He took as his theme, "The work of missions is not a wrecking expedition, but a war of conquest." [31] Robert Wilder, born of missionary parents in India, had just graduated from Princeton and had much to do with the major outcome of the conference—the commitment to overseas service of one hundred of those present. With an associate, Wilder toured American colleges the year following that famous summer conference. More than two thousand volunteers for foreign missions were enrolled, of whom about five hundred were women. In 1888 the Student Volunteer Movement was formally organized, and John R. Mott, Cornell graduate and Methodist layman, took the chairmanship, which he held for some three decades.

Mott, a serious, intense, solid man who won the confidence of Protestant and Orthodox leaders all over the world, was a genius at organization. His central base of operations was in student and international Y.M.C.A. work, but his talents showed clearly in his leadership roles in the Student Volunteer Movement, in the World's Student Christian Federation (of which he was a founder in 1895 and which he served as general secretary for a quarter century), and among denominational missionary boards as they were moving into closer relationships with each other. His influence was felt in the pioneering cooperative agency officially created by the American Protestant missionary boards in 1893 (which later became the Foreign Missionary Conference of North America) and even more in the development of missionary cooperation on a world scale. He presided over the meeting that has since been reckoned as the great milestone of the ecumenical movement, the World Missionary Conference at Edinburgh in 1910, and took the lead in the work that resulted in the formation of the International Missionary Council in 1921 (after 1961 part of the World Council of Churches).[32]

The world missionary crusade into which Mott and the others poured their talents expressed itself in many organizational forms but was largely supportive of the regular denominational channels of outreach. Most of the volunteers who were enlisted by the Student Volunteer Movement worked through the denominational missionary societies. By conservative estimate over twenty thousand of them had served overseas by 1945.[33] The intimate relationship between the volunteer movement and the boards is well illustrated in the life of Robert E. Speer, who after outstanding service as traveling secretary of the S.V.M. was called from his course at Princeton Theological Seminary to become a secretary of the Presbyterian Board of Foreign Missions, where he was to serve in various capacities as a layman for forty-six years. Encouraged by the enthusiasm and commitment of such men, the churches with renewed vigor emphasized missionary work as the way to save souls in distant places and to advance Christian civilization across the globe.

An important clue to understanding the impact on the churches and missionary agencies by the Mott-Speer-Wilder group was their ability to bridge gaps between conservatives and liberals. Though the lines between those movements had not hardened as they later did in the Fundamentalist-Modernist controversy after World War I, the tension was rising, especially among such major denominational families as the Disciples of Christ, the Episcopalians, and the northern branches of the Baptists, the Methodists, and the Presbyterians. Some of those who were in the forefront of the world missionary crusade were very conservative men. Arthur T. Pierson, for example, editor of the *Missionary Review of the World*, was a premillennialist in his views, one who believed in the physical return of the Lord before the coming of the millennium.[34] He could interpret the famous S.V.M. motto—"the evangelization of the world in this generation"—to mean the *preaching* of the gospel everyhere in the world as a necessary preliminary to the return of Christ.

The talk about "Christian civilization" and the interpretation of the kingdom of God as a perfected earthly society did not appeal to such men. Mott and Speer were broader theologically, yet, as their friend Eddy put it, "Both were conservative in mind, theologically, economically, and politically; both emphasized very strongly and almost exclusively the individual and personal side of religion." [35] As laymen deeply devoted to the Christian cause, however, they were not concerned about theological minutiae, and were able to a remarkable degree to bridge the gap between those oriented to the older theology and those informed by the new.

The evangelical liberal forces were then increasing in strength within Protestant missionary ranks. The earlier missionary motivation based on snatching sinners from hell's fires was slowly yielding to that oriented more toward the reform and improvement of all life, present and future. In Beaver's apt wording, for growing numbers of believers "the kingdom here had now tended to displace the kingdom coming at the End from the center of concern." Many of the conservative-minded, living as they were in the optimistic atmosphere of that time, were not oblivious to the appeal of the new, but they wanted to keep it in proper perspective. "The word 'progress' is the key to understanding much of the enthusiasm for missions on the part of theological conservatives and liberals alike and of the humanitarians," Beaver concluded. "There was the remarkable progress of the missions themselves, but still more exciting and inciting to action was the progress which missions had wrought in formerly benighted lands in social change, civilization, economic betterment, and moral improvement." [36]

For the growing liberal elements in the churches, James S. Dennis' massive *Christian Missions and Social Progress* was a seminal and instructive work which helped to hold their interest in missions. Surveying the world scene, Dennis showed how individual and social life was being improved by the many types of movements for rescue, relief, rehabilitation, education, and reform which were being carried out under Christian agencies all over the world. Appealing to impressive compilations of statistics, Dennis combined an evangelical stance with scientific survey in a way which was attractive to many Protestants. "We feel bound to advance the claim that Christian missions have already produced social results which are manifest, and that society in the non-Christian world at the present time is conscious of a new and powerful factor which is working positive and revolutionary changes in the direction of a higher civilization," he declared early in his first volume, and the wealth of evidence that followed made his claim arresting.[37]

The blend of piety and progress which enabled conservatives and liberals to work together in missions was well illustrated at the Ecumenical Missionary Conference in New York in 1900. In a preliminary meeting, William R. Huntington, Episcopal rector in New York, said that the conference "is called 'ecumenical' . . . because the plan of campaign it proposes covers the whole area of the inhabited globe," and that it would be "a reaching after some method in such an attempt to Christianize the non-Christian portion of the inhabited earth as shall be commensurate with the vastness of the undertaking."[38] When that great meeting of missionary representatives from around the world was over, the editorial committee attempted to sum up what had been the dominating spirit of the gathering by saying:

> The Conference . . . was held at a time when the political and commercial expansion of Europe and America had directed the thought of Christendom to distant parts of the earth. America had been brought into immediate contact with Asia by the occupation of the Philippines, Great Britain was engaged in war in South Africa, and the clouds of the coming uprising [the Boxer rebellion] were even then gathering in China. Regrettable as were these disturbances in themselves, they widened the circle of thought, and

> resulted in an increased appreciation of the condition of the non-Christian portions of the world, and deepened the conviction that human progress is inseparably bound up with Christian missions. The great advance, also, made in almost every department of mission work during the closing years of the century, made it desirable that there should be a united consideration of the new conditions which had arisen.[39]

During the meeting, great attention was paid to the civilizing aspects of Christianity. The president of the United States, William McKinley, noted that missionaries have been "among the pioneers of civilization," and Theodore Roosevelt, then governor of New York but soon to be vice-president, mentioned the civilizing role of home missions.[40] Former President Benjamin Harrison, honorary chairman of the conference, expressed the great expectations for the new century which were widely shared among Protestants:

> God has not set a uniform pace for Himself in the work of bringing in the kingdom of His Son. He will hasten it in His day. The stride of His Church shall be so quickened that commerce will be the laggard.[41]

Tensions between liberals and conservatives were somewhat sublimated in the partnership of piety, progress, and civilization which, it was confidently believed, was preparing the way for the kingdom itself. The possibility of a greater sense of self-criticism, which might have come out of a more open confrontation of the parties, was largely suppressed, in considerable measure because of the necessities of the missionary consensus. Deeper differences were not faced lest the causes of denominational peace and Christian civilization suffer.

Mott and Speer were both at the conference, displaying their ability to stand for evangelical unity. In summarizing the significance of the gathering, Speer declared that "it demonstrated the essential unity of the evangelical churches. For above all separating peculiarities the single Spirit of the single Lord lifted the hearts of his servants, and they found themselves to be brethren." Missionary motivation was changing, Speer conceded, but he saw it as a cause for hope, not alarm:

> Considerations of future destiny now occupy less place in the thought of men than considerations of present duty. But could anything be more favorable to the missionary argument than this? Such a change only brings out more clearly the Church's responsibility for the world's evangelization.[42]

Mott, speaking in Carnegie Hall, provided an inclusive interpretation of the S.V.M. motto, "the evangelization of the world in this generation."

> We do not minimize the importance of any missionary work which has been and is being used by the Spirit of God. We rather add emphasis to all the regular forms of missionary work, such as education, medical, literary, and evangelistic. As Dr. Dennis says: "The evangelistic method must not be regarded as monopolizing the evangelistic aim, which should itself pervade all other methods."[43]

Evangelicals of various shades felt themselves part of one crusade for the evangelization, the Christianization, and the civilization of the world.

Many of the more conspicuous leaders of the missionary advance of those years were widely traveled men of profound international sympathies. In their contacts with thoughtful men of other cultures, they were at times reminded of the limitations of the Anglo-American apprehensions of Christian faith. Sherwood Eddy spoke of the personal impact of men like L. P. Larsen, learned Danish missionary. "These Europeans were a living reminder to our sometimes more superficial, yet often imperialistic, Anglo-Saxons that we were only a part, and a humble part, of a great world movement."[44] He described the grief with which Fletcher Brockman, when working among students in China, discovered that most Westerners treated the Chinese with condescension and discrimination, and that some missionaries did too. Missionary leaders admitted that there were serious problems in Western Christianity and Anglo-Saxon civilization. Some saw beyond this, suggesting that churches did not always see clearly the differences between Christian faith and Western civilization. For example, Arthur J. Brown, secretary of the board of Foreign Missions of the Presbyterian Church (U.S.A.), observed early in the century that "in the course of nearly two thousand years, Christianity has undoubtedly taken on some of the characteristics of the white races, and missionaries, inheriting these characteristics, have more or less unconsciously identified them with the essentials."[45] He pleaded for the development of indigenous churches, based on the principles of the gospel, in overseas cultures.

Such views as these were, of course, to spread more widely after World War I, but for the most part evangelical leaders before then rarely doubted the superiority of their version of Christianity and Christian civilization to all other options, and they faced the admitted limitations in Western religion and culture as challenges to be met and overcome on the road to perfection. Paul Varg's judgment on the leaders of the missionary crusade is instructive:

> Bred in comfortable urban middle-class homes, or more often amid the happy circumstances of well-established families in small towns or on farms, this generation had no squeamish doubts about the superiority of American life. Its excellence they attributed to the influence of Protestant Christianity. Nor did they have any difficulty in accepting the then current picture of dark practices of heathen lands so in contrast with the enlightened ways of the Christian world.[46]

Varg cited as examples such men as Mott, Eddy, Horace Pitkin, Congregational martyr of the Boxer rebellion, and Henry Luce, Presbyterian educational missionary in China. These leaders were quite in tune with the prevailing American Protestant sentiments of the time, to which they had themselves contributed not a little. Missionaries were not unique in their confidence in the universal application of Christianity and democracy, for such views were widely held in the America they knew. Public, business, and educational leaders often spoke with much appreciation of the religious and humanitarian work of missions, and supported the movement generously.

The first decade and a half of the twentieth century saw continuing advance in the resources poured into the world mission. By 1910 North American missionaries made up about one-third of the total Protestant world missionary staff of twenty-one thousand, while nearly half of the financial backing for the whole enterprise was raised in the United States and Canada. In men and money, North American missions had surpassed the British as leaders in the Protestant world mission.[47] In part, this was accomplished by the continued emergence of new organizational instruments as they were needed. A Presbyterian layman, John B. Sleman, Jr., was so inspired by the spirit of dedication among students at the 1906 meeting of the S.V.M. that later that year he founded the Laymen's Missionary Movement to challenge the Christian laity to provide financial backing in a similar spirit. The L.M.M. was both an expression of and a contribution to the sense of unity which characterized the missionary thrust. "The whole enterprise is lifted out of a narrow limited perspective, and men of all churches begin to feel something of the larger enthusiasm of the Kingdom of Christ among men," an early publication of the movement announced. "The success of the whole army of Christ in the world becomes the inspiration of every regiment and of every private soldier." [48] With vast mass meetings in many American cities, cultivated by a busy staff, the L.M.M. soon made itself felt in the churches. For example, a Presbyterian comment on the movement in 1910 observed that "it has been so spectacular that none can have failed to remark its appearance." [49]

In 1911 at the twenty-fifth anniversary of the S.V.M., the crusade for the Christianization of the world seemed to be going splendidly. Looking back, J. Ross Stevenson, a conservative Presbyterian minister soon to become president of Princeton Theological Seminary, said: "I am sure we all would agree that during the last quarter century there has been the most marvelous advance in the Kingdom of God that the Church has ever witnessed, surely surpassing any that was accomplished in the centuries that preceded." Then, looking ahead, he added that:

> the resources of the Church, material, mental and spiritual, if properly conserved and directed, are ample for the speedy accomplishment of the evangelization of the entire world; and therefore I say that that which in the beginning was criticized as being a futile dream of a few enthusiasts, has really come to be the established policy of the whole Church in defining our missionary obligation. . . . We are dealing with the prospective leaders who are to have part in a service which is destined, I believe, under God during the next quarter century to be the greatest one that has ever been witnessed in the history of the Kingdom of God.[50]

That same year, when John Mott received an honorary degree of Doctor of Laws from Princeton University, the final phrase of the citation defined him as "a new Crusader bent on the Christian conquest of the world." [51]

The crusading missionary spirit continued to flow unchecked until much of it was redirected and absorbed by World War I. When he thought back on those years, Walter M. Horton, theologian at the Oberlin Graduate School of Theology, recalled that:

> The generation that fought the First World War was led to Christian commitment by a triumvirate of great lay leaders, continuators of the tradition of lay evangelism which formerly centered at Northfield in Dwight L. Moody. No one who went to student conferences or Church mass meetings in those days could be in any doubt as to who the real leaders of American Christendom were. Their names were Mott, Speer, Eddy—the inevitable three to call upon when a Christian movement was to be launched or a national convention held.[52]

The crusade for a Christian civilization in America which they and so many others like them sponsored was set in a world context; not only at home but abroad was the expectation of the victory of Christianization and civilization high among Protestants.

NATIONALISM AND RELIGION

Looking back from the last third of the twentieth century to its first two decades, we can see how the Protestant denominations rather easily idealized the culture and democracy of America. There was a considerable transfer of religious feelings to the civilization and the nation. "This was still a period of fervent devotion, but the object of devotion had been subtly changed under the appearance of enlargement to include a particular system of social, political, and economic life," Sidney E. Mead has observed. "Consequently under the system of official separation of church and state the denominations eventually found themselves as completely identified with nationalism and their country's political economic systems as had ever been known in Christendom." [53] The world setting of American Protestantism did not seriously work against this, for the flow was largely one way. In Varg's judgment, "missionary activity, although an exercise in both an intellectual and a practical philanthropy, was nonetheless subject to the usual egotistical elements and caught in the vortex of nationalistic crosscurrents. In the end American nationalism threatened to triumph over the religious." [54]

Nationalism did not succeed overtly in triumphing over the religious, though its influence was pervasive. For the Protestant leaders and their followers in that period were for the most part religiously sincere and devout men, earnestly seeking to follow God's will as they understood it. Beaver's observation catches the right balance: "Nationalism provided a powerful incentive to the development of the missionary movement, but, nevertheless, it was secondary to the spiritual and theological motivation." [55] The missionary forces, home and foreign, were more involved than they knew in a form of religious nationalism from which they thought the separation of church and state had delivered them. Their religious devotion could and did unwittingly bolster a nationalist spirit. Greatly impressed by the achievements of Western, especially American, civilization, they attributed its remarkable progress primarily to the working of Christianity within it. Though they strove as Christians to keep the priority on spiritual religion and to be aware of the differences between faith and culture, it was not difficult in the spirit of those times to lose the distinction and to see Christian civilization as a main outcome of faith, if not its chief outcome.

Even those who, as Christians, insisted on the priority of faith could unwittingly speak as though they were devotees of culture religion. Referring to the Christian gospel, the Episcopal bishops in 1898 said: "It is a new regenerating force, applied first to the individual man and thence to the mass of men, producing in the first instance a Christian character, and in the second, Christian civilization." [56] Three years later they said: "The end of Christian faith is attained in the glories of Christian civilization." [57] In the early years of the new century, dozens were saying what R. Fulton Cutting, financier and president of the New York Association for Improving the Conditions of the Poor, put into his Kennedy Lectures for 1912 at the New York School of

Philanthropy. "The Church is living too much for Christianity and too little for civilization. She seems to underrate the value of the latter's function," he declared. "We may be perhaps too close to our American civilization to gauge its merits and to estimate the degree to which it may commend Christianity to the pagan world." [58] For those who understood Christianity as the chief force in civilization's progress, it was not illogical to transfer considerable religious feeling to civilization and to give it high priority in their scheme of values.

It took an outsider, the philosopher George Santayana, to see what many American Christians could not see:

> Meantime the churches, a little ashamed of their past, began to court the good opinion of so excellent a world. Although called evangelical, they were far, very far, from prophesying its end, or offering a refuge from it, or preaching contempt for it; they existed only to serve it, and their highest divine credential was that the world needed them.[59]

Such an observation no doubt overlooks the facts of continuing differences and tensions within the Protestant world, but it does dramatize the situation in which churches could rather easily focus their hopes on temporal concerns.

Most of the glorification of American civilization as Christian was rather restrained and qualified, but occasionally it moved toward a religious nationalism which viewed the United States as the center of civilization. As American citizens who had been reared in a tradition of national destiny and who were proud of their country, some Protestants could focus the religious feeling they had for Christian civilization on America in particular. The Pastoral Letter of the Episcopal bishops in 1898 said it simply: "And we are Americans, proud indeed of our traditions of law and liberty as Anglo-Saxons, yet with the hopes and convictions, the privileges and responsibilities of Americans." [60] The resolution of the Northern Methodists which permanently put the national flag on the platform of their General Conference justified the action by declaring that "the Methodist Episcopal Church has ever been loyal and true to the government of the United States and to its symbol, the beautiful banner of stars and stripes, for the integrity of which thousands of its communicants have freely offered their lives, and which stands for Christian civilization everywhere" and that "we believe that our devotion and loyalty thereto should be manifested and emphasized by this General Conference in order that with our loyalty to the King eternal may be advanced our love of country and its institutions." [61]

Popular preaching could even more emphatically portray America as the purest example of Christian civilization. In discussing the preaching of the southern revivalist Sam Jones, William G. McLoughlin has said: "The mixture of Christianity and chauvinism which became increasingly popular in revival preaching after 1890 was perfectly evident in Jones's statements. He asserted that 'we have the most advanced civilization in the world today' and that 'God has given us the greatest country the sun shines on.' " [62] All this was rooted in long historical development, the virtual identification of the Christian way and the American became axiomatic for many, and became a part of Protestant writing and preaching.

By the early years of the new century, then, the long search for a Christian America seemed to many Protestants to be nearing fulfillment in the spread of democratic civilization. All of the American presidents of this period were spokesmen for the advance of Christian civilization. Referring to the foreign policies of McKinley, Roosevelt, and Taft and their associates, Washington Gladden could say: "I cannot doubt that because of these benign interventions of our national government the people of many of the eastern lands must be more ready than they have ever been to listen to the message of the gospel of Christ." [63] For many in the nation and in the churches, Christianity and American civilization seemed so intimately related that religious duties and patriotic feeling appeared to be but the two sides of the same coin of Christendom. Religion and nationalism lived in intimate association, long after the fact of the separation of church and state.

THREATS TO BE FACED AND OVERCOME

The confidence and enthusiasm of Protestant leaders did not mean that they were unaware of serious problems and dangers in American life. There was uneasy recognition that forces were at work in society which were threatening Protestant values. The range of such concerns was wide, and it affected different groups in the Protestant world with varying intensities. The perplexing realities of social and economic problems, the transforming effects of immigration which cascaded to unprecedented heights in the early years of the present century, the numerical growth of Roman Catholicism and Mormonism, the changing patterns of family life and the increase in the divorce rate—such matters worried the Protestant forces. At many types of church gatherings a familiar rhythm was followed: the identification of problem areas, the acceptance of responsibility to do something about them, and the arousing of enthusiasm to get the job done. The analyses of the problem differed, the proposed solutions varied widely, but in arousing enthusiasm Protestant leaders of many types sounded much alike. It was believed that good intentions and an abundance of zeal would with God's help be adequate to handle the difficult problems.

The self-assurance and crusading spirit of the time could almost but not quite conceal deeper currents of unrest and anxiety. A few perceptive observers were aware of them. William Newton Clarke felt that the new century was not going to be the golden age which so many expected, for in 1901 he prophetically suggested that "mankind has entered one of its periods of passion and unrest." [64] The Presbyterian "Narrative of the State of Religion" for 1900 recognized that "a restlessness of varied and peculiar nature is affecting both our churches and our pastors. It is not to be accurately described nor entirely accounted for, but its presence is undoubted and its effects painfully apparent." [65]

Characteristically, however, the anxieties and perplexities were seen to be molehills beside the towering mountain of hope. The Episcopal Address of the Northern Methodist bishops in 1900 provided a startling illustration of this. The bishops indicated an anxious awareness of difficulties before them, especially as they faced the burgeoning urban world:

> The American city is a conglomerate of all races, nations, tongues, faiths, cutsoms, and political ideas; and by this fact, and that of an easily attainable citizenship, it is the menace of the American State and Church. To penetrate this alien mass by an evangelical religion is as difficult as it is imperative. The question of the city has become the question of the race. How to reach the heart of the city and to change its life is, indeed, the question of questions.[66]

But without coming to grips with the problems to which they had quickly pointed, they concluded with a confident affirmation:

> However disquieting some present aspects of morals and religion may be, we nevertheless close this address in joyful confidence. The Church is not fighting a losing battle The Christian area enlarges; the Christian populations gain on the non-Christian; the Church itself was never more sound in its faith, more pure in life, more influential within Christendom, more aggressive and hopeful without.[67]

The techniques of the voluntary crusades, applied with the best of intentions and with much zeal—and, it was believed, under divine leadership—would surely defeat the enemies of Christian civilization.

At certain points, however, the fact that fundamental changes were threatening the vision of a Protestant America could not be disguised. In the matter of Sabbath observance, to pick an example that especially touched evangelical anxieties, there was obvious decline, not only in the world, but among the faithful. Cries of alarm and protest were sounded, but they could not stop the erosion of Sunday practices advocated by Protestant leadership. Indeed, there was great ambivalence among Protestant clergy and laity about Sunday—there was a wish to hold on to aspects of the "Puritan Sabbath," and yet a lack of real will to launch a counter-crusade. Most of the statements intended to stiffen the backbone of the committed only provide evidence of the actual decline. The Methodist bishops laid bare the problem:

> Obviously there is within the Church, as well as in the world without, a serious and rapidly increasing laxity of Sabbath observance. Unnecessary travel, unnecessary work, the Sunday newspaper, social visiting, excursions, and amusements encroach more and more on time which God has consecrated to sacred uses. Hence many among us are weak, and many are dying. The decay of religion is inevitable if the Church does not abide in the right use of the holy day. Let us be fully persuaded that a holy Sabbath eminently ministers to holy character, and that without Sabbath sanctity our people will suffer moral loss, our sanctuaries will be deserted, and our ministries will be ineffective.[68]

A special committee of the Presbyterian (U.S.A.) General Assembly reported that "the present condition of the Sabbath question in the United States of America presents more dark than bright sides, more threatening aspects than hopeful signs, more difficult problems than encouraging features. It is a question of far greater importance in its effects upon the weal or woe of the American Church and the American Nation, and upon all Christian civilization, and deserves more attention than is generally accorded it." Reflecting the nineteenth-century background in which they had been reared, the members of the committee tended to blame other troubles on the neglect of the Sabbath:

> The life and strength, power and potency of the Church are, and always must be, determined by the character of the Sabbath of its environment. When the people who should be in the pews in the sanctuary are absorbed in the pursuit of pleasure or business on the Lord's Day, the Church and the Lord's treasury are the immediate and inevitable sufferers. Other questions are superficial; this is basal. Others affect the limbs; this strikes at the vitals.[69]

While not all would agree with the diagnosis that this was the *basal* question, especially among the liberal and socially minded Christians, there was nevertheless a rather wide Protestant consensus on the importance of the Sabbath. The decline in Sunday observance seemed to threaten the seedbed of Protestant vitality, morale, and finance—the morning and evening services of worship of the local congregations. The voluntary way of maintaining Christian civilization depended on the continual cultivation of local support. Furthermore, Sunday observance was a way of keeping faith with past generations; a way of showing that nothing really vital was lost under the conditions of freedom. The strict Sabbath was one sign of the continued dominance of Anglo-American Protestantism in the culture. Hence anxiety was displayed when it was evident that the patterns of Sunday observance were changing, both in the culture and in the churches. For example, the Episcopal bishops spoke forcefully on the point in their Pastoral Letter of 1901, deploring the increasing disregard among the confessed disciples of the Lord and condemning this "robbery of God." "To one and all alike we appeal that they labour and deny themselves to conserve the sanctity of our American Sunday," they concluded. "Fathers, mothers, churchmen, we your pastors, entreat that you rally to the defence of this mighty citadel of our religion. Americans, we call upon you to rouse to the protection of this palladium of our liberties, our government, our English civilization." [70] These comments were made just as the motor car was beginning to appear in ever greater numbers on American roads!

The decay of the Sabbath patterns of Christendom was evident as church people were carried along by the cultural trends of the times, especially in the cities. Considerable pressure was put on the faithful to hold the line, and there were groups which labored hard for this cause. Yet the overall trend toward relaxation of strict Sabbath observance even by the pillars of the church was not checked. Protestant leaders still believed hopefully that with determination of will and devotion to duty, however, the trend could be reversed. Then the Protestant forces could be more readily rallied to deal with the serious problems of the day as they perceived them.

For Protestant leadership was determined to deal with the many evils confronting American life. The great attention given to the world scene was not exploited as a way of evading American problems. An emphasis that had long been a part of American Protestant mentality—to save America for the world's sake—was renewed. "He does most to Christianize the world and to hasten the coming of the Kingdom who does most to make thoroughly Christian the United States," affirmed Josiah Strong. "I do not imagine that an Anglo-Saxon is any dearer to God than a Mongolian or an African. My plea is not, Save America for America's sake, but, Save America for the world's sake." [71] Looking back on the early days of the S.V.M., Arthur J. Brown could give as part of the reason for its origin the double necessity of having the "best" aspects of America represented abroad and strengthened at home:

> Asia was finding out more about Europe and America than it had known before. We could no longer pose before the non-Christian world as so superior as we had once imagined ourselves to be. Our crimes and vices were read about in

> Persia, Japan, and China. . . . Asiatic gentlemen visited America and returned to tell their astonished countrymen about the Sunday desecration, the saloons, and the brothels of this alleged most Christian nation.[72]

The strong Protestant endorsement of American life was of the "ideal America" and not of all the current practices. It was accompanied by a professed commitment to remedy whatever practices were incompatible with the vision of Christian America.

The gap between the ideal and the real was believed to be narrowing, however, and crusading enthusiasm was confident that it could be closed, almost entirely if not completely. Gaius Glenn Atkins, looking back on those years before World War I, said:

> The first fifteen years of the twentieth century may sometimes be remembered in America as the Age of Crusades. There were a superabundance of zeal, a sufficiency of good causes, unusual moral idealism, excessive confidence in mass movements and leaders with rare gifts of popular appeal. . . . The air was full of banners, and the trumpets called from every camp.[73]

Quite in keeping with individualistic traditions of voluntaryism, reformers focused on those particular causes which were especially appealing to them, and committed themselves to the appropriate agencies and ways of working that they found best among the many options. There was widespread Protestant enthusiasm for the world missionary crusade; particular reform crusades to make America more Christian usually drew more limited but quite devoted constituencies.

Conspicuous among the crusades of the time was the temperance movement. The drive for a temperate America had been gaining strength among most Protestant groups in the nineteenth century, and as the new century opened it pressed toward victory with broadening support from the churches. The formation of the Anti-Saloon League in 1895 focused the struggle for the Eighteenth Amendment into nonpartisan political channels. To arouse public opinion, to seek prohibition legislation in local areas and then in the nation, and to get the laws fully enforced once they had been enacted—these were the aims of the league. In his clarifying study of the relationship between prohibition and progressivism, James H. Timberlake finds that the league in its early days was based on a loose collection of church, local, and county temperance groups, but that it soon developed its own national structure broadly based primarily on church constituencies. He wrote:

> By 1913 the Anti-Saloon League had become transformed into an independent temperance agency with its own organizational structure, its own constituency, its own leaders, and its own methods and policy. From a coalition of existing temperance groups, it had become a national federation of state antisaloon leagues, which, in turn, had become federations of individual churches throughout each state. With a highly centralized yet extremely flexible federal structure, the league, through its closely coordinated state branches, could reach down into thousands of local churches and mobilize at almost a moment's notice a large body of Protestant voters.[74]

Between 1905 and 1915 the number of churches cooperating with the league more than doubled to about 40,000, chiefly Methodist, Baptist, Presbyterian, and Congregational. Majority opinion in these churches saw intemperance as one of the greatest if not the greatest evil in American life, and a great threat to them. Methodists North and South were especially devoted to prohibition; the northern bishops in 1900 could say: "Yet in extent and direful consequences intemperance, the moderate drinking from which it proceeds, and the saloon which ministers to and aggravates it constitute an evil vastly greater than slavery. It is the servant of all evils." [75] Evangelical denominations felt themselves under attack by the liquor habit and all who participated in it. "Of all the weapons used against the Church of Christ, we believe intemperance is the most dangerous and deadly" a report to Presbyterians declared in 1904.[76] The Anti-Saloon League's power was gained by combining rural, small-town, middle-class, and progressive interests (in all of which Protestants were deeply involved) to rescue American civilization from the threatening forces of the city, the immigrant, and the liquor industry. As Timberlake aptly summed it up:

> As local option progressed, it assumed more and more the nature of a conflict between country and city. One reason for this was the growing determination of the old-stock middle classes to clean up the cities and rid them of vice, crime, poverty, and corruption. Unless cleansed, they feared, the cities would undermine the foundations of American civilization and prevent any further progress toward uplift and reform.[77]

Gusfield's studies led him to a similar conclusion:

> The Eighteenth Amendment was the high point of the struggle to assert the public dominance of the old middle-class values. It established the victory of Protestant over Catholic, rural over urban, tradition over modernity, the middle class over both the lower and the upper strata.[78]

Prohibition drew the support of both liberal and conservative Christians (including some liberal Catholics). Many leaders of the social gospel favored the cause in their speeches and writings.

Prohibition was part of the progressive drive to reform American life, to curb big business (of which the liquor interests were a part), and to democratize the nation. It shared in and contributed to the moral idealism of that drive. Robert A. Woods, long a participant in settlement-house work, predicted in 1919 that the Eighteenth Amendment would reduce poverty, nearly wipe out prostitution and crime, improve labor organization, and increase national resources by freeing vast, suppressed human potentialities.[79] The moral enthusiasm of Protestant crusading contributed to the intensity and uncompromising quality of prohibition. When the Eighteenth Amendment went into effect in January of 1920, it was seen as a striking victory for the advance of Christian civilization.

THE GREAT CRUSADE

The Protestant hope for world conquest for Christ and civilization was to be realized primarily by voluntary means, by the spirit, commitment, and sacrifice of those who believed it would soon be realized, with God's help. But when civilization was threatened, then the Protestant forces could include war in their crusading pattern—it happened in 1898, and on a much larger scale it happened in 1917–18. Though there had been much sentiment for peace and a desire to remain neutral, when America finally entered the war in April 1917, the churches generally supported the military effort, and with serious determination.

Lyman Abbott spoke for the majority of American Christians in calling the war a "twentieth century crusade." On the title page of his book by that title, he stated its thesis: "A crusade to make this world a home in which God's children can live in peace and safety is more Christian than a crusade to recover from pagans the tomb in which the body of Christ was buried." He interpreted the war as a struggle of civilization against barbarism: "In strictness of speech there is no war in Europe. There is an international *posse comitatus*, representing more than twenty civilized nations, summoned to preserve the peace and protect the peaceable nations of Europe from the worst, most highly organized and most efficient band of brigands the world has ever known." Along with many others, he idealized American participation in the war as an illustration of its Christian character:

> A nation is made Christian, not by maintaining an established church, nor by building cathedrals, nor by writing a confession of its faith into its constitution. It is made Christian by the spirit of love, service, and sacrifice. When did a nation ever show so much of this spirit of love, service and sacrifice as the American Nation does today? [80]

Beyond the storm of war, however, spiritual leaders discerned the rainbow of a Christian peace; in the midst of war the signs of the coming of the kingdom could be glimpsed by the eye of faith. "When the prisoners in every belligerent land, sitting behind barbed wire fences or surrounded by stockades and guards, are writing tens of thousands of letters to praise the work done by the Y.M.C.A. and done in the name of Christ, here is going on before our eyes a visible preparation for the Christianization of the world," declared W. H. P. Faunce in lectures at Kenyon College.[81]

In a book that was written in the long period of disillusionment and reaction after the war, Ray H. Abrams collected statements uttered by clergymen during the war showing how unqualified and full of hate for the enemy were the endorsements of the war by many Protestant spokesmen.[82] In a careful study, John F. Piper, Jr. has since shown that Abrams did not present the whole picture. There were sizable and responsible elements in Protestantism, clearly influential in the work of the Federal Council of Churches and in the major denominations in its membership, which did not thoughtlessly bless the war nor give in to hatred. Piper has demonstrated that "the Federal Council of the Churches of Christ in America developed and maintained a responsible Christian social policy during World War I," a policy "which was responsible to the basic imperatives of the Christian faith and adhered to it in general through the war."[83] The leaders of the Council were churchmen prominent in the denominations; the views they held were representative of an important range of church opinion. Though with more restraint than has at times been pictured, Protestants nevertheless did largely and strongly support American participation in the war, seeing it as part of the crusade for Christian civilization and as an expression of Christian purpose. "Physical force never wins any permanent victory unless that force be the transient expression of a righteous purpose," exclaimed Dr. Faunce right after the war.[84] Christians were largely united (though with varying degrees of emphasis) in their estimation of the war as an expression of righteous purpose.

The approach of peace found Protestants looking ahead to carrying the crusade to victory. "If there ever was a time in the history of the Christian Church when the establishment of the world-wide kingdom of God should be the dominating thought and purpose of the united body of Christ, that hour has just dawned upon us in these tragic, pregnant days," wrote S. Earl Taylor and Halford E. Luccock, articulating views widely held. "Everywhere we look, in Europe, Asia, Africa, and America, men and nations are in upheaval and we see conditions which demand the concentration of the unifying and guiding forces of Christendom."[85] New crusades of reconstruction were planned. Dr. Faunce succinctly stated the spirit in which they were launched: "Having won the War by moral force, we must rebuild the world on moral principles."[86] Such idealism was soon to encounter some chilling realities, but it was strongly enunciated in evangelical churches as the second decade of the century drew to a close.

This chapter has called attention to the fact that much that the Protestant churches did from 1890 to 1920 was largely a continuation of the familiar patterns of the nineteenth-century search for a Christian America by voluntary means—the missionary enter-

VI

The New Christianity and the Old Hopes (1890–1920)

Much that the evangelical churches did from 1890 to 1920 continued the familiar patterns of nineteenth-century voluntaryism—the missionary advances and the temperance crusade are obvious examples. Two quite closely interrelated movements, however, broke significant new ground in this period—the social gospel and cooperative Christianity.

Both of these movements had roots deep in history and had many direct continuities with the evangelical Protestantism of the nineteenth century. Both the social gospel and cooperative Christianity, however, were also trying to deal in fresh ways with new problems emerging from the relentless pressures of urban growth, industrial proliferation, and intellectual ferment. Those in the vanguard of these two movements wanted to preserve whatever was good in the Protestant ways of the past, but were quite conscious that they were advocating certain new patterns of thought, organization, and action to the degree that some could speak of the emergence of a "new Christianity." The new emphases, they were convinced, did not come from a repudiation of the authentic Christian tradition but from a recovery of it. They believed that certain important aspects of the faith had become obscured in the long course of history.

The social gospel and cooperative movements were not the only Protestant efforts to come to terms with twentieth-century realities, but they were very conspicuous and often controversial ones. They were closely related, but they were certainly not identical. They will be considered separately in this chapter, with particular attention to their relationship to the familiar Protestant hope for a Christian America.

THE SOCIAL GOSPEL

The term "social gospel" did not come into prominence until the early twentieth century. Through the centuries, Christians of many traditions have concerned themselves with the social problems of their times in various ways.[1] The burgeoning of industrialism in the nineteenth century brought about serious maladjustments, and much public attention was focused on social questions. In Europe, a number of social Christian movements arose and a broad literature was produced; the American social gospel was much informed by such developments, especially in England.[2] Though the term has not always been employed so precisely, it is now standard usage to mean by "social gospel" the movement among liberal minded Protestant evangelicals to rally Christian forces to deal with the problems of society which were intensifying in the late nineteenth and early twentieth centuries. Social gospel leaders wanted to renew for their own times the reform spirit that had guided the benevolent empire in the earlier nineteenth century. The difficulties arising out of industrialization and urbanization were their particular concern. They sought to parallel the Protestant emphasis on the individual and his freedom with attention to social realities, especially those of the urban slum and of the condition of labor. The movements' leaders were in most cases evangelical or Christocentric liberals in their theology. They were still working for a Christian America, but they believed that in the changed social situation new ways of thought and action were called for to speed its coming. Their views on public issues were largely shaped by the reformist currents of the progressive movement, then reaching the peak of its influence in American life.

Though the social gospel was the most conspicuous form of corporate Protestant concern for society in this period, it was by no means the only significant expression of it. Among conservatives, there was often serious attention to the problems of the day, but their characteristic approach was to deal with the victims of social maladjustment on an individual basis and to resist as inconsistent with personal freedom the new social emphases. The methods used by "rescue missions" and the Salvation Army were favored by the conservatives, and much was done along such lines.[3] On the other hand, there were also some Protestants, considerably fewer in number, who were drawn to more radical solutions to social problems than those favored by either conservative or liberal social Christians. Radical social Christians often espoused some brand of socialism, usually in a nondoctrinaire, evolutionary form.[4] Though some exponents of the social gospel drew some of their beliefs from socialist ideas and programs, in general they were progressive and reformist rather than reconstructionist or revolutionary in their thought and action.[5]

The first clear articulation of the social gospel in evangelical Protestantism appeared in the 1870's. Washington Gladden, liberal Congregational pastor, was its first prominent spokesman. Influenced by currents of thought associated with the names of Ritschl and Bushnell (he was a personal friend of the latter), Gladden was also an early interpreter of liberal theology who emphasized the doctrine of the coming kingdom of God in history in the not too distant future.[6] In the 1880's the movement burgeoned rapidly. Josiah Strong became an early social gospel spokesman; as secretary of the Evangelical Alliance he was responsible for three significant gatherings in 1887, 1889, and 1893, meetings which did much to arouse evangelical interest in social concerns.[7] Richard T. Ely, Episcopal layman and influential teacher of economics at Johns Hopkins and Wisconsin, wrote a widely read book in 1889, *The Social Aspects of Christianity*.[8] A number of other Christian leaders became concerned with social issues, and fellowships and organizations devoted to these matters began to appear—the Church Association for the Advancement of the Interests of Labor (CAIL, founded in 1887) was a conspicuous early example.

It was in the 1890's, however, that the movement began to play a significant role in the life of the denominations, especially in the Congregational, Episcopal, Baptist, Methodist, and Presbyterian churches (primarily in the northern branches of the latter three). New social Christian spokesmen emerged; the most widely heard and controversial such figure in the 1890's was George D. Herron, Congregational pastor who was called to teach at Iowa College (later Grinnell), and whose startling platform addresses across the country drew large throngs and filled a series of small books.[9] New organizations were formed, some along denominational lines but others cutting across them; of especial importance was the Brotherhood of the Kingdom, in which Walter Rauschenbusch, Baptist pastor and seminary professor who was destined to become the most conspicuous interpreter of the social gospel, was prominent.[10]

The social gospel "came of age" in the first and second decades of the new century, when it became quite influential in the Protestant world. Many liberal pulpits were filled by exponents of the expanding movement, while a flood of its books came from the presses. A number of denominations formed official agencies to deal with socio-economic questions—the Department of Church and Labor of the (northern) Presbyterian Church's Board of Home Missions, under the leadership of a former workingman, Charles Stelzle, was the first in 1903. The fame of Rauschenbusch's *Christianity and the Social Crisis*, which appeared in 1907 on the heels of a financial panic, helped to project the movement into national prominence. Though the self-conscious advocates of the new interpretation never became a majority party in any given denomination, in the years prior to World War I they were highly articulate in pulpit, platform, and press and evoked wide interest in social questions.

The social gospel from its first appearance was critical of the individualism of the earlier evangelicalism, and insisted that the older *personal* ethic was not sufficient for the day of big industry and sprawling cities, for a *social* ethic was also required. Though the movement was concerned with a wide range of questions, its central focus was steadily on the problems of labor and the rights of labor to organize. Gladden's first social gospel book was prefaced by this comment: "Now that slavery is out of the way, the questions that concern the welfare of our free laborers are coming forward; and no intelligent man needs to be admonished of their urgency." [11] In 1886, a year marked by bitter strikes and marred by the disastrous Haymarket riot in Chicago, a year when many Protestants seemed willing to sacrifice labor's rights to the need for law and order, Gladden boldly declared in an oft-quoted paragraph:

> The state of the industrial world is a state of war. And if war is the word, then the efficient combination and organization must not all be on the side of capital; labor must be allowed to make the combinations necessary for the protection of its own interests. While the conflict is in progress, labor has the same right that capital has to prosecute the warfare in the most effective way. If war is the order of the day, we must grant to labor belligerent rights. The sooner this fact is recognized, the better for all concerned. The refusal to admit it has made the conflict, thus far, much more fierce and sanguinary than it would otherwise have been.[12]

The awakening of the churches to the plight of labor and the encouragement of the worker to get a fair share of what he produced were always close to the heart of social gospel interest.

Typical of the hundreds of statements was this one by the corresponding secretary of the Board of Education of the Presbyterian Church (U.S.A.) in 1907:

> Religious leaders have been slow to appreciate the fact that the working man is deserving of sympathy because he has been the sufferer in every phase of the industrial revolution. The introduction of labor-saving machines by which the product has been vastly increased has inured almost exclusively to the interests of the employer. . . . The employer and not the employee has been in the position to invoke the aid of the state in the framing of industrial legislation and the throttling of remedial measures.[13]

Encouraged by such views, some ministerial associations exchanged fraternal delegates with central labor unions.

The social gospel contributed to significant changes in American Protestant mentality; it led many churchmen to take seriously crucial issues in American life and to rethink their philosophies of public life. Many Protestants became much more aware of the way social and economic realities operated in modern industrial society. Even where the movement, with its liberal theological and reformist premises, was specifically rejected, as it was in some churches almost completely, still it raised questions which could not again be easily evaded though its particular answers might be rejected.

The social gospel emphasized the motif of service to humanity—selfless and sacrificial service. A favorite phrase of the movement was "enthusiasm for humanity"—a phrase popularized through a pioneer work by an English social Christian writer, Sir John Seeley, in his *Ecce Homo: A Survey of the Life and Work of Jesus Christ.*[14] Josiah Strong entitled the last chapter of *The New Era* "An Enthusiasm for Humanity." Social gospel advocates were often especially active in institutional churches and social settlements which featured busy programs of service to workingmen, immigrants, and the socially disinherited. "The churches need to feel more of that social compunction which is the high-water mark of modern civilization," said Edward Judson, pastor of an active "institutional" church in New York which carried on a busy program of service activities seven days a week.[15] There was a strong tendency in the movement to minimize to some extent the role of the church, to subordinate it to the coming kingdom. With the characteristic directness which helped to make him famous, Rauschenbusch said of the church: "She does not exist for her own sake; she is simply a working organization to create the Christian life in individuals and the kingdom of God in human society." [16]

The notes of humanization, of sacrificial service, and of the servant role of the church were, however, accommodated to the familiar quest for a Christian civilization. The social gospel advocates were men of their time who operated largely within the patterns of the quest for a Protestant America. The new social Christianity had a vision of a vastly better human society, but it was essentially the old vision of a religious nation socialized. One of the influential pioneers among the new voices, William Jewett Tucker, president of Dartmouth, was sensitive (as most socially oriented Christians were) to the gap between the principles espoused and their social applications, but both principles and applications were intended to revivify and rescue a Christian civilization. He explained: "Here lies the ready task of the new Christianity, to set Christendom in order—its cities, its industries, its society, its literature, its law." [17]

To set Christendom in order, to save Christian civilization by infusing it with principles of justice and love according to the teaching and example of Christ—this was a major goal of the social gospel. Gladden stated the program clearly in the early 1890's:

> Every department of human life—the families, the schools, amusements, art, business, politics, industry, national politics, international relations—will be governed by the Christian

> law and controlled by Christian influences. When we are bidden to seek first the kingdom of God, we are bidden to set our hearts on this great consummation; to keep this always before us as the object of our endeavors; to be satisfied with nothing less than this. The complete Christianization of all life is what we pray and work for, when we work and pray for the coming of the kingdom of heaven.[18]

The social gospel's goal was in many ways in continuity with the old dream of a Christian America. Toward the climax of his career, when the social gospel had won an accepted place, Gladden declared, "If we want the nations of the earth to understand Christianity, we have got to have a Christianized nation to show them. Small samples will not serve. The real question is, after all, what Christianity is able to do for the civilization of a people." [19] Josiah Strong made explicit his understanding of the relation between the social gospel and the hope of the winning of the world by Protestants in many places, as in these words: "If the church is willing to teach by her example that Christianity is divorced from philanthropy and reform and social science and the progress of civilization, or that these are broader than Christianity, she must be content to occupy a little place and never dream of conquering the world for Christ. But if she aims at universal conquest, she must show a universal interest in human affairs." [20] The influence of a "benevolent" and perhaps largely unconscious imperialism was operating in such attitudes. Much social gospel thought and action looked toward the future and sought to come to terms with new social realities, but it was set in the matrix of the continuing search for a Protestant nation.

The idea of the kingdom of God, so central in the thought of the social gospel, was not consciously conceived or presented merely as an idealized Christendom; the social hope was more complex than that. Statements of the hope of the coming kingdom normally implied dimensions of transcendence which could not be wholly caught within history. Most doctrines of the kingdom did not see the reality as becoming completely immanental in a perfected social order on earth. Rauschenbusch was careful at this point, especially in his mature theological reflection: "The kingdom of God is divine in its origin, progress and consummation." [21] Careful expressions of the hope of the coming of the kingdom of God emphasized that it is always present and always future, always coming, never fully exhausted in a given social order. But the social gospel was a movement which stressed preaching and encouraged action; those especially concerned about implementing its tenets tended to sweep aside the qualifications and to interpret the kingdom of God as a perfect social order soon to come in history. Harry F. Ward, a Methodist seminary professor who was one of the social gospel's most effective early evangelists, saw it this way:

> While the theologians were emphasizing the transcendent aspects of the kingdom of God, the statesmen of the Church were ever seeking to give it visible form. . . . His Kingdom is to come on earth by intensive conquest—by the power of a love, mighty to save the whole of life, a transforming leaven able to reach the heart of society as well as of men, to capture its motives and motor powers. This was the purpose of Jesus, and his followers must consciously undertake the task of realizing his vision.[22]

As the social gospel came of age, it attracted a number of popularizers who wrote without the theological precision of the more reflective. One such was a professor at Illinois Wesleyan, who cried that "the western religious world has during the last few years been roused to a pitch of exultant enthusiasm over the Christian ideal of the coming Kingdom of God upon the earth. This social version of the Christian faith dreams of an ideal world that is to be gradually realized." [23] Gradually, yes, for the process had been long—yet now the time was at hand, the kingdom of God on earth was very near. The transcendent elements that had been strongly emphasized in the millennialist doctrine of the coming kingdom as stressed by nineteenth-century evangelicals were now pushed into the background; the kingdom would soon come in history in near if not full completeness, and it would come largely through the efforts of men. "The Church's great purpose is to transform human society into the Kingdom of God by regenerating individuals and reconstructing all human relations in accordance with the will of God," exclaimed William S. Chase of Brooklyn at the (Episcopal) Church Congress.[24] The concern for civilization, which in the early nineteenth century had been secondary to the religious mission, was now often being put first, with religious mission as a means to the end of the Christianization of civilization. The priorities had subtly been reversed; men were being exhorted to be religious for the sake of civilization. Often unconsciously, an idealized Americanism had become the real center of interest for many Christians.[25]

The stress on the complete Christianization of American life left many Protestants largely oblivious to the fact that the number of Jews, though small in proportion to the total population, was rapidly increasing. The Jewish population increased threefold in the first two decades of the twentieth century, largely because of immigration from Russia. It was also difficult for Protestants accustomed to thinking of themselves as the religious majority, to come to terms with the growing numbers of Americans who were quite disinterested in organized religion, both among the working classes and among intellectuals. They usually looked at such persons either in a patronizing or a fearful way. Insofar as social gospel leaders discussed such matters, they usually spoke of winning as many as possible to their point of view, expecting to gather enough to carry the day. As a sensitive student of American life, Walter Rauschenbusch was not unaware that significant elements of the population could not accept Christianization. His way of attempting to meet the objection was to magnify the person of Jesus Christ and to exalt his moral teachings apart from the trappings of institutional religion. He could still confidently claim that most Americans still explicitly followed Jesus: "To the great majority of our nation, both inside and outside of the churches, he has become the incarnate moral law and his name is synonymous with the ideal of human goodness. To us who regard him as the unique revelation of God, the unfolding of the divine life under human forms, he is the ultimate standard of moral and spiritual life." He knew that outside these groups were growing minorities, and he sought to broaden the concept of Christianization to include as many of them as possible:

> But very many who do not hold this belief in a formulated way or who feel compelled to deny it, including an increasing portion of our Jewish fellow-citizens, will still consent that in Jesus our race has reached one of its highest points, if not its crowning summit thus far, so that Jesus Christ is a prophecy of the future glory of humanity, the type of Man as he is to be. Christianizing means humanizing in the highest sense. I ask the consent of both classes to use his name for the undertaking which he initiated for us. To say that we want to moralize the social order would be both vague and powerless to most men. To say that we want to christianize it is both concrete and compelling.[26]

So he (and the social gospel generally) related their efforts to deal creatively with economic, industrial, and urban problems to the Protestant hope for a specifically Christianized social order. With great confidence in God, in themselves, and in the vitality of their churches, they believed it could be done; indeed, as they hopefully saw it, it *was* being done. Their great hope, their confidence in the future, led them to seize avidly the evidence that supported their views but to be selective in facing that which challenged them. So great was their hope that they confused future possibilities with contemporary realities, and too easily saw what they hoped would happen already coming to be. Their strategy was often superficial because their reading of the situation they faced was too limited, too onesided; disillusionment and frustration were to follow later.

From the perspective of the later twentieth century, the Christian social hopes of the early decades seem naive indeed. "A considerable part of the life of civilized society is controlled by Christian principle," said Gladden. "We have come to a day in which it does not seem quixotic to believe that the principles of Christianity are soon to prevail; that all social relations are to be Christianized."[27] Rauschenbusch, though more realistic than many of his colleagues, could nevertheless make his oft-quoted and frequently criticized statement in 1912 that of the five great sectors of the social order, four had been largely Christianized: family, church, school, and politics! As he saw it, these had passed through constitutional changes so that they could be accounted to some degree as part of the organism through which the spirit of Christ could do its work in humanity. He could say, for example, that "the teaching profession as a whole is under the law of Christ" and that "our political communities are constitutionally on a Christian footing."[28] The unredeemed sector remaining to be Christianized was business. Here the drive for Christian civilization faced its greatest problem, as Rauschenbusch viewed it, for unless the economic order could also be brought under subjection to the moral principles of Christ, the already Christianized sections would be negatively affected. The concentration of the social gospel on economic questions, especially on the just relations of labor and capital, is disclosed with great clarity at this point. This was the fresh contribution of the social gospel, but it was set axiomatically in the familiar pattern of extending and improving a specifically Christian civilization.

The social gospel, of course, specifically repudiated any notion of a Christian society with *formal* or legal religious establishment. The commitment to religious freedom was wholehearted. Gladden spoke for the movement in agreeing that America was not a Christian nation in any legal sense, for a compulsory faith is a contradiction in terms. "And while we have no desire to see the establishment of any form of religion by law in this land," he explained, "most of us would be willing to see the nation in its purposes and policies and ruling aims becoming essentially Christian. . . . It must be, in spirit and purpose and character, a Christian nation." [29] Social gospel thought characteristically understood the Christian spirit as the key element in the development of democracy, and thus interpreted the spread of democratic ways as "Christianization." Richard T. Ely was more explicit than most social gospel writers when he insisted on the central importance and the divine nature of the state, explaining that this meant "that God works through the State in carrying out His purposes more universally than through any other institution; that it takes first place among His instrumentalities." Therefore he found that "the main purpose of the State is the religious purpose. Religious laws are the only laws which ought to be enacted." Hence he urged all Christians to see to it "that they put as much as possible, not of doctrine or creed into the State constitution, but of Christian life and practice into the activity of the State, working, to be sure, to change the constitution in so far as this may stand in the way of righteousness. The nation must be recognized fully as a Christian nation." [30] All this was to be done without limiting anyone's freedom!

One of the fullest discussions of the state and democracy was produced by Samuel Zane Batten, who with Rauschenbusch was conspicuous for progressive leadership in the Northern Baptist Convention. The three great facts of the modern world, he argued in 1909, were the state, democracy, and Christianity—the latter was "the most potent force in our modern civilization." The state "is the one organ great enough and varied enough to express and correlate the varied powers and talents of mankind, the one medium through which all men can cooperate in their search after social perfection," while democracy "is the one idea of human society that is befriended by the universe, legitimated in history, in accord with the Christian spirit, and inevitable in the future." He presented democracy as less a form of government than a confession of faith in "human brotherhood based on the divine Fatherhood." He argued for a "great social synthesis" which would sweep family, church, and state into the larger whole of the kingdom of God. The way to do this was clear, he declared, "since the Christian ideal is absolute in its requirements, and the Christian law is universal in its sweep, it follows that Christian citizenship is confronted with the task of creating a truly Christian civilization." He insisted that the coming great synthesis of state, democracy, and Christianity was not utopian, for it was realizable. Neither was it theocratic, for "the Christian order of society is inspirational rather than institutional." [31] Batten was saying with some precision what many were expressing more generally as he delineated the ideal of a socialized Christian society in which the concerns of the Protestant majority operating through the channels of persuasion would control the society. By a consensus of enthusiasm would the kingdom be brought near.[32] The position was summed up succinctly in somewhat different terms by a layman, R. Fulton Cutting, in 1912. The new ideal of the church, he explained, was "the actual uplift of Society in all phases of its moral life; the scientific embodiment of her theology in a comprehensive ministering to the souls, minds and bodies of men. She must Christianize civilization practically and the civil authorities of the democratic state are the tools she herself so aptly fashioned." [33] The social gospel's commitment to democracy was frequently stated; through democracy enlightened Christians could share in the building of the kingdom of God on earth.

It has been noted that the social gospel movement was strong primarily in the northern denominations. Yet the ferment of the social gospel was not unknown in the South. Kenneth K. Bailey has found that:

> between the turn of the century and World War I, the three major southern white Protestant groups underwent significant changes in program and outlook. Absorbed at the turn of the century in evangelism and little mindful of social needs beyond blue laws and prohibition, they emerged during the next fifteen years as advocates of social justice, proclaiming the Christian obligation to fashion Christ's kingdom on earth. . . . Southern Protestant social pronouncements mirrored the Progressive Movement in tenor and phraseology.[34]

The pronouncements did not often lead to social action, however, and strong opposition was accorded even to the expression of progressive views. Yet the impact of social Christian ideas was felt everywhere within American evangelical Protestantism in the early years of the present century. In fairness, it must be added that even where it was the strongest, the social gospel was more a pulpit and platform movement than it was one devoted to social or political action.

There was much implicit internationalism in social gospel thought. Evangelical liberal and social gospel forces shared in the world missionary enthusiasm of the time, and of course believed that the coming kingdom would be finally worldwide in scope. The international aspect was intensified by World War I. President Faunce of Brown, for example, extended the social gospel crusade to the world, saying that the Church "is divinely and imperatively summoned now to lead, to set men dreaming of the day of God, to unite men in erecting the great new structure of international life." [35] As the war was justified by making the world safe for democracy, so the peace could be justified and safeguarded by making the world safe for Christian democracy. In Faunce's words: "To place underneath the world-order the steady perception that all nations are members one of another is the first step in Christianizing the relation of states." [36] In a popular presentation, two Methodist authors explained that Jesus Christ was the world's first and greatest democrat. "A safe democracy will come in these belated nations when Christ comes. It will come with the Great Democrat, not before." [37] The social gospel envisioned the triumph of Christianized democratic civilization throughout the world.

In many ways a "new Christianity," the social gospel was also continuous in many respects with the dream of a Christian America. There were important differences in the new movement's challenge to the old individualism, and in its acceptance of liberal theological views and progressive attitudes toward labor and industry. But in its unreflective clinging to the idea of the triumph of Protestant civilization, it exhibited real continuity with the earlier nineteenth century.

COOPERATIVE CHRISTIANITY

Along with the missionary movement, the social gospel played a prominent role in the development of closer cooperation among the denominations in the twentieth century. The informal devices which the denominations had founded for cooperation in the previous century were not proving adequate to the demands of the new one, especially in the effort to deal seriously with the burgeoning cities at home and with difficult missionary problems abroad. Increasingly regularized and official cooperation among churches was seen to be necessary if the evangelical message was to be carried into the unfriendly environments of troubled cities and distant non-Western lands. The missionary crusade, the social gospel, and the rise of councils of churches and other officially sponsored cooperative agencies bore an intimate relationship to each other.

Early in the 1890's, Josiah Strong called for federation among churches at various levels (especially local) so that the social task of Christianity could be more fully accomplished. He said: "There are increasing indications that if the churches do not soon organize for the prosecution of social reforms they will lose their opportunity of leadership and with it their great opportunity to regain their lost hold on the masses and to shape the civilization of the future."[38] Washington Gladden had long advocated closer cooperation among the churches. In the early 1880's he wrote an imaginative account, *The Christian League of Connecticut*, which attracted wide attention for it pictured how successful a local association of churches could be in dealing with missionary and social problems. A decade later he wrote a sequel, *The Cosmopolis City Club*, this time focusing on the urban problem; his book provided impetus for the formation of several associations for municipal improvement.[39] Strong and Gladden both referred primarily to quite localized federations, but the problems churches faced were clearly national and world in scope, and the desirability of official church cooperation by national church bodies was seen as increasingly necessary.

By the dawn of the new century there were many voices saying that "some adequate and far-reaching method for the unification of Christian effort in reform should at once be inaugurated and that such unification can best be effected by aggressive, organic cooperation of the great governing bodies of the Evangelical Churches of Christendom."[40] In 1901 a "National Federation of Churches and Christian Workers" was formed under the leadership of Elias B. Sanford, a Congregational pastor who was especially interested in "institutional" churches. The denominations were not officially represented in this federation, but under Sanford's leadership steps were taken to call a conference in 1905 at which officially appointed representatives of the churches would be present. At that gathering, delegates of twenty-nine communions drafted plans to form the Federal Council of Churches of Christ in America, which came into being in 1908.[41]

In his welcoming address to the representatives at the first meeting of the council, William H. Roberts, stated clerk of the General Assembly of the Presbyterian Church (U.S.A.), emphasized the blending of missionary, social, and cooperative emphases in the life of the new agency. He neatly conjoined the familiar concerns for the spread of Christianity and its world victory with the new interests in economic justice and Christian unity. Explaining that the Federal Council would seek "the thorough Christianization of our country," Roberts declared that:

> The essential spirit of our Nation is thus that of Jesus Christ, and it is the duty of the American Churches to make that spirit more Christian, to awaken yet greater national interest in the welfare of all earth's peoples, to provide men and means in increasing ratios for the work of spiritual salvation, and to hasten the day when the true King of Men shall everywhere be crowned as Lord of all. This council stands for the hope of organized work for speedy Christian advance toward World Conquest. . . . It is marvelous how the presence of the common enemy in heathen lands has brought Christian men to realize their need of unity in thought and work. Face to face with the corruption and degradation of heathenism, they realize in a very distant manner that this world is a lost world apart from Jesus Christ.[42]

The conquest was to be by sheer weght of numbers, by the enthusiasm and commitment of Christian forces—the familiar accents of nineteenth-century Protestantism. In this remarkable statement, Roberts was revealing the broad consensus that allowed the conservative and liberal elements of the main line evangelical denominations to work together for Christian civilization at home and abroad. Though the new council was especially concerned with Christian work in the nation, for the Foreign Missions Conference of North America (1893) was responsible for cooperation in overseas work, the interests and experiences of the churches abroad gave added impetus for federation at home.

A number of prominent social gospel leaders were deeply involved in the work of the Federal Council from its early days; those who have already been mentioned in this chapter as having worked with the council were Batten, Faunce, Gladden, Rauschenbusch, Stelzle, Strong, Tucker, and Ward. Also conspicuous in the early years was Frank Mason North, Methodist pastor and mission leader, author of the Christian social hymn, "Where cross the crowded ways of life"; for him "the dream of a united Church has no field for its actualization nearer or more appealing than our great American cities." [43] Later to be the third president of the Federal Council, North had been prominent in the formation of the Methodist Federation for Social Service in 1907, out of which came a statement which became known as "the social creed of the churches." Adopted by the General Conference of the Methodist Episcopal Church in 1908, these social ideals were also adopted by the Federal Council at its first meeting later that year, and further expanded in 1912 to put the Federal Council on record as deeply concerned with the rights and just treatment of all men, especially of workingmen.[44]

Though the Federal Council grew slowly in the early years, its influence soon began to be felt in the denominations. A Presbyterian report for 1910, for example, after examining the many difficulties facing churches in the new century, said:

> All these new questions can not be solved by one Church alone, nor one denomination alone. There must be a combination of the Churches—a united, persistent effort to lift society, in both Church and State, or the Republic is doomed. Realizing this, the Church bodies formed the Federal Council of Christ in America, popularly called the Inter-Church Federation. The work of the Inter-Church Federation is the rousing in all our churches and citizens to the solving of the great religious and social problems of our day.

Then, in a typical example of the way denominational leaders could sweep into one statement some of the old moral concerns with the new social ones, the report specified the problems: "such as the distribution of charity, the alleviation of poverty, better care for the aged than the almshouse, the reduction of the number of saloons, the cure of the awful ills of social impurity, moral education in the public school, the furnishing of lectures, good times and clean shows for the boys and girls, the young and the old, without the awful temptations that now cluster around the dance hall, the pool-room and the saloon; the bringing of the Gospel message into every home, American and foreign." [45]

The Federal Council was only one of a number of agencies in which the blending of mission, social, and cooperative motifs was evident. The Foreign Missions Conference of North America, the Missionary Education Movement (1902), the Home Missions Council (1908), and other agencies exhibited similar concerns. The rise of the councils of churches and other cooperative agencies at local, state, and national levels was an important development in the Protestant effort to deal with the emerging social realities of the twentieth century. The councils contributed to the development of the ecumenical spirit and were in tune with many of the currents of their time.[46] But it must also be noted that they developed under the rubrics of the crusade for the full Christianization of American civilization. This stance was maintained in cooperative Protestant circles all during the World War I period into the immediate postwar years. As one of the most articulate Protestant voices of those years put it: "Slowly, irresistibly, the world is moving toward a federation of all churches in the common task of Christianity and a league of all civilized states in the tasks of civilization." [47] The relationship between the two was understood to be very close indeed.

BLACK PROTESTANTS: SEPARATE AND UNEQUAL

In the flood of literature emanating from social gospel and co-operative Christian sources there was relatively little reference to Negro life, problems, and religion. The search for justice and re-conciliation to which the "new Christianity" was dedicated was truncated by the axioms of the "old-Protestantdom" with its overtones of Anglo-Saxon world leadership. The relegation of

Negro Christianity to second-class status deprived the white Protestant world of resources, insights, and judgments that were sorely needed. Idealistic and well-intentioned white Protestants moved in an atmosphere tainted by racism and imperialism—and they were cut off from those who might have helped them to see it.

Actually, Protestantism was generally a more powerful force in the black community than it was in the white. Just prior to World War I, of a total population of about ten million Negroes, some two million were members of Baptist churches (in which children were not counted in membership) and one and a half million were communicants of Methodist churches. It has been widely observed that the black churches served much more important roles in the life of their people than was true for the white. "The Negro church is not merely a religious institution, but comprises all the complex features of the life of the people," declared the dean of Howard University in 1913. "It furnishes the only field in which the Negro has shown initiative and executive energy on a large scale." [48] There is much evidence to show that black Protestants took their Christian and democratic heritages very seriously; August Meier has concluded that "Negroes never abandoned their emphasis upon the Christian and humanitarian and democratic elements in the American tradition," and that "their outlook never became as secular as that of many of their fellow Americans." [49] And somewhat ironically, at a time when white Protestant leadership was deploring its inability to reach large numbers of the working classes, black churches were filled with them. Many of the latter were agricultural workers, of course, but as the migration to southern and later to northern cities increased, growing numbers of industrial workers were found in Negro congregations. "The Negro church is the only Protestant church in America which has kept hold of the common laborer, and it is the largest and strongest organization among Negroes," said the editor of the

Christian Recorder of Philadelphia in 1913.[50] The vast world of Negro Christianity, however, was little known in the white churches.

On the whole, the major denominations offered little effective resistance to the passage of Jim Crow legislation and to the disenfranchisement of Negroes in the South. Within the Negro bodies, of course, these developments were watched with anxiety. The black churches also had a dream of the triumph of Christian civilization in America; the rhetoric of world Christian conquest was familiar to them. But Negro Christians were painfully aware of the relegation of blacks to second-class status in the civilization they knew. For them "Christian civilization" had a long way to go—but they characteristically had hope that it would improve.

The Bishops' Quadrennial Address at the Centennial Celebration of the African Methodist Episcopal Church in 1896, for example, voiced the hope in familiar terms: "May we not suppose that America, made up as she is of all races and kindreds, is to be the battle ground where the enemy of mankind shall be dethroned, and the kingdom of Christ shall be permanently established to the fulfillment of said prophecy?" Not only in the United States but in the world would the victory come: "But now kingdoms are tumbling and empires are falling before the giant sway of Republican reform, and ere the close of another century we predict that there will not be a king, monarch or emperor known in civilization but that the Christian world will be united into one international Republican family, with Christ as their King."[51] But at the very same session, a fraternal delegate from the African Methodist Episcopal Church said candidly:

> We are to brace up under the Jim-Crow-Car pressure, the ill treatment at eating counters, the insults at health and pleasure resorts and the absolute refusal to be admitted into the restaurants and hotels of the land, especially the South land, though you be a gentleman and possess the means to pay your way.

> These things, with a thousand more, are perpetuated upon us in a so-called Christian land and by a Christian people, many of whom preach identically the same doctrine which we preach, and proclaim aloud that "of one blood God has made all men for to dwell upon the face of the earth, etc."

But Dr. Evans Tyree concluded as so many others did:

> America has put herself on the defensive more than once for the sake of others far away, but her black sons have suffered and died by the hundreds within her own dominion and and none have come to their rescue. These are things we see with much sorrow, but we shall live and die loyal to the stars and stripes, in obedience to law and order.[52]

The basic tension between appreciation for Christian civilization and its terrible shortcomings was expressed again and again. In 1904 at the General Conference of the African Methodist Episcopal Church, the Episcopal Address rejoiced in missionary and cooperative advance:

> The Gospel has gone into all lands, and is winning its way into the life and thought of the people of whatever nationality or tongue. . . . The Euphrates and the Ganges, the Nile, the Niger, and the Congo have become attractive centers to civilizing and Christianizing forces. . . .
>
> The pronounced tendency to unity of spirit and cooperation in Christian work, and, indeed, to organic union, is hailed with delight.[53]

The same conference was reminded in detail about the sweeping disenfranchisement of blacks then going on in Christian America; the president of Morris Brown College in Atlanta rehearsed the methods—all too familiar to his audience—of the way Negroes were deprived of their votes, and he noted some of the outcomes. For instance, he said: "In 1890 the vote for the President in South Carolina was 170,956, but in 1900, under the revised Constitution, the number was only 50,815." [54] The bishops qualified their confidence in the future as expressed in the address quoted above by some shorter-range disillusionment as they reflected on the loss of civil and political rights:

> To an extent that neither we nor the greater portion of the victorious North were prepared to believe, we have been bereft of such portions of these that but shreds of our former new self remain. To enter into detail would bring our Address to a level that does not become a deliverance to so august a body, especially in view of the fact that all, by a sad and trying experience, know to their hurt.[55]

The plight of Negro leadership was poignantly described by a fraternal messenger from the Colored Methodist Episcopal Church, H. S. Doyle. He said:

> We stand between embittered peoples, inflamed by race hatred on the one side and goaded to desperation on the other. The one will strike us down if we attempt to save our people—our own people will strike us down if we attempt to restrain them from retaliation. Between these antagonisms, precarious indeed is our position.

He urged continual struggle for rights, for as he and many other blacks saw it: "This is our civilization. We live in it and must adjust ourselves to our environment or go down in extermination." [56]

Negro churchmen were deeply troubled during the Wilson regime as they observed the spread of segregation in the departments of government.[57] The northern churches did little effective to help. Ray Stannard Baker noted in 1913 that "the North today has no feeling but friendship for the South," and hence did not seriously resist Negro disenfranchisement. Indeed, he concluded, "the North, wrongly or rightly, is today more than half convinced that the South is right in imposing some measure of limitation upon the franchise."[58] Though northern church leaders were vehement in their condemnation of lynchings and criticized the reduction of Negro rights and the passage of Jim Crow legislation, they were also men of their time and largely shared the views of the white majority. Northern churches which had long resisted segregation of their institutions in the South now finally gave in.[59] Those devoted to social and cooperative Christianity were often among the more progressive and enlightened white voices of their time, but even such persons were more influenced by racial stereotypes and attitudes than they were aware.

The social gospel movement, concerned primarily with the plight of industrial labor, largely ignored the special problems of the blacks. Thomas F. Gossett has stated that "the Social Gospel clergymen spoke out much more strongly in the area of specific economic injustices—the abuse of the laboring class in unhealthful working conditions, long hours, and poor wages, for example—than they did on matters of racial injustice."[60] He accounts for this in part because these men were genuinely uncertain in the area of race theory. It is clear that much of the energy and attention of the social gospel leaders was being absorbed by their crusade against the wrong they saw being done to working people in the northern cities. Washington Gladden on many occasions observed that much had been done for the Negro at the time of emancipation, and that the next great problem was the plight of the workingman. He did not entirely ignore the racial situation in his work, but he did not dwell on it. "I can see how the black man has been from the beginning the victim of wrongs unspeakable, at the hand of the whites," he said in an address on the Emancipation Proclamation.[61] He expressed hope that the two races could live together in peace and mutual respect.

Josiah Strong frequently emphasized the superiority of the Anglo-Saxons in his work, and he has been especially criticized for his racism. Several contemporary scholars have concluded that Strong's views were not as rigid and racist as they have sometimes been interpreted to be. They explain that for Strong the term "Anglo-Saxon" was not defined in terms of a racial strain, for Anglo-Saxon superiority, as he saw it, came in part from the mixed origins. Strong, especially in his later career, defined "Anglo-Saxon" more in terms of the dual tradition of civil liberty and spiritual Christianity, into the privileges of which all other groups can be admitted.[62] In his writing after 1890, Strong criticized the Anglo-Saxons for their mistreatment of "weaker" races, and of the weak members of their own race. He called attention to the universalism of the gospel, noting that Jesus "revealed the brotherhood of the race, and made every member of it—Jew and Gentile, Greek and barbarian, bond and free—eligible to citizenship in the kingdom of God." [63] Though Strong's views were not as racist as they sometimes appeared, nevertheless an ambivalence remained and he could easily be misunderstood.[64] He continued to picture the Anglo-Saxon as born into a position of dominance, arising out of qualities acquired through centuries of struggle. He said: "Among races, as among individuals of the same race, there will be permanent differences of temperament and tendency, of adaptation and skill. And these inherent differences, together with those of climate and of natural resources, will afford a permanent basis for the organization of a world industry and a world commerce." [65] As a prominent leader in social and cooperative Christianity, Strong was for the extension of Christian civilization, of which the chief custodian was Anglo-Saxon Protestantism.

While few social gospel leaders spoke as Strong did about Anglo-Saxon superiority, there was some reflection of his views among them, and they did not venture far in the field of racial problems. Rauschenbusch believed that Christianity was anti-ethnic in character, but felt that the North could not solve the problem for the South. He admitted that the race problem was so difficult that he rarely mentioned it.[66] On the whole the social gospel had a high estimate of the civilization it wished to make more fully Christian; it believed that the best hope for the Negro was to educate himself and to strive to live up to the standards of that civilization. This fitted in well with the goals advocated by Booker T. Washington of Tuskegee, who was usually warmly endorsed whenever mentioned in social gospel materials.[67]

As interdenominational agencies such as the Federal Council developed, they normally included Negro denominations as members, but they also wanted the support of southern white churches. At the meeting in New York in 1905 at which the plans for the Federal Council were completed, the one major spokesman to deal with the race problem was a bishop of the Methodist Episcopal Church South, and a believer in Negro disenfranchisement and segregation. At the founding meeting in 1908, there was no serious attention to the race problem. Until after World War I, the council did not deal significantly with racial matters, though it encouraged missionary and education work among Negroes. There was little in the period to brighten the picture presented by the fraternal delegates of the African Methodist Episcopal Zion Church, J. Harvey Anderson, to the African Methodist Episcopal Zion Church in 1904:

> Contact of the Negro with white church organizations is beneficial in some ways, but generally from a pecuniary standpoint it is not imperative, it limits him in almost every respect which it is not here necessary to explain. He must play second fiddle in almost everything and in almost every relation, and is considered a dependent member of the organization, in no way necessary to its existence, and only a contingent source of contributions of credit, strength and efficiency. He is not permitted to lift himself to equality in any way whatever, but in isolated cases only, and even then must submit to allow his supposed supervisors to do it.[68]

The contrast between the hardheaded realism of the black denominations and the sentimental paternalism of the white about racial matters as revealed in the records of the church assemblies of the time vividly shows how wide the gap between these evangelicals was.

Voices of protest and criticism resounded within the black churches. For example, when a number of southern states passed laws preventing whites from teaching in Negro schools, a report of the woman's convention at the National Baptist Convention said prophetically:

> States that passed these infamous laws repudiate Christian civilization and the idealism that is the boast and dream of American reformers and social workers. A country that is too full of prejudice to Christianize, socialize and evangelize those right at their door has no business sending missionaries to heathen lands. If there isn't at least enough sentiment abroad in this land to keep measures of this kind from passing, then it will not be many years before American Christianity as a vital force will become a farce.[69]

When the Negro community rallied to support American participation in World War I, there was hope that the commitment of the nation to idealism and democracy would be sincere. Patterns in the North and the South seemed to change but little, however. "The Negro cannot understand how enlightened people can retire behind the influence of ideals, custom and prejudice, and still define their relation to Christianity as that of Christians," wrote John H. Grant after the war. "The Negro believes that the spirit and power of Christianity has been meanly and sparingly applied to the solution of the problem growing out of the relationship of the white and black man of the South. In fact he does not see where it has ever been applied."[70] In similar vein, as he reviewed the years from 1890 to 1920, a sensitive Negro church historian, Carter G. Woodson, with primary reference to the North in this instance, said: "The North, then, if it ever wakes from its lethargy, will probably accept either the principles of Jesus of Nazareth as they have been preached and practiced by the Negroes, or the Anglo-Saxon-chosen-people-of-

God faith for which many misguided white communicants have jeopardized their own lives and have taken those of Negroes unwilling to worship at the shrine of race prejudice." [71]

Unfortunately, social gospel and cooperative Christian movements, which did break significant new ground in their areas of primary concern, were quite typical of the dominant patterns of nineteenth-century Protestantism at other points. White Protestants set out to make "still more Christian" a civilization which they already assessed highly and in which they saw themselves as the best examples and guides for the future. But they tried to deal with new realities by the old techniques of seeking consensus and launching crusades for the conquest of American life. Social and cooperative movements did develop important new perspectives and strategies for twentieth-century Protestants. Their adherence to older views about the Christian nature of Western civilization and the dreams of its world victory, however, kept them from seeing some of the deeper meanings of industrial, population, and intellectual changes going on about them. A radically pluralized and urbanized society required significantly different and varied ways of relating faith to culture. Ironically, the conviction that their civilization was so fully democratic and Christian that it was almost ready for the kingdom was one of the things which prevented them from hearing clearly the voices of their fellow black evangelicals, who might have helped them to broaden and correct their bright vision.

VII
The Second Disestablishment

President Woodrow Wilson, a son of the manse, could speak eloquently about a nation under God. Never did his rhetoric seem more consonant with the aspirations of vast numbers of Americans than at the heady moment of victory in 1918. It seemed as though the great new era, so long promised, was at last at hand. A more fully democratic and Christian civilization in America and in the world appeared to be within reach. True peace and genuine brotherhood at home and abroad seemed attainable.

The churches had participated vigorously in the "great crusade" of the war and now were anxious to see the realization of the goals for which the sacrifices had been evoked. A great door of opportunity for democratic civilization and true religion throughout the world was opened, as many church leaders saw it. They called on the churches to make the most of the situation. "At the present moment it appears as though the immediate effect of the war has been to strengthen the church as an organization, at least in all the Allied and in many of the neutral countries," wrote Tyler Dennett, at that time a publicist for church causes. He reported that the church seemed to be strengthened organizationally as it emerged from the war:

> All religious organizations took on a new importance in the eyes of government shortly after the war began. The churches, like the press, offered direct and open channels for

> communicating with the people, for stimulating patriotism, and for education in war aims. They also offered exceptional facilities, through existing fraternal relations with the religious groups in other countries, for international propaganda.[1]

Christians of many denominations were anxious to seize the opportunities that the armistice brought so that the long cherished dream of a more Christian civilization might become reality. The time and the circumstances seemed right.

Soon after his return from the peace conference, President Wilson presented the proposed peace treaty to the Senate on July 10, 1919 concluding with these words:

> Our participation in the war established our position among the nations and nothing but our mistaken action can alter it. . . . We answered the call of duty in a way so spirited, so utterly without thought of what we spent of blood or treasure, so effective, so worthy of the admiration of true men everywhere, so wrought out of the stuff of all that was heroic, that the whole world saw at last, in the flesh, in noble action, a great ideal asserted and vindicated, by a Nation they had deemed material and now found to be compact of the spiritual forces that must free men of every nation from every unworthy bondage. It is thus that a new role and a new responsibility have come to this great Nation that we honor and which we would all wish to lift to yet higher levels of service and achievement.

His peroration blended the themes of providence and progress:

> The stage is set, the destiny is disclosed. It has come about by no plan of our conceiving, but by the hand of God who led us into this way. We cannot turn back. We can only go forward, with lifted eyes and freshened spirit, to follow the vision. It was of this that we dreamed at our birth. America shall in truth show the way. The light streams on the path ahead, and nowhere else.[2]

The very familiarity of the rhetoric made this call sound authentic to the majority of idealistic churchgoers.

American churches generally tended to believe in a League of Nations as provided for in the Treaty of Paris, seeing it as an important instrument for securing the coveted goal of permanent world peace. In the year following the war, the churches significantly contributed to the shaping of the prevailing opinion in the nation that the United States should enter the league. The Federal Council of Churches, for example, declared in 1919: "In international relations, a League of Nations is, in effect, an attempt to apply Christian principles to the dealings of nations with one another." [3] The respected Robert E. Speer was quite sensitive to the political aspects of the question, but nevertheless he boldly said: "What we speak of today as the League of Nations is an indispensable and unavoidable implicate of all our Christian faith and endeavor in the world." [4] The league seemed to offer the channels through which the Christian world vision could find fulfillment. Hence many church spokesmen deplored the partisan politics which were threatening the nation's entry into league membership. A National Committee on the Churches and the Moral Aims of the War secured the signatures of nearly 15,000 clergymen drawn from a wide denominational spectrum to this statement: "We, the undersigned clergymen, urge the Senate of the United States to ratify the Paris Peace Treaty, embodying the League of Nations Convenant, at the earliest possible date without amendments or such reservations as would require resubmission of the Treaty to the Peace Conference and Germany." [5] But their hopes were soon to be dashed.

THE INTERCHURCH WORLD MOVEMENT

To sustain Protestant idealism, and to seize the opportunties that appeared so bright at war's end for a more Christian America and world, an extensive crusade was launched. Just after the armistice of November 11, 1918, a call went out from the Executive Committee of the Board of Foreign Missions of the Presbyterian Church in the United States for a gathering of representative Protestant churchmen to plan for a united drive for world evangelism and a cooperative advance which would be adequate to the unprecedented challenge of the postwar world. One hundred and thirty-five prominent members of mission boards and related agencies met in New York on December 17, 1918 and took the first steps toward organizing the Interchurch World Movement.[6] The gathering was led in worship by Robert E. Speer —a sign that the trusted leadership of prewar evangelism and mission supported this new thrust. The group then heard reports from the various denominational "forward movements," many of which were then being conducted with conspicuous success for the raising of vast sums of money for missionary and benevolent causes.[7] It was believed that a united campaign could reach hitherto unattainable goals.

Those present were in a mood to believe that the most formidable tasks could be accomplished through serious cooperative effort. The spirit of commitment and sacrifice that had marked church support of the war effort was still running high, while the sense of exhilaration stemming from the victory made anything seem possible. "No one who was present in the upper room on that momentous December day when the Interchurch World Movement was born can forget the thrill of expectation which stirred those who had gathered there," said William Adams Brown of Union Theological Seminary in New York, chairman of the Committee on the War and the Religious Outlook and secretary of the General War-Time Commission of the Churches. The participants were not naive idealists, he recalled, but were responsible veteran workers who knew the weaknesses and limitations of the bodies they served.

> But they had seen a vision—the vision of a united church uniting a divided world, and under the spell of what they

> saw all things seemed possible. Difficulties were waved aside, doubters were silenced. In the face of an opportunity so unparalleled there seemed but one thing to do, and that was to go forward.[8]

A Committee of Twenty was named to perfect the plans and to seek official support.

Moving swiftly, the committee drew up specifications for the movement, the purpose of which was "to present a unified program of Christian service and to unite the Protestant churches of North America in the performance of their common task, thus making available the values of spiritual power which come from unity and coordinated Christian effort and meeting the unique opportunities of the new era." [9] The various "interboard agencies" for mission and education which served to correlate the work of the denominational boards enthusiastically endorsed the crusade in January 1919. A massive program for survey, education, and publicity was undertaken, in preparation for an extensive and coordinated fund drive in 1920. John R. Mott was elected chairman of the executive committee, while S. Earl Taylor became general secretary of the movement. Taylor had been directing the Methodist Centenary Movement; like Mott he was a Methodist layman well known for his work with the Student Volunteer Movement, the Laymen's Missionary Movement, and the Young Men's Christian Association.

The denominations as such were soon drawn into the crusade. For example, in successfully urging the Northern Baptist Convention to support the movement, Frank W. Padelford reported that though the previous understanding of missions was a worthy ideal, it had been "completely dwarfed" by the newer concept. "Our business," he explained, "is to establish a civilization that is Christian in spirit and in passion, the world around, in Borneo as much as in Boston." [10] To such appeals as these some thirty evangelical denominations responded.

The paid staff of the "Interchurch" (as it was often called) mushroomed in a way that surprised even its most ardent proponents—by May 1920 there were 2612 employees at work, the majority of them at the headquarters in New York.[11] The staffs of the other interdenominational agencies were tiny by comparison—something massive and exciting had appeared on the scene. Spurred by the publicity minded general secretary, the movement sent out a vast amount of information and promotional material. It combined scientific and evangelical approaches in its work as it launched comprehensive surveys into American and world human and religious needs in the interest of nothing less than the complete evangelization of all of life.

The great financial drive which was to provide the sums required for a mighty denominational and interdenominational advance was scheduled for the spring of 1920. An immediate financial goal of some 336 million dollars—a breathtaking and unprecedented amount—was set. As the year opened, all seemed to be progressing well. An impressive World Survey Conference under Interchurch auspices was held in January at Atlantic City; the seventeen hundred workers heard the movement called "one of the most glorious achievements in the history of the church, the proper and inevitable response of God's people to the appalling needs of our age." [12] Victory in this crusade to Christianize America and the world seemed to be within reach.

That January, too, the prohibition amendment went into effect—a long-sought goal of much of the Protestant world seemed to be permanently realized. This was a dramatic example of the power of the churches when mobilized by what they regarded as a clear moral issue. Though many forces, secular and religious, worked together toward the ratification of the amendment, which was part of the general program of the progressive movement, the evangelical churches felt it was a victory for them especially. In the words of an indefatigable prohibition leader, Southern Methodist bishop James Cannon, Jr.: "In any discussion of 'why' the Eighteenth Amendment was ratified, it cannot be too strongly emphasized that the prohibition movement in the United States has been Christian in its inspiration and has been dependent for its persistent vitality and victorious leadership upon the active and, finally, upon the practically undivided support of American Protestants, with support from some Roman Catholics."[13] Encouraged by this achievement, evangelicals hoped to overcome all the obstacles that lay between them and a Christian America. As Robert Speer had declared when the prohibition amendment was ratified:

> Thirty years ago was there one of us here in this room who believed that we would see the saloon abolished in the American nation? There are many of us in this audience tonight who will live to see other institutions of lust and evil and sin absolutely extirpated from American life. But what we are being told today is just what Christians have known from the very beginning, that any generation might have the Kingdom of God if it would open itself to the full inpouring of the will and power of God.[14]

The generation represented at that huge World Survey Conference in Atlantic City early in 1920 was determined that the kingdom should be theirs, very soon.

Though the saloon had come to symbolize for the evangelical mind much that stood in the way of a better world, its closing was but one of the needed forward steps. The Protestant crusaders were convinced that many other important advances were going on, in the work of missions at home and abroad, in the progress of Christian education, and in the social witness of the churches.

CHANGING MOODS

Though the Protestant mood was buoyant as 1920 began, developments in the nation and in the churches were bringing about a quite changed atmosphere and situation. American entry into the League of Nations had been blocked by the Senate in November 1919, and was finally rejected on March 19, 1920. The political partisanship and bickering that prevented passage of the treaty saddened many Americans, who felt that their sacrificial support of the war was being betrayed. The sense of national unity and purpose that had seemed so strong at the close of the war was also being weakened by the spread of an atmosphere of suspicion and distrust, directed often without much discrimination against dissenters and foreigners. Postwar periods of inflation and unemployment brought privation and bitterness; there were a number of stormy strikes; racial tension erupted in ugly urban riots. The "red scare" that resulted in the arrest of some 6000 alleged leftist suspects on New Year's Day of 1920 at the aegis of Attorney General Palmer dramatically illustrated the swift alteration of national mood.

In the sharply changed atmosphere, the idealistic interpretation of the war fell under increasing criticism as its professed goals seemed to remain unfulfilled and its cost and brutality appeared to growing numbers to have been in vain. The sense of disillusionment deepened as world reaction to the global struggle began to be heard, much of it unflattering to the West and to Christendom. As William Adams Brown described a shift in world opinion:

> Noticeable among the effects of the war has been the loss of confidence in Western leadership. The war which has shattered so many ideals has given an irreparable blow to European prestige. The early respect for the superior knowledge of the foreigner, the willingness to take his counsel and follow his advice, which was apparent in the earlier relations of the East with Europe, has been sadly shaken. Asiatics and Africans fought in Europe against white men during the war and have carried back to their homes a very different report of the state of European civilization from that which has been

> given to them by the missionaries. They have seen its weakness as well as its strength and are not likely to forget what they have seen.[15]

Brown concluded that people who hitherto had been content to accept western models determined now to make their own judgments and to order their lives in their own way.

There were serious difficulties at home and sharp criticism from abroad—a discouraging turn of events. Gabriel A. Almond once observed that "American action has tremendous *élan* which often works wonders, but when it doesn't work and when secondary improvisations are similarly thwarted, the bubble of optimism often collapses and gives way to moods of defeatism and deflation." [16] Surprisingly soon after the end of the war there spread across the nation a sense of disillusionment that was to pervade many aspects of life in the third decade. As Arthur S. Link has sharply put it, "the 1920's were a period made almost unique by an extraordinary reaction against idealism and reform." [17] In light of later reactions against idealistic reformism, the twenties may not look quite so distinctive, but at the time the challenge to the optimistic crusading spirit had a strong negative effect in the church world.

College students were quick to sense and to express the sweeping change of mood. When John R. Mott addressed the Eighth Convention of the Students Volunteer Movement at Des Moines right after Christmas 1919, he began by saying: "What a different world it is from that upon which delegates gazed at the last convention, held in Kansas City just six years ago. What an old world that was. How absolutely different is the world which we view today." But the burden of his message was not much changed; as before he called the conferees "to Christianize the impact of our western civilization upon the non-Christian world." [18] His friend Sherwood Eddy had a more difficult time. When he spoke at the same gathering in the prewar tradition of the Student Volunteer Movement, some of the students disclosed their feelings to him frankly, saying: "Why do you bring us this piffle, these old shibboleths, these old worn-out phrases, why are you talking to us about the living God and the divine Christ?"[19] Eddy thereupon threw aside his prepared second address, and spoke instead in support of the League of Nations and social reform before turning again to spiritual reform. In the new national situation, the old progressive evangelicalism with its crusading passion was losing something of its power and appeal.

The war had brought irreversible changes to American life. Industralization had leapt ahead, major population shifts had occurred, cities had expanded, moods had changed as naturalism and pragmatism had broken the sway of the older idealism. Evangelical leaders had felt themselves to be in the vanguard of progress in the early years of the twentieth century; understandably, they hoped to resume the advance that the war had interrupted. More than that—they hoped to reach new heights. Secure in the continuing patterns of church life which had not been seriously disturbed by the war, they were not always aware of the discontinuties the conflict had released in other aspects of American life. The crusading techniques, once so effective, had lost their freshness for the many young people who sensed they were living in a quite new situation.

The change of mood soon affected the older generation also. Tyler Dennett, who became director of the Interchurch Publicity Department, did speak enthusiastically on the way the war had strengthened the church as an organization, as has been noted, but he went on to say that "at the same time here seems to have been a weakening of religious convictions and a cooling of spiritual fervor."[20] In January of 1920—the same month of the peak of enthusiasm at the Interchurch's Atlantic City meeting—the Executive Secretary of the Home Missions Council declared:

> Spiritual gains, which seemed to be promised through the unifying and sacrificial elements of war, have not remained as permanent possessions. We are broken into classes and

> groups, and pitted against each other in rivalry for leadership and for possessions. Even the Church has shown a recurrence of intense denominational self-consciousness and a disposition to exalt human agencies and rely upon material resources.[21]

At the meeting in which Alfred Williams Anthony uttered those remarks, the Home Missions Council pledged its support of the Interchurch World Movement, in the hope that the dangers might be overcome by the massive effort.

There were those in the churches who did not want to go along, however. More conservative elements in the denominations were pulling away under militant leadership from the broad evangelical consensus of the cooperative agencies and attacking liberalism aggressively. The World's Christian Fundamentals Association, organized in 1919, put great emphasis on such doctrines as the inerrancy of the scriptures, the virgin birth, the substitutionary atonement, and the premillennial, imminent return of Christ. Troubled by many of the drifts of modern life, the fundamentalists by an appeal to the authority of Scripture hoped to hold evangelical churches firmly on the familiar course. If correct doctrines were followed, then they believed that Christian family and congregational life would rest on a secure foundation. As they found the liberal spirit pervading their own denominational houses, however, the fundamentalists in some communions organized fellowships to press for their interpretations of the faith. A divisive spirit was appearing in both denominational and interdominational circles.

The changed situation proved disastrous to the Interchurch World Movement. As the problems and tensions that had emerged in 1919 cast shadows across the future that had recently looked so bright, those committed to the movement saw it as a last chance to bring the nation back to its ideals. In the first four months of 1920 a barrage of publications was directed to the American public and hundreds of meetings prepared the way for the financial drives. As the campaign crested in early May, the denominational subscriptions (which were counted as part of the movement's total goal) were coming in quite well, but the hoped-for sum of forty million dollars from the "friendly citizens" outside the immediate clientele of the churches was falling far short—only three million had been subscribed. This was especially serious because the machinery of the Interchurch Movement itself was to be financed from this forty million. The movement had been functioning wholly on borrowed money underwritten by the participating denominations. Nearly eight million had been spent by mid-May 1920.[22] A second attempt to reach the "friendly citizens" failed almost completely, and in the several denominational gatherings which met at that time the growing group of fundamentalist critics found an opportunity to press their criticisms. By summer the movement collapsed—the great crusade was prematurely over.[23]

There were many efforts to explain the movement's collapse. Its goals had never been stated very clearly. The lines of representation from the churches had not been very carefully worked out. The crusade began as an interdenominational thrust which then had to be related to the denominations, a difficult matter which was not always adequately handled. Planned in an era of good feeling among the denominations, the movement was faced by an upsurge of theological strife and an intensification of the denominational spirit. Possibly also the Interchurch's incisive but controversial report on the unsuccessful steel strike of 1919, a report which contributed significantly to the elimination of the twelve-hour day in the steel industry, may have harmed the campaign, though it was not published until the summer of 1920, after the movement had been fatally wounded.[24] The underlying causes of failure were much deeper; they were rooted in the shift in American life that was displacing evangelical Protestantism as the primary definer of cultural values and behavior patterns in the nation. The hopes for a Christian America as envisioned by nineteenth-century evangelicals were fast fading in the face of the realities of postwar America; the enthusiasm and morale needed to sustain the crusade were undermined. In some sections, especially in the south, the older Protestant patterns persisted for a longer period and of course in all sections there were those who were hardly aware of what was happening. For those who had eyes to see, a dramatic sign that a major change in American cultural and religious patterns was taking place was the failure of the Interchurch World Movement. In Eldon Ernst's words:

> The collapse of the Interchurch World Movement, and especially the lack of response by so-called "friendly citizens" to the Movement's appeal for support, helped open Protestants' eyes to the fact that they and their churches no longer commanded the authority, power, influence, or even respect which they had hitherto enjoyed in America. The long-developing pattern of a rising urban, non-Protestant, non-Puritan secularized American population, which had caused increasing alarm to Protestant leaders since the Civil War, had begun to come of age after World War I.[25]

Even though the churches tried quickly to return to business as usual after the movement's collapse, the old buoyancy was lacking. In a book published in 1920 but written before the issue of American entry into the League of Nations had been settled, Tyler Dennett put boldly what many were suspecting: "The so-called Christian nations are approaching moral and spiritual bankruptcy as is clearly revealed by the apathy of public opinion on the great moral issues which underlie the Treaty and the League." [26] To confess that the "Christian" nations were nearing "spiritual bankruptcy" was to declare that the fundamental assumptions on which the hope of a Christian America had been based were losing their credibility. The confident belief that America was basically Protestant and was progressing toward the kingdom of God had been an important foundation for evangelical Protestant crusading. But that foundation was crumbling under the pressures of population shifts, intellectual changes, and increased pluralism.

There were other signs of the shaking of the foundations besides the failure of the Interchurch World Movement. Not only the progressive evangelicalism of the cooperative Christian forces, but the individualistic evangelism of professional revivalism lost its potency in the postwar decade. Billy Sunday, the baseball evangelist, a popular and bombastic figue who had barnstormed through America early in the century drawing vast audiences and attracting much publicity, lost much of his power. A careful study of him by William G. McLoughlin came to this conclusion:

> By the time the war ended, Sunday had begun to lose his grasp on the American public. His rhetoric and demagogic technique had not changed, but his audiences had. The great crusades for liberty abroad and Prohibition at home were over. The movies, the radio, the automobile, and organized sports provided better entertainment than the tabernacle. People were tired of the symbols which Sunday flaunted; they were tired of world-saving, civic cleanups, and personal salvation, and they were tired of professional evangelism.[27]

Crusades for a Christian America, whether under progressive or conservative leadership, were proving difficult to sustain.

THE RETURN TO "NORMALCY"

It is much easier to see the deeper meaning of the events of those stormy days in retrospect than it was at the time. It was not until another time of troubles came a few years later that many Protestants began to sense what really had happened. At the time, it was possible to blame the fall of the Interchurch Movement on the haste with which it had been planned, or on the rising spirit of denominationalism, or on the national letdown after the discipline and sacrifice of war. The mood of many in the churches, reflecting the spirit pervading the nation in the new decade, was to get back to business as usual, to return to normalcy, to move again along familiar channels. William Adams Brown resumed a well-known theme in 1922 when he declared: "But while jealously guarding the principle of the separation of state and church, the American people are equally insistent upon the fact that their country is a Christian nation." [28] He listed the old familiar proofs, such as the opening of Congress with prayer, the respect paid to the church by presidents, the Thanksgiving Day proclamations, and military chaplaincies. A few years later Robert Speer emphasized that the Christian character of western countries should be reasserted. He did argue for the development of indigenous churches, no longer tied to western culture, *abroad*. He explained that "foreign missions, indeed, are not charged with the task of Christianizing the world." As for the United States and other western nations, however, he insisted that "the Christian Church in the nations which have regarded themselves as Christian ought to seek to secure the Christian character and Christian actions of the State." [29]

There were many other patterns of return to normality as many interests restated their particular programs for a Christian America in the postwar world. Battle cries from the past were sounded again. There were those, for example, who tried to renew the fight for a Christian Sabbath. One editor sounded this call:

> Presbyterians all, Christians all, you have need to marshal all your forces, all your strength of prayer and works, to save the Christian Sabbath. The Christian Sabbath in America is doomed unless you act concertedly, unless you act at once. If the Christian Sabbath is once lost to America, America is doomed.
>
> America acquired world leadership through the faith and vision and fidelity of its Christian founders. Decay of other nations followed departure from sacred standards.[30]

He urged a joint Protestant effort to save the Sabbath from the wicked ones who had planned its downfall.

Others urged a new unity of Anglo-Saxon Protestantism. An Episcopal rector in New York believed that "the increase in the power of the Roman Catholic Church in American life is largely due to the weakness of the Protestant churches, and that unless that weakness can be overcome by some genuine religious co-operation among the Protestant churches—the result of true spiritual unity—the Roman Catholic Church may dominate the religious life of this country." To forestall this and other dangers, Leighton Parks recommended his own church as a comprehensive center for English peoples and ideals:

> Most thoughtful men are agreed that in the crisis of the world today the future of civilization largely depends upon the faithful and earnest cooperation, the mutual understanding and reciprocal respect of these two great branches of the English-speaking peoples of the world. . . .
>
> Is there not need then, for just such a church as this—a church which will influence the life of the people of this great land so as to cement the spiritual union of the great race of which we form so important a part? [31]

There were those who put their Anglo-Saxonism in cruder form. The Imperial Wizard of the revived Ku Klux Klan, for example, said in 1926:

> There are three of these great racial instincts, vital elements in both the historic and the present attempts to build an America which shall fulfill the aspirations and justify the heroism of the men who made the nation. These are the instincts of loyalty to the white race, to the traditions of America, and to the spirit of Protestantism, which has been an essential part of Americanism ever since the days of Roanoke and Plymouth Rock. They are condensed into Klan slogan: "Native, white, Protestant supremacy." [32]

The Klan was not affiliated with any denomination, of course, though many of its members were.

In addition to such particular ways of trying to maintain the familiar styles of Protestant America, there was a more general return to the normalcy of adjusting to the main tendencies in the culture. The twenties turned out to be the decade of business, the decade of prosperity. Many churches quickly adapted methods of efficiency in packing their product. From his perspective as advertiser, layman Bruce Barton wrote a best seller, *The Man Nobody Knows*, in 1925. He presented Jesus as a young executive who put together the best management team in history. After a few years of such blending of Christian faith with the mentality of the period, an Episcopal bishop reacted vehemently. "America has become almost hopelessly enamoured of a religion that is little more than a sanctified commercialism; it is hard in this day and in this land to differentiate between religious aspiration and business prosperity," declared Charles Fiske of the diocese of Central New York. He said, "Our conception of God is that he is a sort of Magnified Rotarian." Criticizing the tendency to substitute efficiency for virtue, he added, "I hope I may be forgiven a note of exaggeration that is necessary to make my meaning clear when I say that Protestantism, in America, seems to be degenerating into a sort of Babsonian cult, which cannot distinguish between what is offered to God and what is accomplished for the glory of America and the furtherance of business enterprise."[33] Such criticism would not of course fit many struggling churches, rural or urban. But others succumbed to the temptations of prosperity. Overall, Protestantism was profiting not a little from the good times of the twenties, as is indicated by growing financial support and a marked increase in the value of church property.[34]

SPIRITUAL RECESSION

The desired return to the normalcy of the confident, crusading Protestantism of the prewar period did not occur, however. The realities of postwar life were proving difficult to understand and address within the familiar styles of Protestant thought and piety. The very adequacy of the patterns themselves was being questioned by the children of those who once held them sacrosanct. By the mid-twenties, a spiritual depression was troubling Protestantism, an event that began several years before the economic depression was touched off by the stock market crash of 1929.[35] Decline in missionary enthusiasm, giving, and personnel was manifesting itself by 1926: a danger sign for a faith that defines itself in missionary terms.[36] One observer noted that "interest in missions was waning before the depression. All through the decade of the 1920's the foreign missionary enterprise was being questioned and it was failing to attract the vigorous support which it formerly enjoyed."[37] The once-potent Student Volunteer Movement had lost its touch; though approximately 2700 students had volunteered for foreign missions in 1920, only 252 offered themselves in 1928.[38] The peak year of missionary giving in the postwar period was 1921, after that there was a rather steady overall decline.[39]

Home missions felt the pinch, too. Nearly two years before the financial crisis of 1929, the executive secretary of the Home Missions Council reported that "almost all major denominations are now in a period of financial stringency in the conduct of mission work. . . . There has been more or less a retrenchment all along the line, and new work has been for several years practically at a standstill."[40] Local churches were suffering in a number of ways. Sunday school enrollments were declining, and the traditional Sunday evening service was becoming harder to maintain, especially in cities.[41] Various methods of evangelism were not working too well; one analyst plotted an "evangelical index line" which showed a sharp downturn in the winning of converts in a number of major denominations through the decade.[42] The status of the ministry declined in the postwar period; early in the decade George A. Coe reported a widespread conviction that there was a debilitating inertia among ministers.[43] After reviewing the evidence, Paul A. Carter came to the conclusion that "the clergy, then, in the decade of the 20's, was committed on the whole to a ministry to the middle class, but it was a clergy too low in public esteem to reach even that class effectively with its message."[44]

The "spiritual recession" that is being traced here is of course so labeled in relation to the earlier period of confidence and advance, and to a later period of recovery and renewal. All through this difficult time the vast network of denominational and interdenominational life continued. Yet there was a loss of morale and enthusiasm. The intellectual atmosphere was prevailingly uncongenial to religion, oscillating between questioning and hostile moods. The advances in science encouraged a popular "scientism" in which other approaches to reality were minimized if not repudiated. At the close of the decade a famous teacher of preachers observed that this tended to breed a sceptical attitude, for "an exclusive devotion to scientific method ends almost inevitably in a kind of intellectual disillusion."[45] Many decades later James Ward Smith observed that "the disillusion of the 1920's is often attributed to World War I and to Prohibition. I cannot but feel that this is a superficial reading of the period." He suggested that "the real source of our disillusionment with art and religion after World War I was our optimism that science could solve all human problems."[46] To be sure, the various theological movements of the period took differing attitudes toward science. Liberal parties generally welcomed and related to scientific developments, while groups on the conservative spectrum tended to resist them, especially when dogmatic assertions seemed to be threatened. But all groups suffered from the critical attitude toward religion which accompanied the popularization of the scientific perspective. A philosopher reported that "there is today a widespread and increasing belief that the minimum essentials of Christian supernaturalism . . .

have been rendered antiquated, false, and absurd by our modern knowledge."[47] All this played a role in religion's loss of confidence and morale; in his first book Reinhold Niebuhr exclaimed that "a psychology of defeat, of which both fundamentalism and modernism are symptoms, has gripped the forces of religion."[48] The erosion of the belief that progress depended upon religion was very disturbing to those who had long been confident of it.

The prestige of Protestantism was further lessened by the bitter controversy between fundamentalists and modernists. The fundamentalist forces attempted to oust the liberals from places of influence in a number of major denominations—the northern Presbyterian and Baptist struggles were especially intense.[49] The leadership of William Jennings Bryan brought the movement much publicity, especially in the tragi-comic anticlimax of the great orator's career when he was ridiculed by Clarence Darrow at the famous Scopes trial in Dayton, Tennessee, in 1925.[50] A law prohibiting the teaching of evolution was upheld, but the fundamentalist movement was discredited and soon receded.[51] Neither side really won; as the most widely known liberal preacher of the time, Harry Emerson Fosdick spoke of the "collapse of the late controversy," he insisted that it could not be "remotely construed as the victory of progressive ideas and policies."[52] With its bitter polemics and personal attacks, the struggle further harmed organized religion in a time of disllusionment and spiritual hunger.

There were moments when it seemed as though Protestantism was maintaining its old power. The nomination in 1928 of Alfred E. Smith for president evoked much of the old rhetoric about Protestant America, for Smith was a Roman Catholic and opposed to prohibition. In his informative book on the election of 1928, Edmund A. Moore recapitulated the main points in the campaign against Smith: "Whether viewed in its special aspects—Prohibition, Tammany, and Romanism—or as a comprehensive whole, the determination to save 'Anglo-Saxon civilization' in this campaign was unique."[53] A publication of the Anti-Saloon League for use in Ohio at the peak of the campaign summarized the issue as it appeared to many: "If you believe in Anglo-Saxon Protestant domination; if you believe in those principles which have made the country what it is; if you believe in prohibition, its observance and enforcement, and if you believe in a further restricted immigration rather than letting down the bars still lower, then whether you are a Republican or a Democrat, you will vote for Hoover rather than Smith."[54] Mrs. Elizabeth H. Tilton, a Yankee reformer, saw the contest to be "between two levels of civilization—the Evangelical, middle-class America and the Big City Tammany masses."[55]

Against this background, the overwhelming defeat of Smith could be (and often was) cited as evidence that the Protestant character of the nation had in fact not been seriously affected. Careful study of the election, however, has suggested that religion and prohibition really had less to do with Hoover's victory at the polls than the fact of prosperity—though the former were more extensively and heatedly discussed during the campaign. Moore observed that the heart of the matter lay elsewhere, for "Hoover was a very strong candidate, and prosperity was the political prize and possession of the Republican party. . . . For the country as a whole, prosperity was the key issue."[56] A detailed analysis of the election returns by Ruth C. Silva has claimed "statistical proof that the so-called liquor, religious, and metropolitan issues had no significant relation to Smith's electoral strength." By making many comparisons, as between the votes for dry, Protestant, rural Democrats, and Smith's, Silva concluded that religious, prohibition, and metropolitan considerations "were not ordinarily controlling factors and that their role in the presidential election of 1928 should be described in the most circumscribed terms."[57] Further, Congress had failed to reapportion itself after the census of 1920 had shown that the majority of the population had become urban, so that the election of

1928 was on the basis of the 1910 apportionment—not until 1932 was the change made. Of course many people were influenced in voting by the candidates' religion and by their views on prohibition, but the evidence does suggest that such considerations overall were not finally decisive for the election's outcome, and that 1928 was a "Republican year" in which the issue of prosperity was central.

At that moment, however, the image of a dry, Protestant civilization seemed secure. Only with the passage of time and the shock of events would some at last see that the direction of social change, demographic trends, and urban patterns was against the dominance of an acculturated Protestantism with its partly exorcized notions of Anglo-Saxon superiority and its rural nostalgia. Meanwhile the uneasy awareness that deep-flowing currents were running against the Protestant hope for a Christian America contributed to the anxieties, doubts, and depression of the Protestant world. Social realities were moving in a different direction from Protestant theories. The comment of the Lynds on the basis of their famous study of an Indiana city in the mid-twenties is revealing: "In theory, religious beliefs dominate all other activities in Middletown; actually, large regions of Middletown's life appear uncontrolled by them." [58]

Anglo-American Protestantism had so long depended upon its environing culture for coherence and a sense of unity and direction that the increasing divergence of evangelical patterns and American civilization left it in a somewhat depressed, uncertain state. H. L. Mencken's comment in 1925 that "Protestantism in this great Christian realm is down with a wasting disease" might be dismissed as the jibe of a hostile critic, but Bishop Fiske was no less forceful when three years later he spoke of "a sad disintegration of American Protestantism." [59] One Unitarian writer who spoke of the deep-seated infection in American education, literature, morals, and religion was struck by "the appearance of intense effort and uncertain purpose; of energy without peace; of fevered occupation with details unguided by any sense of the whole."[60] The loss of the sense of the whole—that is what troubled much religious life in the twenties. The belief that American civilization was basically Christian and was progressively moving toward the kingdom was becoming more and more divorced from reality, and appeared to be more and more of an illusion. Winthrop S. Hudson's summary of the plight of Protestantism in the twenties is apt:

> Nothing is more striking than the astonishing reversal in the position occupied by the churches and the role played by religion in American life which took place before the new century was well under way. By the nineteen twenties, the contagious enthusiasm which had been poured into the Student Volunteer Movement, the Sunday School Movement, the Men and Religion Forward Movement, the Laymen's Missionary Movement, the Interchurch World Movement, and other organized activities of the churches had largely evaporated.

Hudson noted that the practices of church attendance and Sabbath observance, once a strong testimony to the influence of religious faith, "were no longer sustained and enforced by the moral conscience of the community."[61] Community moral conscience, of course, had for centuries been informed largely by Protestant assumptions. By the twenties the force of a public conscience informed by religion was in fact diminishing, especially in the cities, even though it was still maintained in theory. Denominations industriously and with considerable success cultivated their own constituencies and launched building campaigns as prosperity returned, but the loss of the sense of overall coherence, unity, and direction was reflected in the spiritual recession of those years. Protestant churches had long depended on their common dedication to the Christianization of American civilization as the great goal that gave them a sense of partnership and purpose, but as the hope of the coming kingdom on earth dimmed during a time of decline in idealism and spiritual vitality, they did not easily or unitedly find their way to deeper resources of faith.

ECONOMIC DEPRESSION

It was on a Protestantism weakened by the spiritual decline of the twenties that the weight of the economic depression fell, slashing budgets, reducing memberships, halting benevolent and missionary enterprises, dismissing ministers, closing churches. When the Lynds restudied Middletown ten years after the original survey, they found that "the city had been shaken for nearly six years by a catastrophe involving not only people's values, but in the case of many, their very existence." Virtually everybody in the community had been hit in some way, for "the great knife of the depression had cut down impartially through the entire population, cleaving open the lives and hopes of rich as well as poor." [62] Churches struggled along as best they could. It was a bitter, difficult, discouraging time. In the midst of it, the prohibition experiment, which Hoover had called "noble in motive," came to an end.

One of the expectancies of the depression period within the churches was that there would be a revival of religion. In his study of religion during the depression, Samuel C. Kincheloe reported that "some religious leaders actually hailed the depression with rejoicing since they had the idea that previous depressions had 'driven men to God' and felt that the time was overdue for men again to be reminded of the need to let the spiritual dominate the materialistic order." [63] An editorial in the *Christian Century* pointedly commented on the absence of such a revival in 1935: "It must be a subject of at least occasional reflection on the part of thoughtful people that this period of depression has brought forth no revival of religion. We are accustomed to expect revivals in such periods." The editorial also observed that "the Christian church has come into the depression wholly unprepared to take account of it, and to minister to the deepest human need which it discloses." It did discern some signs of hope for renewal—but from unconventional places.[64]

Revival in the old pattern simply did not materialize. Revivalism as it had been developed through the nineteenth and into the twentieth centuries had been in the context of a civilization understood to be Protestant in a general sense. Much of its power was drawn in fact from its community nature and from its confident assumption that in calling men to God it also enlisted them directly in the forces which strengthen the Christian character of a civilization. To answer the call was important, therefore, both for the individual and for society. The appeal was usually couched in highly individualistic terms; paradoxically, the appeal was effective because it reflected the prevailing opinion of the community at large.

When the spiritual and general depressions had run their courses, however, during which the effects of demographic and urban trends were felt in public life, there were few American cities in which Protestant forces had a significant enough hold on the larger community to speak for it religiously. The outward forms of the old influence often persisted, but the realities had changed. The Lynds had found the gap between religious theory and actual practice wide in Middletown in the mid-twenties; ten years later it had markedly widened: "The gap between religion's verbalizing and Middletown life has become so wide that the entire institution of religion has tended to be put on the defensive; and the acceptance of a defensive role has tended to mean that it is timid in jeopardizing its foothold in the culture by espousing unpopular causes, when they appear in the economic order, in questions of world peace, and in the elements of contradiction in local institutions."[65] Revival was not likely in such a defensive setting, nor did it come through the old channels.

Other institutions were filling some of the roles the churches had once pre-empted. Edwin S. Gaustad has observed that between the two World Wars:

> The school, not the church, would now Americanize ethnic minorities and culturally deprived groups. The school, not the church, would now give instruction in prudence and morality—the basic niceties that became known as "citizenship." The school, not the church, would now plan and plot how to refashion and reform the society of America, holding national meetings and instituting ambitious programs to this end.[66]

The divided and weakened churches had difficulty making much impact during national crises. Gilman Ostrander has noted that "the depression found the Protestant churches at the nadir of their influence, outside the rural area of the nation, and the New Deal consequently was a secular movement such as the nation had not witnessed since the days of Jeffersonian republicanism." [67] The wheel had turned full circle!

It would be easy to overdraw the picture, to minimize the strength of the Protestant traditions in certain sections of the country (as in much of the South), and to overlook the role of strong congregations in the common life of a community. In national affairs the churches did participate significantly at many points.[68] The social Christian tradition proved to have strength and relevance in a difficult time.[69] Important work in the cause of civil liberties and in supporting the rights of labor was being done. And in many of the smaller, newer religious movements which were usually looked down on by the main line denominations as "sects," there was remarkable vitality and growth. Holiness, Pentecostal, and Adventist groups were numerically small compared to the large communions, but often were able to offer religious alternatives to those dissatisfied with the religious and cultural patterns that had long been dominant.[70] What is being emphasized here is not that the Protestant churches were lethargic and inactive, for they were not, but that their special identification with American civilization was drawing to an end. The "second disestablishment" of religion was well along. The continued use of the rhetoric of a Christian America was increasingly out of place. When it was used, it often produced a sense of unreality that has troubled institutional religious life ever since.

Of course, there were many serious and sincere attempts to restate the old alignment, often in modified forms. In 1937, Henry Sloane Coffin of Union Theological Seminary urged church and state to become partners in education, for "normally the morality which the State enacts in its law is part of the ethics which the Church inculcates in her teaching." Because of the divine aspect of the church's life, she cannot enter into a compromising relation, he declared, but "if the State will take her on her own terms, and accord her liberty to teach her Gospel, she becomes the State's ablest helper in producing useful and loyal citizens." [71] In a book written in the 1960's in which Protestants were urged to accept the passing of "Protestantdom," Martin E. Marty observed how strong the hold of the past still was: "Few Protestants, at least, would like to go back to the formal, legal bases of placed Christianity—though many of them still desire an informal, semilegal status for it." [72] The attempt to hold on even to such shadows of past conventions has been increasingly unrealistic since the 1930's.

In the early nineteenth century, to sum up, resurgent evangelical Protestantism, reacting against the difficulties of the revolutionary period, had set out to make America a Christian nation, and to do this by voluntary means through persuasion. Some of the things that then transpired have been the burden of this book. A religion and a civilization became interrelated in many ways. The religion impressed itself on the civilization so that the latter in part became its carrier. The religion also became so attached to the civilization that as the latter changed it was difficult for many Protestants to sense to what degree they had become a religion of the culture. By the mid-thirties, however, some conspicuous Protestant leaders were calling for the disentanglement of Protestantism and American civilization; they were asking for a reversal of what had long been axiomatically accepted. Instead of the church having Christianized civilization, they found that the civilization had captured the church. In a book published in 1935 entitled *The Church Against the World*, Francis P. Miller, a Presbyterian layman who was chairman of the World Student Christian Federation, seeking to relate his knowledge of the plight of European churches in the 1930's to the American situation, declared:

> The plain fact is that the domestication of the Protestant community in the United States within the framework of the national culture has progressed as far as in any western land. The degradation of the American Protestant church is as complete as the degradation of any other national Protestant church. The process of degradation has been more subtle and inconspicuous, but equally devastating in its consequences for faith.[73]

Miller appealed to the churches to distinguish more clearly between their primary tasks and their secondary ones. First must come preoccupation with those elements in the Christian faith that have an absolute and eternal value, Miller insisted, while the realization of the special ends of American national culture was a secondary matter.

In the same book, H. Richard Niebuhr, professor of ethics at Yale, traced in broad historical outline (which fit the American situation rather aptly) the process whereby a church gets tied to a culture:

> A converted church in a corrupt civilization withdraws to its upper rooms, into monasteries and conventicles; it issues forth from these in the aggressive evangelism of apostles, monks and friars, circuit riders and missionaries; it relaxes its rigorism as it discerns signs of repentance and faith; it enters into inevitable alliance with converted emperors and

> governors, philosophers and artists, merchants and entrepreneurs, and begins to live at peace in the culture they produce under the stimulus of their faith; when faith loses its force, as generation follows generation, discipline is relaxed, repentance grows formal, corruption enters with idolatry, and the church, tied to the culture which it sponsored, suffers corruption with it. Only a new withdrawal followed by a new aggression can then save the church and restore to it the salt with which to savor society. . . . The task of the present generation appears to lie in the liberation of the church from its bondage to a corrupt civilization.[74]

This was a clear call for ceasing to value civilization for civilization's sake, a call for evangelical Protestantism to redefine its ministry and mission for a new period in the nation's history. Two years later Samuel McCrea Cavert, general secretary of the Federal Council of Churches, reviewing the world religious scene, said,

> in the main the Church seems headed for an era of conflict with contemporary culture, no longer of easy domestication within it.
>
> The conflict is less apparent in America but we would be deluding ourselves if we thought it be absent. We can no longer discuss the relation of Church and State, even in America, on the basis of the old assumptions which have held the field down to our own day.

He questioned whether the church was justified in principle or as a matter of strategy to force its moral standards on the members of the community who do not voluntarily accept them. He asked: "On what ground can we expect the government of a country in which half the people are not even nominally Christians, to lay down policies which are specifically related to Christianity?"[75]

Though many only later became aware of it, during the depression period the "Protestant era" in American history came to a close. The voluntary effort to maintain a Protestant America had failed. For some, this seemed to mean the loss of religion itself; for others, it meant the freeing of religion from an alliance that was outdated and had become dysfunctional.

SINCE 1935

The Protestant era in American life had come to its end by the mid-thirties. Though 1935 is being suggested as marking the end of one period and the beginning of another, of course historical transitions can rarely be precisely dated, and certainly this one cannot. Spokesmen for the older perceptions and goals continued to appear long after the middle of the fourth decade. In many cases they were not unaware of changes, but it took time and the emergence of the shattering events of the forties, fifties, and sixties to convince people that the familiar landscape had been decisively altered.

To say that the Protestant era in American life ended in the thirties does not at all mean that Protestant faiths and institutions have not carried on through the years of war and peace since then. The churches maintained their faith and work through times of advance and decline, drawing millions of the population into loyalty and support. But they have had to adjust to the loss of a vision that once provided inspiration and direction. Because that overarching dream was so often referred to in a rather generalized way, its fading has given many Protestants a sense of uneasiness and guilt without their really being able to say why. The decline of the Protestant attempt to turn America into a Christian nation has left the nation with a complex heritage of impressive achievements and visible limitations. Significant changes in any of the nation's major religious subcultures are important, not only for those who belong to it, but also for the life of the nation as a whole. Either to mourn, to praise, or to condemn indiscriminately what has passed is not as helpful as an effort to understand it for what it was and for what it tried to do, and for what its continuing influence on the nation and its churches is.

Many of the contemporary problems that are usually treated under the "church and state" rubric have come to us out of the "Protestant era" of American history. Laws relating to Sunday closings, for example, are largely an inheritance from the Puritan and evangelical phases of American historical experience. They have been upheld by the courts as a safeguard for labor and for health, but they were enacted for other reasons. Such matters as tax exemption for church property, prayer and Bible reading in the public schools, the use of public property for religious displays, the evaluation of the fitness of candidates for public office largely on the basis of religious affiliation and personal moral stands, and a host of other pressing questions are the heritage of Protestant predominance in the earlier era of American history. Most of the birth control laws that raised church-state issues in the last part of the twentieth century were not the product of massive Catholic immigration but of the earlier Protestant era. They were framed in a time that daily grows more remote; they need rethinking and reworking for a strikingly different period.

Since 1935, the debate over the relation of church and state has often been clouded by lack of clear recognition that the Protestant era of American history has indeed come to an end. If some Protestants continue to think and work as though the virtual identification of their religion and American civilization is still viable, or that with a little more effort America will become a Christian nation in their terms, they will be seriously hampered in playing a creative role for human good that a religious movement can exercise in a modern cultural situation. For Protestants (or others) to think that they have to defend viewpoints and practices that once may have been understandable but are now outmoded is needlessly to handicap themselves in serving the present and facing the future. For non-Protestants or post-Protestants to continue to see mainly the blunders of the past and not some of the present directions of the various religious communities might be to dismiss spiritual resources helpful to the health of a people. The recognition that an era did come to an end some years ago can be liberating for all.

The passing of the Protestant era has allowed many to see more fully the meaning of the highly pluralistic character of American religion. Ever since disestablishment there has been general recognition of the facts of religious pluralism, but often it has been widely understood to be an essentially "Protestant pluralism" which tolerated "minority" groups of quite different backgrounds. This general definition of the situation was long accepted, not only by the evangelical leaders who conceived the Protestant denominations as cooperating in a broad religious united front, but also by many spokesmen of the minority churches. After the demographic, social, and intellectual transformations of American life had exerted their powerful effect, it became easier to see with greater clarity the realities of a religious pluralism that had always been more diversified than the evangelical mind had realized. Still, many were startled when Will Herberg declared in 1955: "Protestantism today no longer regards itself either as a religious movement sweeping the continent or as a national church representing the religious life of the people; Protestantism understands itself today primarily as one of the three religious communities in which twentieth century America has come to be divided."[76] Actually, the reference to the "three communities," though surprising to many at the time, was oversimple. Religiously, America is a Catholic-Jewish-Orthodox-Protestant-Mormon-Pentecostalist-New Thought-Humanist nation, to list only some major options. Most of these options are further subdivided into a number of quite divergent types.[77] Furthermore, much of the pluralism of religion has been "internalized" in most of the larger churches, so that they themselves embrace a wide range of religious styles. Though certain broad denominational distinctives can be discerned, many of the main divisions cut across them. In Protestant life, for example, the cleavage between fundamentalist and modernist (or conservative evangelical and ecumenical, in recent terminology) has been one of the most visible. The slackening of the Protestant drive for a Christian America has weakened the framework within which the various parties could work together. The tensions between the evangelistic and social action perspectives sharply reappeared in the 1960's, threatening to disrupt some of the households of faith.[78] Somewhat paradoxically, the diminishing drive has made it easier for Protestant churchmen to be more tolerant to other religious groups. The latter are no longer seen as threats to the achievement of certain cultural goals which have become vague or have in fact been given up, both because of the internal diversity of Protestantism and because of the fading of the dream.[79]

There have been some remarkable developments, surprising achievements, and disappointing failures in the Protestant world since 1935. The theological renewal and the controversies relating to its rise and fall, the postwar revival and decline of religion, new ecumenical trends, and new kinds of encounters between black and white churches—these are some of the major themes. These movements are all complex, and all have interrelationships with developments in other parts of the world. Detailed researches, biographies, and analyses on which satisfying historical interpretations of these currents can be based are now in process or await attention. But these and other developments cannot be fully understood apart from the history and the decline of the Protestant quest for a Christian America. A once-powerful vision does not fade overnight; it continues to evoke expectations. When they cannot be fulfilled, frustrations and disillusionments follow. Even when it is recognized intellectually that a once dominant synthesis has gone, the feelings and habits it produced linger on. Such major themes in Protestant history since 1935 as theological renewal, religious revival, ecumenical trends, and black church advance provide illustrations.

The renewal movement in theology which swept stormily through American Protestantism in the 1930's and after is usually known as neo-Protestantism or neo-orthodoxy, though in its American style it was usually broader than the European neo-orthodox, dialectical, or crisis theology movements which predated and influenced it. In American neo-orthodoxy, the contributions of the many-sided, broadminded Niebuhr brothers were especially prominent. As in Europe, the work of the biblical theologians with their emphasis on the unity of the Bible as a witness to divine revelation was appropriated, and such classical Christian emphasis as God's sovereignty, man's sinfulness, and the primacy of faith were stressed.[80] Much of the early thrust of the movement derived from its critique of what was often called culture Protestantism. Neo-orthodoxy was devoted to the recovering of Christianity's own source of authority and direction, that it might stand apart and serve as a leaven in human society. "The paradox of religion is that it serves the world best when it maintains its high disdain for the world's values," said Reinhold Niebuhr in 1927.[81] For many years he, with others, battled against the compromises both liberal and conservative religion had made with the culture, seeking a sound theological basis for a relevant Christian service to society.

The achievements of these efforts at theological recovery were impressive. An evaluation of the movement offered in the mid-sixties, after it was well past the peak of its influence, said:

> In the past 45 years of theological reawakening the significance and weightiness of the tradition and vocabulary to which we are heir were rediscovered. This was accordingly a time of great constructiveness, given vitality by the sense that the deeper meaning of the Christian faith, after almost having been lost, was once again being appropriated.[82]

Many reasons for the rather swift decline of neo-orthodoxy have been advanced. In part, and often in the face of its deeper insights, there was a tendency for some of those who were part of the general movement to slip partially back into a state of mind which sought to view Christianity as holding the keys to civilization. One of the recent critics, William A. Clebsch, has suggested that "the devotees of the so-called theological renaissance in America fell into a trap of their own manufacture, the trap of thinking that the best way to proclaim Christianity was to claim for it everything." [83] Clebsch was especially critical of its tendency to raise ancient questions, and to return subtly to dogmatism. For "in claiming for it everything" the movement suggested the possibility of a new cultural synthesis, an updated theology for American civilization. As it strengthened Protestantism's intellectual resources, old temptations were raised again as some began to dream of a new synthesis of religion and culture. Neo-orthodoxy's own deeper insights about the proper tension between faith and culture have been used to criticize some of the denominational and interdenominational programs that movement in fact helped to produce.[84] As the work of understanding historically and theologically this whole important development goes on, it must be remembered that it arose just as the dream of a Protestant America was eroding, and was in part an attempt to fill the gaps left by that decline. Both its contributions and its limitations can be fully understood when seen from that perspective, along with others.

A somewhat chaotic theological scene followed the decline of the neo-orthodox effort. Theological trends in the 1960's were very varied and complex; secular and radical positions sparred for a hearing with new movements of liberal and natural theologies and fresh articulations of confessional and evangelical options. Some were saying, in ways that were heard by those who stood in other theological alignments, that the old ways of doing theology would no longer serve. Harvey Cox, for example, criticized Protestant doctrines of the church as almost entirely past-oriented. They "have come to us from the frayed-out period of classical Christendom and are infected with the ideology of preservation and permanence." He noted that the synthesis of Protestant and bourgeois culture is over, yet concluded that "in their organization, their theology, and their ways of relating to the world, our churches today are for the most part merely richer and shinier versions of their nineteenth-century parents." [85]

The various theological stances at the close of the 1960's seemed either to be over-reacting to styles of relating faith to culture which were in fact rapidly eroding, or still to be cast too much in the mind sets and vocabularies of past perspectives. Radical theologies tended to be too negative in their emotional reaction to what was really over; conservative theologies seemed to be too concerned about clinging to formulations relevant to another time in history. Frank facing of the achievements, limitations, and decline of the Protestant quest for a Christian America may help to free theology for a creative and constructive period.

The postwar revival of religion was also a complex phenomenon; it operated on a broader and more popular level than the theological renewal. Many things contributed to it: efforts to restate the faith in fresh terms, anxieties over the state of a world locked in cold war, desires for security and peace in a troubled world. Herbert W. Schneider focused scholarly attention on it in 1952, reporting that "during the dark 30's" came the "beginning of an offensive which has grown steadily since then." He called attention to the fact that practically all major types of religion had staged a significant "comeback." [86] The theological renaissance itself contributed to the general revival of religion, though the latter was much broader. An important part of the religious resurgence was the regrouping of the fundamentalists, who cast off some of their earlier intransigence and as "conservative evangelicals" organized the National Association of Evangelicals (1942).

As the revival crested in the 1950's, it attracted much attention. It had many strands, such as the refurbished revivalism of Billy

Graham, the "positive thinking" of Norman Vincent Peale, and the enriched and deepened products of the denominational bureaucracies. Many lives were significantly touched by the recovery of religion; congregations expanded and many new ones were founded.

Critics of the movement noted that in certain respects the revival was an effort to recover lost ground. A. Roy Eckardt believed that much of the postwar resurgence was folk religion, which was utilitarian, fostered individual security, and aided brotherhood and social solidarity.[87] Folk religion became something of a surrogate for the earlier commitment to Protestant civilization. Will Herberg found that the religious revival to a considerable extent was a search for identity and conformity in mass society, and was directed heavily toward supporting "the American way of life" as its highest value.[88] The Protestant revival can be seen as a many-sided and often very sincere effort of a heterogeneous movement to regain a sense of its unity, direction, and place in the culture.

After the revival had begun to recede, Martin E. Marty analyzed "the new shape of American religion," finding it had been not so much a revival of historic faith as a revival of *interest* in "religion-in-general."[89] A "religion of democracy" was emerging as America's *real* religion, in part a sociological replacement of the old dream of Christian America. Some argued openly for this; J. Paul Williams, for example, believing that "the duty to strengthen public morals" is among the most important of religion's responsibilities, and finding that churches and synagogues "play less determining roles in American culture than in former decades," argued that "governmental agencies must teach the democratic ideal *as religion*."[90] To be sure, most of these who supported the religious revival did not espouse such a position, but many were clearly interested in the renewal for the sake of what it could do for the nation.

The critiques of the revival of religion when it was still current show an awareness that Protestantism was seeking something which had been lost. The recovery did not run deep for it did not clearly recognize that what was missing was the former close identification with American civilization. Had it been able to see that, it might have been able to face more fundamental questions, rather than trying to replace what historical circumstances had made irreplaceable. As it was, the revival as a general phenomenon rather quickly passed. A thoughtful epitaph was written in the 1960's by Edward A. Farley. As the revival waned, he found that Christian faith or piety was not passing away, but "that one *historical* piety (Protestant piety) is passing off the scene. . . . As I look at the evidence, it seems to say that a certain historical form of Christian piety (Victorian Protestant piety) is going. Faith itself remains, searches for, and in part finds new forms—some idolatrous, some innocuous, and some seemingly genuine." [91] For a good many people, however, both inside and outside the churches, the passing of the form seemed to mean the end of faith. To fail to see the rise and decline of the religious revival against the background of previous revivals, and in part as an attempt to restore or to provide a substitute for something that had passed, might be to misunderstand it entirely.

The development of the ecumenical movement since 1935, a story interwoven with that of the theological renaissance and the religious revival, has been remarkable indeed. The increase in the size, number, and influence of many local councils of churches; the consolidation of major cooperative agencies into the National Council of Churches in 1950; the reunion of a number of divided denominational families and the formation of a United Church across confessional lines; the launching of the Consultation on Church Union in 1962 and its movement toward a Plan of Union involving nine major Protestant denominations; and the dramatic entrance into ecumenical dialogue and cooperation by Roman Catholicism, highlighted by the pontificate of John XXIII and the Second Vatican Council (1962–1965)—these are but main headings of an interesting and complex history.[92] Cooperative and ecumenical agencies of many types often originally had a pan-Protestant character; only slowly have some of them been able to broaden out to include as full equal partners Orthodox and Catholic Christians, and representatives of some of the smaller Protestant bodies.

As has been suggested previously,[93] some of the earlier cooperative activity was an effort on the part of Protestants to replace the sense of unity once carried by the general culture. There continue to be those inside and outside of ecumenical activity who fear that it is but an attempt of Christians to regroup in order to maintain special privileges, to hold on to or win back what was a place of security if not dominance in national life. When Eugene Carson Blake offered the "Proposal" which led to the founding of the Consultation on Church Union, one scholar criticized it because he feared that it invited "Christians in the United States to form a club or trust of the well-established, respectable, English-extraction denominations at the expense of union with the least of Christ's brethren, be they Christian or not." [94] The consultation itself, beginning with its first meeting in 1962, and soon involving six white and three black denominations struggled hard to avoid any such implication, yet such comments as Paul L. Lehmann's that the consultation is too much concerned "with the Church in the act of saving itself" are heard.[95] It is my own opinion that the consultation through the 1960's successfully resisted the most serious of such dangers, but the very fact that it has had to be so careful shows how the historical experience of the Protestant quest for a Christian America with its white, Anglo-Saxon overtones shadows the ecumenical effort. Referring to certain ecumenical trends in an "inter-religious" direction, Harvey Cox has suggested that "it would be too bad if Catholics and Jews, having pushed for the de-Protestantizing of American society and having in effect won, should now join Protestants in reconstructing a kind of tripartite American religion with Americanized versions of Moses, Luther, and Saint Thomas sharing the haloes in its hagiography." [96] A new "religiondom" might try to replace old Christendom.

One of the ugliest aspects of American Protestantism has been the patronizing and condescending attitudes of whites toward blacks. Such attitudes too often accepted and even contributed to racial injustice, usually despite public statements to the contrary. For example, an interesting study has shown how a liberal and ecumenical Protestant weekly, the *Christian Century*, only slowly moved away from a "mildly held Anglo-Saxonism" between the world wars. "Its mind set inclined it to view Jews with suspicion and Negroes with condescension." [97] The churches only slowly and in some places hardly at all improved in their racial practices. Shortly after World War I the Federal Council took leadership in the struggle renouncing "the pattern of segregation in race relations as unnecessary and undesirable and a violation of the Gospel of love and human brotherhood" and pledging to "work for a non-segregated Church and a non-segregated society." [98] The gap between resolution and practice, however, can be a very wide one. A sociological study of Detroit's religious situation in the late 1950's provided much evidence for the conclusion that "segregation tends to be the rule in the urban North almost as much as in the rural South." [99] Only slowly and against considerable opposition were black Christians given responsibility in the major denominations; the Methodist union of 1939 was marred by the provision for a separate jurisdiction for Negroes.[100] The civil rights movement of the 1950's and the emergence of a black power emphasis within the black churches has enabled many white Christians to see their past in a new perspective.[101]

The criticisms by black Christians of the limitations which they have seen in the traditional Protestant design for a Christian America reveal how much it was related to white cultural patterns. There is a demand that the past be seen clearly for what it was so that errors not be repeated. Joseph R. Washington, Jr. has declared that "the eradication of white folk religion is indispensable because it is the undeniable demand of this historical era which can no longer be disregarded." [102] In a significant essay, Vincent Harding has remarked parenthetically that one of the blessings of the black power movement

> is the honesty it has already forced into the black-and-white dialogue in America. It has not produced hate; it has rather revealed hate and called upon both whites and blacks to admit its sorrowful depths. There are, of course, large segments of the society who still fear this radical honesty, but it is likely that they also fear true religion.[103]

The massive background of the (white) Protestant effort to mold a Christian civilization carried with it certain serious limitations, some of which continue to cast their spell long after the main patterns have dissolved.

The theological renaissance, ecumenical advance, and the emergence of outspoken black witness have together helped the Protestant world to recognize and move away from Anglo-Saxonism. E. Digby Baltzell has written a fascinating book, *The Protestant Establishment*, in which he has argued that the large corporation executive suite in America is still largely composed of those of Anglo-Saxon Protestant background. His work is a study of this tight, closed, country-club caste of wealth and power. In a way, the book is wrongly named—"The Anglo-Saxonist Establishment" might have been more accurate. For he observed that "Anglo-Saxonism is a debilitating denial of our Anglo-Saxon traditions," and agreed that "as everyone knows, of course, the values of Christianity have often been in conflict with those of the country club." [104] Many congregations of various denominational backgrounds have continued to avoid that conflict, however, trying to hold on to some of the shattered fragments of a nineteenth-century dream. What Baltzell has called in oversimple terms "the Protestant establishment" is in part a degenerate and secularized form of what was once a powerful vision of religion and civilization in real partnership. Officially, at least, most responsible church leadership respects the concepts of the establishment about which Baltzell has written, though romanticized versions of the Protestant past continue to exert considerable influence.

The Protestant effort to make American civilization Christian has had a long, complicated history with many fascinating and some unpleasant chapters. The record has had many tales of courageous individuals and corporate Christian contributions, and is marred by unfortunate compromises. The realities of twentieth-century life have brought revolutions in thought and have vastly multiplied the number of non-Protestants in the culture. Protestant churches have struggled to redefine their role and mission, handicapped often by a sense of failure because things are not what they used to be. Despite the mistakes which nineteenth-century evangelical Protestants made—and it is far easier for us to see their limitations than it is our own—they struggled earnestly with the problems of how to make faith a force in the common life, or how to live a life of commitment to a religious vision without denying the freedom of others. Twentieth-century Americans still live with many of the outcomes of their successes and their failures, and still face, often in quite different ways, the same basic problems of religion and society which they encountered then. At their best, they looked and worked toward the future, and they struggled to translate their dreams into reality. From the successes and failures there is much to learn.

Bibliographical Note

The primary and secondary sources for the study of the historical relationships between religion and civilization in America are vast, but happily there are some very useful guides into these materials. Indispensable is the solid work of Nelson R. Burr, in collaboration with James Ward Smith and A. Leland Jamison, *A Critical Bibliography of Religion in America*, vol IV: *Religion in American Life* (Princeton, 1961). Helpful at many points is Edwin S. Gaustad's *Historical Atlas of Religion in America* (New York, 1962). There is still value in Peter G. Mode's *Source Book and Bibliographical Guide for American Church History* (Menasha, Wis., 1921), though more recent and comprehensive is the work by H. Shelton Smith, Robert T. Handy, and Lefferts A. Loetscher, *American Christianity: An Historical Interpretation with Representative Documents* (2 vols.; New York, 1960, 1963). Two sets of interpretive esays have been especially suggestive for this study: *The Lively Experiment: The Shaping of Christianity in America* (New York, 1963) by Sidney E. Mead, one of those seminal books to be consulted again and again; and *The Shaping of American Religion* edited by James Ward Smith and A. Leland Jamison, vol. I: *Religion in American Life*, containing contributions by some of the leading interpreters of American religion. The best one-volume coverage of American religious history is by Winthrop S. Hudson, *Religion in America* (New York, 1965). A classic theological interpretation of Christianity in America is by H. Richard Niebuhr, *The Kingdom of God in America* (New York, 1937); see also Sydney E. Ahlstrom, *Theology in America: The Major Protestant Voices from Puritanism to Neo-Orthodoxy*, The American Heritage Series (Indianapolis, 1967). An effort to reinterpret the religious history of the United States from a functional and secular point of view is by William A. Clebsch, *From Sacred to Profane America: The Role of Religion in American History* (New York, 1968). A fresh, stimulating overall interpretation of Protestantism in the United States is by Martin E. Marty, *Righteous Empire: The Protestant Experience in America* (New York, 1970). The present state of the discipline of American church history has been analyzed in a symposium edited by Jerald C. Brauer, *Reinterpretation in American Church History*, vol. V: *Essays in Divinity* (Chicago, 1968).

As the notes of the present volume should show, I have sought to shape and test my interpretations through study of primary sources, especially for the nineteenth and early twentieth centuries, and have referred to the writings and actions of many individuals who played a role in and commented on developments discussed here. In the effort to understand more fully Protestant ideas about civilization and the role of religious institutions in it, I have found researches in the records of denominational gatherings revealing. Documents issuing from such assemblies often have a useful representative character that the observations of a single person rarely have. The way in which the published records of a denomination have been titled has varied from time to time and is often cumbersome; in the footnotes I have adopted standard short title forms for referring to such records, and have supplied the year in which the meeting being discussed occurred. The minutes of the quadrennial General Conference of the Methodist Episcopal Church (and of the Methodist Episcopal Church, South), of the triennial General Convention of the Protestant Episcopal Church, and of the annual general assemblies of the various branches of the Presbyterian Church have been especially useful. The pastoral letters of the Episcopal bishops and the "Narratives of the State of Religion," prepared through most of the nineteenth century for the Presbyterian general assemblies, have provided important clues. The minutes of the national conventions of the congregationally ordered denominations have proved to be somewhat less helpful, in part perhaps because such gatherings could not speak officially for the congregations; samplings in the minutes of the National Council of the Congregational Churches, and of the proceedings of the Southern Baptist Convention (and of the Northern Baptist Convention after its founding in 1907) seemed to indicate this. On the whole I have looked mainly into the annals of the major evangelical churches; some work in the proceedings of the General Conferences of the United Brethren in Christ, a body of German Methodist background, suggested that the major generalizations applied to the smaller evangelical bodies too.

Though this book deals mainly with the views and actions of white evangelical Protestants, there is some attention to the implications of this experience for black evangelicals. Some sampling of the records of the African Methodist Episcopal Church, the General African Methodist Episcopal Zion Connection, and the National Baptist Convention has convinced me how necessary further detailed attention to these and to other similar materials is needed.

The records of meetings of nondenominational and interdenominational gatherings have also been instructive; especially important for this volume have been *National Perils and Opportunities: The Discussions of the General Conference, held in Washington, D.C., . . . 1887, under the Auspices and Direction of the Evangelical Alliance* (New York, 1887), and *Ecumenical Missionary Conference, New York, 1900: Report of the Ecumenical Conference on Foreign Missions, . . .* (2 vols.; New

York, 1900). The reports of the meetings that resulted in the Federal Council of Churches are important for twentieth-century history; see especially Elias B. Sanford, ed., *Federal Council of the Churches of Christ in America: Report of the First Meeting . . .* (New York, 1909), and Sanford, *Origins and History of the the Federal Council of the Churches of Christ in America* (Hartford, 1916).

Though I have sought to base my intepretations on primary sources, I have been led to relevant sources and have received insights as to their meanings by many scholars of American social, intellectual, and religious history. For an understanding of the interplay between religion and civilization in America, the following writings are recommended.

I. COLONIAL AND REVOLUTIONARY PERIODS

Bridenbaugh, Carl. *Mitre and Sceptre: Transatlantic Faiths, Ideas, Personalities, and Politics, 1689–1775.* New York, 1962.

——— *Myths and Realities: Societies of the Colonial South.* Baton Rouge, 1952.

Gaustad, Edwin S. *The Great Awakening in New England.* New York, 1957.

Gewehr, Wesley M. *The Great Awakening in Virginia, 1740–1790.* Durham, 1930.

Goen, Clarence C. *Revivalism and Separatism in New England, 1740–1800.* New Haven, 1962.

Heimert, Alan. *Religion and the American Mind: From the Great Awakening to the Revolution.* Cambridge, Mass., 1966.

——— and Perry Miller, eds. *The Great Awakening: Documents Illustrating the Crisis and Its Consequences.* The American Heritage Series. Indianapolis, 1967.

McLoughlin, William G. *Isaac Backus and the American Pietistic Tradition.* The Library of American Biography. Boston, 1967.

Miller, Perry. *Errand into the Wilderness.* New York, 1956.

——— *The New England Mind.* 2 vols. New York, 1939, 1953.

——— and Thomas H. Johnson. *The Puritans.* New York, 1938.

Morgan, Edmund S. *The Puritan Family.* Boston, 1944.

———. *Visible Saints: The History of a Puritan Idea.* New York, 1963.

Sweet, William W. *Religion in Colonial America.* New York, 1942.

Tolles, Frederick B. *The Atlantic Community of Early Friends.* London, 1952.

Trinterud, Leonard J. *The Forming of an American Tradition: A Re-examination of Colonial Presbyterianism.* Philadelphia, 1949.

Wright, Conrad. *The Beginnings of Unitarianism in America.* Boston, 1955.

Wright, Louis B. *The Cultural Life of the American Colonies, 1607–1763.* New York, 1957.

——— *Religion and Empire: The Alliance between Piety and Commerce in English Expansion, 1588–1625.* Chapel Hill, 1943.

2. THE PERIOD FROM 1800 TO 1860

Barnes, Gilbert H. *The Antislavery Impulse, 1830–1844.* New York, 1933.

Beaver, R. Pierce. *Church, State, and the American Indians.* St. Louis, 1966.

Berkhofer, Robert F., Jr. *Salvation and the Savage: An Analysis of Protestant Missions and American Indian Response, 1787–1862.* Lexington, Ky., 1965.

Billington, Ray A. *The Protestant Crusade, 1800–1860: A Study of the Origins of American Nativism.* New York, 1938.

Bodo, John R. *The Protestant Clergy and Public Issues, 1812–1848.* Princeton, 1954.

Cross, Whitney R. *The Burned-over District: The Social and Intellectual History of Enthusiastic Religion in Western New York, 1800–1850.* Ithaca, N.Y., 1950.

Foster, Charles I. *An Errand of Mercy: The Evangelical United Front, 1790–1837.* Chapel Hill, 1960.

Griffin, Clifford S. *Their Brothers' Keepers: Moral Stewardship in the United States, 1800–1865.* New Brunswick, N.J., 1960.

Harrell, David E., Jr. *Quest for a Christian America: The Disciples of Christ and American Society to 1866.* Nashville, 1966.

Howe, Mark DeWolfe. *The Garden and the Wilderness: Religion and Government in American Constitutional History.* Chicago, 1965.

Kennedy, William B. *The Shaping of Protestant Education: An In-*

terpretation of the Sunday School and the Development of Protestant Educational Strategy in the United States, 1789–1860. Monographs in Christian Education, no. 4. New York, 1966.

Litwack, Leon F. *North of Slavery: The Negro in the Free States, 1790–1860.* Chicago, 1961.

Lynn, Robert W. and Elliott Wright. *The Big Little School: Sunday Child of American Protestantism.* New York, 1971.

Maclear, James F. "'The True American Union' of Church and State: The Reconstruction of the Theocratic Tradition," *Church History*, XXVIII (1959), 41–62.

Mathews, Donald G. *Slavery and Methodism: A Chapter in American Morality.* Princeton, 1965.

Miller, Perry. *The Life of the Mind in America: From the Revolution to the Civil War.* New York, 1965.

Nichols, James H. *Romanticism in American Theology: Nevin and Schaff at Mercersburg.* Chicago, 1961.

——— ed. *The Mercersburg Theology.* A Library of Protestant Thought. New York, 1966.

Sanford, Charles L. *The Quest for Paradise: Europe and the American Moral Imagination.* Urbana, Ill., 1961.

Smith, H. Shelton, ed. *Horace Bushnell.* A Library of Protestant Thought. New York, 1965.

Smith, Timothy L. "Protestant Schooling and American Nationality, 1800–1850," *Journal of American History*, LIII (1966–67), 679–695.

——— *Revivalism and Social Reform in Mid-Nineteenth-Century America.* New York, 1957.

Staudenraus, P. J. *The African Colonization Movement, 1816–1865.* New York, 1961.

Sweet, William W. *Religion in the Development of American Culture, 1765–1840.* New York, 1952.

——— ed. *Religion on the American Frontier, 1783–1840.* 4 vols. New York and Chicago, 1931–46.

Tuveson, Ernest L. *Redeemer Nation: The Idea of America's Millennial Role.* Chicago, 1968.

Tyack, David "The Kingdom of God and the Common School," *Harvard Educational Review*, XXXVI (1966), 447–69.

Weisberger, Bernard A. *They Gathered at the River; The Story of the Great Revivalists and Their Impact upon Religion in America. Boston,* 1958.

Wright, Louis B. *Culture on the Moving Frontier.* Bloomington, Ind., 1955.

3. THE PERIOD FROM 1860 TO 1920

Abell, Aaron I. *The Urban Impact on American Protestantism, 1865–1900.* Cambridge, Mass., 1943.
Bailey, Kenneth K. *Southern White Protestantism in the Twentieth Century.* New York, 1964.
Cauthen, Kenneth. *The Impact of American Religious Liberalism.* New York, 1962.
Cross, Robert D., ed. *The Church and the City, 1865–1910.* The American Heritage Series. Indianapolis, 1967.
Du Bois, W. E. Burghardt. *The Negro Church.* Atlanta, 1903.
Farish, Hunter D. *The Circuit Rider Dismounts: A Social History of Southern Methodism, 1865–1900.* Richmond, 1938.
Findlay, James F., Jr. *Dwight L. Moody: American Evangelist, 1832–1899.* Chicago, 1969.
Frazier, E. Franklin. *The Negro Church in America.* New York, 1967.
Geyer, Alan. *Piety and Politics: American Protestantism in the World Arena.* Richmond, 1963.
Gossett, Thomas F. *Race: The History of an Idea in America.* Dallas, 1963.
Grimes, Alan P. *The Puritan Ethic and Woman Suffrage.* New York, 1967.
Gusfield, Joseph R. *Symbolic Crusade: Status Politics and the American Temperance Movement.* Urbana, Ill., 1963.
Higham, John. *Strangers in the Land: Patterns of American Nativism, 1860–1925.* New Brunswick, N.J., 1955.
Hofstadter, Richard. *The Age of Reform: From Bryan to F.D.R.* New York, 1955.
Hopkins, Charles H. *The Rise of the Social Gospel in American Protestantism, 1865–1915.* New Haven, 1940.
Hudson, Winthrop S. *American Protestantism.* The Chicago History of American Civilization. Chicago, 1961.
——— *The Great Tradition of the American Churches.* New York, 1953.
Kinzer, Donald L. *An Episode in Anti-Catholicism: The American Protective Association.* Seattle, 1964.

Loetscher, Lefferts A. *The Broadening Church: A Study of Theological Issues in the Presbyterian Church since 1869*. Philadelphia, 1954.

MacKenzie, Kenneth M. *The Robe and the Sword: The Methodist Church and the Rise of American Imperialism*. Washington, D.C., 1961.

McLoughlin, William G. *Modern Revivalism: Charles Grandison Finney to Billy Graham*. New York, 1959.

Marty, Martin E. *Righteous Empire: The Protestant Experience in America*. New York, 1970.

May, Henry F. *The End of American Innocence: A Study of the First Years of Our Own Time, 1912–1917*. New York, 1959.

——— *Protestant Churches and Industrial America*. New York, 1949.

Meier, August. *Negro Thought in America, 1880–1915: Racial Ideologies in the Age of Booker T. Washington*. Ann Arbor, 1963.

Murray, Andrew E. *Presbyterians and the Negro: A History*. Philadelphia, 1966.

Piper, John F., Jr. "The Social Policy of the Federal Council of the Churches of Christ in America During World War I," unpub. Ph.D. thesis, Duke University, 1964.

Reimers, David M. *White Protestantism and the Negro*. New York, 1965.

Sandeen, Ernest R. *The Roots of Fundamentalism: British and American Millenarianism, 1800–1930*. Chicago, 1970.

Smylie, John E. "National Ethos and the Church," *Theology Today*, XX (1963), 313–31.

——— "Protestant Clergymen and America's World Role, 1865–1900: A Study of Christianity, Nationality and International Relations," unpub. Th.D. thesis, Princeton Theological Seminary, 1959.

Spain, Rufus B. *At Ease in Zion: Social History of Southern Baptists, 1865–1900*. Nashville, 1967.

Timberlake, James H. *Prohibition and the Progressive Movement, 1900–1920*. Cambridge, Mass., 1963.

Varg, Paul H. *Missionaries, Chinese and Diplomats: The American Protestant Missionary Movement in China, 1890–1952*. Princeton, 1958.

Weisenburger, Francis P. *Ordeal of Faith: The Crisis of Church-Going America, 1865–1900*. New York, 1959.

——— *Triumph of Faith: Contributions of the Church to American Life, 1865–1900*. Richmond, 1962.

Woodson, Carter, G. *The History of the Negro Church.* Washington, D.C., 1921.

Woodward, C. Vann. *The Strange Career of Jim Crow.* Rev. ed. New York, 1957.

4. THE PERIOD SINCE 1920

Brown, William A. *The Church in America: A Study of the Present Condition and Future Prospects of American Protestantism.* New York, 1922.

Carter, Paul A. *The Decline and Revival of the Social Gospel: Social and Political Liberalism in American Protestant Churches, 1920–1940.* Ithaca, N.Y., 1954.

Cavert, Samuel McCrea. *The American Churches in the Ecumenical Movement, 1900–1968.* New York, 1968.

——— *Church Cooperation and Unity in America, A Historical Review: 1900–1970.* New York, 1970.

Cole, Stewart G. *The History of Fundamentalism.* New York, 1931.

Cone, James H. *Black Theology and Black Power.* New York, 1969.

Cox, Harvey. *The Secular City: Secularization and Urbanization in Theological Perspective.* New York, 1965.

Eckardt, A. Roy. *The Surge of Piety in America: An Appraisal.* New York, 1958.

Ernst, Eldon G. "The Interchurch World Movement of North America, 1919–1920," unpub. Ph.D. thesis, Yale University, 1968.

Farley, Edward A. *Requiem for a Lost Piety: The Contemporary Search for the Christian Life.* Philadelphia, 1966.

Furniss, Norman F. *The Fundamentalist Controversy, 1918–1931.* New Haven, 1954.

Gatewood, Willard B., Jr., ed. *Controversy in the Twenties: Fundamentalism, Modernism, and Evolution.* Nashville, 1969.

Harland, Gordon. *The Thought of Reinhold Niebuhr.* New York, 1960.

Haselden, Kyle. *Mandate for White Christians.* Richmond, 1966.

——— *The Racial Problem in Christian Perspective.* New York, 1959.

Herberg, Will. *Protestant-Catholic-Jew: An Essay in American Religious Sociology.* Garden City, N.Y., 1955.

Hill, Samuel S., Jr. *Southern Churches in Crisis.* New York, 1967.

Hough, Joseph C. *Black Power and White Protestants: A Christian Response to the New Negro Pluralism.* New York, 1968.

Kegley, Charles W. and Robert W. Bretall, eds. *Reinhold Niebuhr: His Religious, Social, and Political Thought.* New York, 1956.

Kincheloe, Samuel C. *Research Memorandum on Religion in the Depression.* New York, 1937.

Lee, Robert. *The Social Sources of Church Unity: An Interpretation of Unitive Movements in American Protestantism.* New York, 1960.

Lenski, Gerhard. *The Religious Factor: A Sociological Study of Religion's Impact on Politics, Economics, and Family Life.* Garden City, N.Y., 1961.

Lynn, Robert W. *Protestant Strategies in Education.* Monographs in Christian Education, no. 1. New York, 1964.

Marty, Martin E. *The New Shape of American Religion.* New York, 1959.

——— *Second Chance for American Protestants.* New York, 1963.

Mays, Benjamin E. and Joseph W. Nicholson. *The Negro's Church.* New York, 1933.

Meyer, Donald B. *The Protestant Search for Political Realism, 1919–1941.* Berkeley, Cal., 1960.

Miller, Robert M. *American Protestantism and Social Issues, 1919–1939.* Chapel Hill, 1958.

Moore, Edmund A. *A Catholic Runs for President: The Campaign of 1928.* New York, 1956.

Nash, Arnold S., ed. *Protestant Thought in the Twentieth Century: Whence and Whither?* New York, 1951.

Niebuhr, H. Richard, Wilhelm Pauck, and Francis P. Miller. *The Church Against the World.* Chicago, 1935.

Schneider, Herbert W. *Religion in 20th Century America.* Cambridge, Mass., 1952.

Silva, Ruth C. *Rum, Religion and Votes: 1928 Re-examined.* University Park, Pa., 1962.

Spike, Robert W. *The Freedom Revolution and the Churches.* New York, 1965.

Van Dusen, Henry P. *et al. Church and State in the Modern World.* New York, 1937.

Washington, Joseph R., Jr. *Black Religion: The Negro and Christianity in the United States.* Boston, 1964.

——— *The Politics of God.* Boston, 1967.

Notes

I COLONIAL ESTABLISHMENTS OF RELIGION

1. *The Cultural Life of the American Colonies, 1607–1763* (New York, 1957), p. 72.
2. *Errand into the Wilderness* (New York, 1956), p. 105.
3. See John A. F. New, *Anglican and Puritan: The Basis of Their Opposition, 1558–1640* (Stanford, Calif., 1964). The literature on the history of English Puritanism is vast; e.g., see William E. Haller, *The Rise of Puritanism* (New York, 1938); Marshall M. Knappen, *Tudor Puritanism: A Chapter in the History of Idealism* (Chicago, 1939); and Patrick M. Collinson, *The Elizabethan Puritan Movement* (London, 1967).
4. *A Loss of Mastery: Puritan Historians in Colonial America* (Berkeley, Cal., 1966), p. 10.
5. *The Quest for Paradise: Europe and the American Moral Imagination* (Urbana, Ill., 1961), p. 52.
6. William Haller, *Foxe's Book of Martyrs and the Elect Nation* (London, 1963). See also Winthrop S. Hudson, ed., *Nationalism and Religion in America: Concepts of American Identity and Mission* (New York, 1970), pp. 153–66.
7. *A Loss of Mastery*, p. 16.
8. The story has been told in detail by Edward McNall Burns, *The American Idea of Mission: Concepts of National Purpose and Destiny* (New Brunswick, N. J., 1957).
9. The evidence is summarized by R. Pierce Beaver, *Church, State, and the American Indians* (St. Louis, 1966), chap. 1.
10. *The Quest for Paradise*, p. 106.
11. *The Social Ideas of Religious Leaders, 1660–1688* (London, 1940), p. 87. Cf. his *Private Property: The History of an Idea* (London, 1951).
12. See Wallace Notestein, *The English People on the Eve of Colonization, 1607–1630* (New York, 1954), chaps. 4–7.

13. *Myths and Realities: Societies of the Colonial South* (Baton Rouge, 1952), p. 169.
14. See, e.g., E. Franklin Frazier, *The Negro Church in America* (New York, 1964), pp. 6–7.
15. See Nelson R. Burr, *A Critical Bibliography of Religion in America*, vol. IV: *Religion in American Life* (Princeton, 1961).
16. *Errand into the Wilderness*, p. 101. See also Louis B. Wright, *Religion and Empire: The Alliance between Piety and Commerce in English Expansion, 1558–1625* (Chapel Hill, 1943).
17. *Early Puritanism in the Southern and Island Colonies* (Worcester, Mass., 1960).
18. For example, see Bernard Bailyn, *The New England Merchants in the Seventeenth Century* (Cambridge, Mass., 1955); Darrett B. Rutman, *Winthrop's Boston: Portrait of a Puritan Town, 1630–1649* (Chapel Hill, 1965).
19. See "Dale's Laws" of 1610, and miscellaneous other items of pertinent legislation, reprinted in H. Shelton Smith, Robert T. Handy, and Lefferts A. Loetscher, *American Christianity: An Historical Interpretation with Representative Documents* (2 vols.; New York, 1960–63), I, 41–44, 48–51. See also George M. Brydon, *Virginia's Mother Church, and the Political Conditions under Which It Grew* (2 vols.; Richmond, 1947–52), I, chap. 1.
20. *From Sacred to Profane America: The Role of Religion in American History* (New York, 1968), pp. 157–58.
21. On the S.P.G., see Alfred W. Newcombe, "The Appointment and Instruction of S.P.G. Missionaries," *Church History*, V (1936), 340–58; Samuel C. McCulloch, "The Foundation and Early Work of the Society for the Propagation of the Gospel in Foreign Parts," *Historical Magazine of the Protestant Episcopal Church*, XX (1951), 121–35; C. F. Pascoe, *Two Hundred Years of the S.P.G.* (2 vols.; London, 1901); Frank J. Klingberg, *Anglican Humanitarianism in Colonial New York* (Philadelphia, 1940).
22. *Culture on the Moving Frontier* (Bloomington, Ind., 1955), p. 170.
23. Quoted by Carl Bridenbaugh, *Mitre and Sceptre: Transatlantic Faiths, Ideas, Personalities, and Politics, 1689–1775* (New York, 1962), p. 152.
24. The late Perry Miller devoted much attention to these matters in his many books and articles; see esp. *Orthodoxy in Massachu-*

setts (Cambridge, Mass., 1933), *The New England Mind* (2 vols.; New York, 1939–53), and the useful collection of some of his key articles, *Errand into the Wilderness.* More recent works show his influence even as they suggest revisions; cf., e.g., Edmund S. Morgan, *Visible Saints: The History of a Puritan Idea* (New York, 1963), and Rutman, *Winthrop's Boston.*

25. The Cambridge Platform has been printed in many forms; in full in Williston Walker, *The Creeds and Platforms of Congregationalism* (New York, 1893), pp. 194–237. It appears in condensed form in Smith, Handy, Loetscher, *American Christianity,* I, 129–40, from which the above quotations from Chapter XVII, "Of the Civil Magistrates Power in Matters Ecclesiastical," pp. 139–40, are taken.
26. The whole story has been competently told by Robert G. Pope, *The Half-Way Covenant: Church Membership in Puritan New England* (Princeton, 1969).
27. For details, see, e.g., R. Freeman Butts, *The American Tradition in Religion and Education* (Boston, 1950), esp. chap. 2.
28. See Thomas O'Brien Hanley, *Their Rights and Liberties: The Beginnings of Religious and Political Freedom in Maryland* (Westminster, Md., 1959).
29. On Roger Williams, founder of Rhode Island, see Ola E. Winslow, *Master Roger Williams: A Biography* (New York, 1957); Perry Miller, *Roger Williams: His Contribution to the American Tradition* (Indianapolis, 1953); Edmund S. Morgan, *Roger Williams: The Church and the State* (New York, 1967). The eighteenth-century leader in the Baptist fight against Congregational establishments was Isaac Backus; see William G. McLoughlin, *Isaac Backus and the American Pietistic Tradition* (Boston, 1967), and McLoughlin, ed., *Isaac Backus on Church, State and Calvinism: Pamphlets, 1754–1787* (Cambridge, Mass., 1968).
30. On the Quakers, see Rufus M. Jones *et al., The Quakers in the American Colonies* (London, 1911), and Frederick B. Tolles, *The Atlantic Community of the Early Friends* (London, 1952). On William Penn, see Tolles and E. Gordon Alderfer, eds., *The Witness of William Penn* (New York, 1957). Winthrop S. Hudson has shown how many of the ideas first fully developed by seventeenth-century dissenters later were used by Enlightenment thinkers; cf. his articles, "John Locke: Heir of Puritan

Political Theorists," in George L. Hunt, ed., *Calvinism and the Political Order* (Philadelphia, 1965), pp. 108–29, and "William Penn's *English Liberties:* Tract for Several Times," *William and Mary Quarterly*, 3rd ser., XXVI (1969), 578–85.

31. *The European Mind (1680–1715)* (London, 1953), p. xviii.

32. On the general impact of the Enlightenment, especially on religion, see Basil Willey, *The Seventeenth-Century Background* (New York, 1934), and *The Eighteenth-Century Background* (New York, 1940); Gerald R. Cragg, *From Puritanism to the Age of Reason* (Cambridge, Eng., 1950), and *Reason and Authority in the Eighteenth Century* (Cambridge, Eng., 1964); Roland N. Stromberg, *Religious Liberalism in Eighteenth-Century England* (New York, 1954); Herbert M. Morais, *Deism in Eighteenth-Century America* (New York, 1934).

33. "Many Mansions," *American Historical Review*, XLIX (1963–64), 315.

34. Cf. this comment by Peter Gay: "One of the most significant social facts of the eighteenth century, a priceless gift from the enlightened style to the Enlightenment of the philosophies, was the invasion of theology by rationalism: Jesuits gave fair and even generous hearing to scientific ideas, Protestant divines threw doubt upon the miraculous foundations of their creed, and churches everywhere tepidly resisted the philosophy of the philosophes with their own bland version of modern theology." *The Enlightenment: An Interpretation. The Rise of Modern Paganism* (New York, 1966), p. 22.

35. Bernard Bailyn has shown that many ideas stressed by Enlightenment thinkers were popularized on the American scene by the tradition of radical dissent which had arisen in seventeenth-century England and was developed in the eighteenth century by a number of British writers well known in America. Stressing such key concepts as natural rights and the contractual basis of society and government, this "Whig interpretation of history" provided a harmonizing force which related to each other various important streams of thought on the American scene—Enlightenment emphases, classical lore, Puritan covenant theology, and common law precedents. Bailyn, ed., *Pamphlets of the American Revolution, 1750–1776* (Cambridge, Mass., 1965), I, 27–37. For the background, see Caroline Robbins, *The Eighteenth-Century Commonwealthman: Studies in the Trans-*

mission, Development of English Liberal Thought from the Restoration of Charles II until the War with the Thirteen Colonies (Cambridge, Mass., 1959).

36. An interesting and late illustration is the role some Unitarian leaders, such as Joseph Tuckerman, a pioneer "inner city" missionary, played in a constitutional convention in Massachusetts in 1820 in defending the provisions for church establishment. See Daniel T. McColgan, *Joseph Tuckerman: Pioneer in American Social Work* (Washington, D.C., 1940), pp. 54–57.
37. The literature on the Great Awakening is vast. For example, see Edwin S. Gaustad, *The Great Awakening in New England* (New York, 1957); Alan Heimert and Perry Miller, eds., *The Great Awakening: Documents Illustrating the Crisis and Its Consequences*, The American Heritage Series (Indianapolis, Ind., 1967); Wesley M. Gewehr, *The Great Awakening in Virginia, 1740–1790* (Durham, 1930); C. H. Maxson, *The Great Awakening in the Middle Colonies* (Chicago, 1920); Darrett B. Rutman, ed., *The Great Awakening: Event and Exegesis* (New York, 1970).
38. Conrad Wright, *The Beginnings of Unitarianism in America* (Boston, 1955), esp. chap. 2.
39. C. C. Goen, *Revivalism and Separatism in New England, 1740–1800* (New Haven, 1962); McLoughlin, *Issac Backus and the American Pietistic Tradition.*
40. Gerald J. Goodwin has argued that George Whitefield's role was especially troublesome for most Anglicans; he seemed to be "a dissenter in a churchman's surplice" who took the nonconformist side in the historic controversies over church government, liturgy, and theology. "The Anglican Reaction to the Great Awakening," *The Historical Magazine of the Protestant Episcopal Church*, XXXV (1966), 343–71.
41. Frazier, *The Negro Church in America*, p. 8.
42. *The Testimony of the Presidents, Professors, Tutors and Hebrew Instructor of Harvard College in Cambridge Against the Reverend Mr. George Whitefield, And His Conduct* (Boston, 1744), p. 14.
43. *An Humble Attempt to Promote Explicit Agreement and Visible Union of God's People in Extraordinary Prayer, for the Revival of Religion and the Advancement of Christ's Kingdom on Earth . . .*, in *The Works of President Edwards* (4 vols.; New

York, 1868), III, 463. For the general setting, see Ernest L. Tuveson, *Redeemer Nation: The Idea of America's Millennial Role* (Chicago, 1968), esp. p. 53.

44. *Thoughts on the Revival of Religion in New England*, in *Works*, III, 314–15.

45. *Journal of the First Session of the Senate of the United States* (New York, 1789), p. 145. The story is told in detail by R. Freeman Butts, *The American Tradition in Religion and Education*, pp. 79–91. See also such studies from varying points of view as Wilber G. Katz, *Religion and the American Constitutions* (Evanston, Ill., 1964); Philip B. Kurland, *Religion and the Law of Church and State and the Supreme Court* (Chicago, 1962); William H. Marnell, *The First Amendment: The History of Religious Freedom in America* (Garden City, New York, 1964); Joseph Tussman, ed., *The Supreme Court on Church and State* (New York, 1962).

46. *The Garden and the Wilderness: Religion and Government in American Constitutional History* (Chicago, 1965), pp. 18, 31.

47. *Travels; in New-England and New-York* (4 vols.; New Haven, 1822), IV, 403.

48. *The Case of the Episcopal Churches in the United States Considered* (Philadelphia, 1782), p. 8.

49. See E. H. Humphrey, *Nationalism and Religion in America* (Boston, 1924); Clara O. Lovelend, *The Critical Years: The Reconstitution of the Anglican Church in the United States of America, 1780–1789* (Greenwich, Conn., 1956); Leonard J. Trinterud, *The Forming of an American Tradition: A Re-examination of Colonial Presbyterianism* (Philadelphia, 1949).

50. *Religion and the American Mind: From the Great Awakening to the Revolution* (Cambridge, Mass., 1966), p. 398.

51. *Issac Baukcs and the American Pietistic Tradition*, p. 148.

II "A COMPLETE CHRISTIAN COMMONWEALTH"

1. See Edwin Scott Gaustad, *Historical Atlas of Religion in America* (New York, 1962), esp. p. 52.

2. For example, William Warren Sweet, *The Story of Religion in America* (rev. ed.; New York, 1950), chaps. 14, 15; Winthrop S. Hudson, *Religion in America* (New York, 1965), chaps. 5, 6; Smith, Handy, Loetscher, *American Christianity*, I, chaps. 10,

11; Perry Miller, *The Life of the Mind in America* (New York, 1965), esp. bk. I.

3. For example, see Timothy Dwight, *The Nature, and Danger, of Infidel Philosophy* (New Haven, 1798); Charles C. Cuningham, *Timothy Dwight, 1752–1817: A Biography* (New York, 1942); James K. Morse, *Jedidiah Morse: A Champion of New England Orthodoxy* (New York, 1939).
4. Catharine C. Cleveland, *The Great Revival in the West, 1797–1805* (Chicago, 1916); Charles R. Keller, *The Second Great Awakening in Connecticut* (New Haven, 1942); William Warren Sweet, *Revivalism in America: Its Origin, Growth and Decline* (New York, 1944); Bernard A. Weisberger, *They Gathered at the River: The Story of the Great Revivalists and Their Impact Upon Religion in America* (Boston, 1958).
5. William G. McLoughlin, *Modern Revivalism: Charles Grandison Finney to Billy Graham* (New York, 1959); Whitney R. Cross, *The Burned-over District: The Social and Intellectual History of Enthusiastic Religion in Western New York, 1800–1850* (Ithaca, N.Y., 1950).
6. On Unitarianism, see Conrad Wright, *The Beginnings of Unitarianism in America;* on Mercersburg theology, see James H. Nichols, *Romanticism in American Theology: Nevin and Schaff at Mercersburg* (Chicago, 1961), and *The Mercersburg Theology,* A Library of Protestant Thought (New York, 1966), a collection of source materials edited and introduced by Nichols.
7. The significance of voluntaryism for American church life has been sensitively probed by Sidney E. Mead, *The Lively Experiment: The Shaping of Christianity in America* (New York, 1963), esp. chap. 8.
8. *Works* (2 vols.; Andover, Mass., 1837), II, 243.
9. *The Limitations of Human Responsibility* (Boston, 1838), p. 80.
10. *Extracts from the Minutes of the General Assembly, of the Presbyterian Church, in the United States of America,* 1819, p. 172. On the form of reference to denominational records, see Bibliographical Note, p. 228.
11. *Ibid.*, 1820, p. 316.
12. *A Pastoral Letter to the Clergy and the Laity of the Protestant Episcopal Church in the United States of America, from the Bishop of the Same,* 1826, pp. 10–11, 20.
13. See, for example, H. Richard Niebuhr, *The Kingdom of God in*

America (New York, 1937), esp. pp. 150–163; Ralph H. Gabriel, *The Course of American Democratic Thought: An Intellectual History Since 1815* (New York, 1940), pp. 34–37; Leroy E. Froom, *The Prophetic Faith of Our Fathers* (4 vols.; Washington, D.C., 1950–54), esp. vol. IV; Ernest R. Sandeen, *The Roots of Fundamentalism: British and American Millenarianism, 1800–1930* (Chicago, 1970), chap. 2.

14. *Journals of the General Conference of the Methodist Episcopal Church*, 1808, p. 77.
15. *Extracts from the Minutes of the General Assembly, of the Presbyterian Church, in the United States of America*, 1815, p. 232.
16. *Ibid.*, 1819, p. 178.
17. Ernest L. Tuveson has found the familiar terms for these main positions—"premillennialist" and "postmillennialist"—not too helpful, and adopted the term "millenarian" for those expecting the literal, physical return of Christ, and "millennialist" for those espousing the more gradualist, progressive position (*Redeemer Nation*, p. 34).
18. From the *Millennial Harbinger*, I (January 1830), I, quoted by David E. Harrell, Jr., *Quest for a Christian America: The Disciples of Christ and American Society to 1866* (Nashville, 1966), p. 42.
19. See Cross, *Burned-over District*, chap. 17; cf. Francis D. Nichol, *The Midnight Cry* (Washington, D.C., 1944).
20. *Works*, II, 246.
21. *A Pastoral Letter to the Clergy and Laity of the Protestant Episcopal Church in the United States of America, from the Bishops of the Same*, 1828, p. 10.
22. For example, Harrell has explained: "It is true that Disciples were first concerned with establishing the Kingdom of Christ on earth, but this spiritual preoccupation had tremendous social implications. They thought and wrote a great deal about what society ought to be like" (*Quest for a Christian America*, p. 19).
23. *Works*, II, 283, 305.
24. *Journals of the General Convention of the Protestant Episcopal Church in the United States of America, 1784–1814* (Philadelphia, 1817), p. 355.
25. *The Americans, in Their Moral, Social and Political Relations* (2 vols. in 1; Boston, 1837), pp. 163–65.

26. *Extracts from the Minutes of the General Assembly, of the Presbyterian Church in the United States of America,* 1815, p. 233.
27. *Ibid.*, 1819, pp. 171–72.
28. David Tyack, "The Kingdom of God and the Common School," *The Harvard Educational Review,* XXXVI (1966), 455. The Tocqueville quotation is from *Democracy in America* (Bradley ed., 2 vols.; New York, 1945), I, 303.
29. Tyack, "Kingdom of God and the Common School," p. 469.
30. "Protestant Schooling and American Nationality, 1800–1850," *Journal of American History,* LIII (1966–67), 687.
31. *Quest for a Christian America,* p. 219.
32. *The Shaping of Protestant Education* (New York, 1966), p. 30.
33. *Journals of the General Conference of the Methodist Episcopal Church,* 1840, p. 102.
34. John Lathrop, *A Discourse Before the Society for "Propagating the Gospel Among the Indians, and Others, in North-America." Delivered on the 19th of January, 1804* (Boston, [1804]), p. 35.
35. *Salvation and the Savage: An Analysis of Protestant Missions and American Indian Response, 1787–1862* (Lexington, Ky., 1965), pp. 5–6.
36. *Quest for a Christian America,* p. 199.
37. *The Lively Experiment,* pp. 53–54.
38. *The Works of William E. Channing, D.D.* (11th complete ed., 6 vols.; Boston, 1849), I, 282. For a good general discussion of voluntaryism, see D. B. Robertson, ed., *Voluntary Associations: A Study of Groups in Free Societies: Essays in Honor of James Luther Adams* (Richmond, 1966).
39. " 'The True American Union' of Church and State: The Reconstruction of the Theocratic Tradition," *Church History,* XXVIII (1959), 56–57. I find the use of the term "theocratic" by Maclear, and also by John R. Bodo, *The Protestant Clergy and Public Issues* (Princeton, 1954), misleading. It was hoped that many of the values of colonial establishment, which itself could not technically be called theocracy, might be continued in the new century of freedom. The dream of theocracy had been given up and was replaced by a vision of Christian civilization to be won by voluntary means.
40. See, e.g., Gilbert H. Barnes, *The Antislavery Impulse, 1830–1844* (New York, 1933); Charles C. Cole, Jr., *The Social Ideas of the Northern Evangelists, 1836–1860* (New York, 1954); Cross, *The*

Burned-over District; Charles I. Foster, *An Errand of Mercy: The Evangelical United Front, 1790–1837* (Chapel Hill, 1960); Clifford S. Griffin, *Their Brothers' Keepers: Moral Stewardship in the United States, 1800–1865* (New Brunswick, N.J., 1960); Timothy L. Smith, *Revivalism and Social Reform in Mid-Nineteenth Century America* (New York, 1957); Alice F. Tyler, *Freedom's Ferment: Phases of American Social History to 1860* (Minneapolis, 1944). Among the great national voluntary societies were the American Board of Commissioners for Foreign Missions (founded 1810), the American Education Society (1815), the American Bible Society (1816), the American Colonization Society (1817), the American Tract Society (1825), the American Sunday School Union (1817–24), the American Temperance Society (1826), and the American Anti-Slavery Society (1833).

41. *Sermons, Delivered on Various Occasions*, vol. II: *Beecher's Works* (Boston, 1852), p. 95.
42. *Extracts from the Minutes of the General Assembly, of the Presbyterian Church, in the United States of America*, 1815, pp. 237–38.
43. *Ibid.*, 1817, p. 24.
44. *Journals of the General Conference of the Methodist Episcopal Church*, 1832, p. 410.
45. *Ibid.*, 1840, p. 171.
46. *The Limitations of Human Responsibility*, pp. 90–91.
47. *Extracts from the Minutes of the General Assembly, of the Presbyterian Church, in the United States of America*, 1817, p. 27.
48. *Journal of the General Conference of the Methodist Episcopal Church*, 1844, p. 181. Yet this was the year in which Methodists split sectionally over the slavery issue! See below, pp. 62–63.
49. *Culture on the Moving Frontier*, p. 138. He noted that a Mormon pledged gold dust for the chaplain's salary; this is a highly unusual development at that time, for though evangelicals cooperated with each other on occasion, they usually regarded Mormonism with great distaste as a dangerous superstition. See below, pp. 74, 215.
50. For example, see Walter B. Posey, *Religious Strife on the Southern Frontier* (Baton Rouge, 1965).
51. Referring primarily to foreign missions, R. Pierce Beaver has observed, "Nationalism provided a powerful incentive to the

development of the missionary movement, but, nevertheless, it was secondary to spiritual and theological motivation." "Missionary Motivation through Three Centuries," in Jerald C. Brauer, ed., *Reinterpretation in American Church History*, vol. V: *Essays in Divinity* (Chicago, 1968), p. 139.

52. The story is briefly told in Bodo, *The Protestant Clergy and Public Issues*, pp. 39–43.
53. *Extracts of the Minutes of the General Assembly, of the Presbyterian Church, in the United States of America*, 1815, p. 256.
54. Quoted from Johnson's "Sunday Observance and the Mail," reprinted in Joseph L. Blau, ed., *Cornerstones of Religious Freedom in America* (rev. ed.; New York, 1964), p. 120.
55. *Journal of the General Conference of the Methodist Episcopal Church*, 1844, p. 130.
56. *Writings of Professor B. B. Edwards, with a Memoir by Edwards A. Park* (2 vols.; Boston, 1853), I, 62.
57. *Extracts from the Minutes of the General Assembly, of the Presbyterian Church, in the United States of America*, 1818, p. 13.
58. From Miller's introductory essay in John Holmes Agnew, *A Manual of the Christian Sabbath* (Philadelphia, 1834), p. xxxv. Sabbatarians usually argued that without Sabbath rest prosperity would fail. See especially the hundreds of pious examples given by Justin Edwards, *The Sabbath Manual Nos. I, II, III, and IV* (New York, n.d.).
59. *Issac Backus and the American Pietistic Tradition*, p. 212.
60. Tyler, *Freedom's Ferment*, p. 312.
61. *Extracts from the Minutes of the General Assembly, of the Presbyterian Church, in the United States of America*, 1818, p. 54.
62. *Journals of the General Conference of the Methodist Episcopal Church*, 1828, p. 359.
63. "Address to the Young Men of the United States on Temperance," *The Temperance Volume; Embracing the Temperance Tracts of the American Tract Society*, no. 244, (New York, n.d.) p. 5.
64. See, e.g., John A. Krout, *The Origins of Prohibition* (New York, 1925); Joseph R. Gusfield, *Symbolic Crusade: Status Politics and the American Temperance Movement* (Urbana, Ill., 1963, 1966).
65. *The Limitations of Human Responsibility*, p. 80.
66. Quoted in "Bishop Hobart's Estimate of the Church of England: A Review of *The United States of America Compared with*

Some European Countries, Particularly England" (New York, 1825), pages torn from a book and bound as a pamphlet in the Union Theological Seminary Library, New York, pp. 120–21.

67. *The Lively Experiment*, p. 63.

68. "From the Covenant to the Revival," in James Ward Smith and A. Leland Jamison, eds., *The Shaping of American Religion*, vol. I: *Religion in American Life* (Princeton, N.J., 1961), p. 354. Miller added: "They summoned sinners to the convulsions of conversion; what in fact they were doing, even though few quite understood, was asserting the unity of a culture in pressing danger of fragmentation." I would say that they were in fact and in intention summoning sinners to conversion, but that they were also, often without much conscious awareness, attempting to maintain and to extend a distinctly Protestant society by the methods of persuasion.

69. *A Pastoral Letter to the Clergy and Members of the Protestant Episcopal Church in the United States of America, from the Bishops of the Same*, 1832, pp. 9–10.

70. *Writings of Professor B. B. Edwards*, I, 490.

71. *The Duty of Freemen to Elect Christian Rulers . . .* (Philadelphia, 1828), pp. 12, 14. The sermon produced a considerable negative reaction among workingmen; cf. Arthur M. Schlesinger, Jr., *The Age of Jackson* (Boston, 1945), pp. 137–43.

72. *Lectures to Professing Christians* (New York, 1837), p. 90.

73. *Memoir of the Rev. Samuel J. Mills* (New York, 1820), pp. 106–7.

74. The story has been told in full detail in the standard work of Ray A. Billington, *The Protestant Crusade, 1800–1860: A Study of the Origins of American Nativism* (New York, 1938).

75. Beecher's sermon in Boston in 1834 contributed to the mood in which the burning of the Ursuline Convent in Charleston could occur; see also his *Plea for the West* (Cincinnati, 1835), which sought to save that section from "Romanism"; Bushnell's widely read tract, *Barbarism the First Danger: A Discourse for Home Missions* (New York, 1847), saw Romanism as the "second" danger.

76. *Protestant Crusade*, p. 181.

77. *Religion in America; or, An Account of the Origin, Progress, Relation to The State and Present Condition of the Evangelical Churches in the United States* (New York, 1844), p. 283. A

critical abridgment of this work, edited by Henry Warner Bowden, was published in 1970; cf. p. 268.

78. The story has been competently retold by P. J. Staudenraus, *The African Colonization Movement, 1816–1865* (New York, 1961).

79. See, e.g., Leon F. Litwack, *North of Slavery: The Negro in the Free States, 1790–1860* (Chicago, 1961), chap. 6.

80. Donald G. Mathews, *Slavery and Methodism: A Chapter in American Morality* (Princeton, 1965), p. 26.

81. *Journal of the General Conference of the Methodist Episcopal Church*, 1816, pp. 169–70.

82. *Extracts from the Minutes of the General Assembly, of the Presbyterian Church, in the United States of America*, 1818, pp. 28–29.

83. *Ibid.*, 1819, p. 163.

84. Quoted from a letter of Rice to William Maxwell, printed in the latter's *A Memoir of the Rev. John H. Rice* (Philadelphia, 1835), pp. 306–8, by Ernest T. Thompson, *The Spirituality of the Church: A Distinctive Doctrine of the Presbyterian Church in the United States* (Richmond, 1961), p. 20.

85. See C. Bruce Staiger, "Abolitionism and the Presbyterian Schism of 1837–1838," *Mississippi Valley Historical Review*, XXXVI (1949–50), 391–414, and Elwyn A. Smith, "The Role of the South in the Presbyterian Schism of 1837–1838," *Church History*, XX (1960), 44–63.

86. For a brief guide to the vast literature on this topic, see Burr, *A Critical Bibliography of Religion in America*, vol. IV: *Religion in American Life*, pp. 683–93.

87. For example, Harrell shows how deeply Disciples of Christ were torn by the slavery controversy, and concludes that "In fact, if not in theory, the Disciples of Christ were divided by the Civil War" (*Quest for a Christian America*, p. 173).

88. *The Great Tradition of the American Churches* (New York, 1953), p. 108.

89. "The Protestant Quest for a Christian America, 1830–1930," *Church History*, XXII (1953), 12, reprinted under the same title as a Facet book, Richard C. Wolf, ed. (Philadelphia, 1967), p. 10.

90. *Barbarism the First Danger*, p. 32.

III DEFENDING PROTESTANT AMERICA

1. *Confederate Morale and Church Propaganda* (Gloucester, Mass., 1964 [c. 1957]), pp. 42, 93.
2. *Minutes of the General Assembly of the Presbyterian Church in the Confederate States of America*, 1864, p. 293.
3. *Sermons, Speeches and Letters on Slavery and Its War* (Boston, 1869), pp. 358–59. For full documentation, with analysis of the ranges of opinion, see Chester E. Dunham, *The Attitude of the Northern Clergy Toward the South, 1860–1865* (Toledo, Ohio, 1942).
4. *At Ease in Zion: Social History of Southern Baptists, 1865–1900* (Nashville, 1967), p. 20.
5. *Proceedings of the Southern Baptist Convention*, 1866, p. 82.
6. *The Circuit Rider Dismounts: A Social History of Southern Methodism, 1865–1900* (Richmond, 1938), p. 111.
7. *Journal of the General Conference of the Methodist Episcopal Church, South*, 1866, p. 34.
8. *Quoted from the Appendix to the Journal of the General Conference of the Methodist Church, South*, 1866, pp. 25–28, by Farish, *Circuit Rider Dismounts*, p. 55.
9. Baptists and Presbyterians remain divided to this day; the Methodist schism was finally healed in 1939.
10. *Southern Churches in Crisis* (New York, 1967), p. 16.
11. *Southern White Protestantism in the Twentieth Century* (New York, 1964), p. 4.
12. This mater is considered in some detail below, pp. 110–16.
13. For example, see W. E. B. Du Bois, ed., *The Negro Church* (Atlanta, 1903); E. Franklin Frazier, *The Negro Church in America;* Benjamin E. Mays and Joseph W. Nicholson, *The Negro's Church* (New York, 1933); G. Myrdal, *An American Dilemma* (2 vols.; New York, 1944), chap. 40; David M. Reimers, *White Protestantism and the Negro* (New York, 1965); Carter G. Woodson, *The History of the Negro Church* (Washington, D.C., 1921).
14. *Journal of the General Conference of the Methodist Episcopal Church, South*, 1886, pp. 18–19.
15. *At Ease in Zion*, p. 50.
16. Mays and Nicholson, *The Negro's Church*, p. 279.

17. *Journal of the General Conference of the Methodist Episcopal Church, South*, 1882, p. 176.
18. For example, see H. Paul Douglass, *Christian Reconstruction in the South* (Boston, 1909); Henry L. Swint, *The Northern Teacher in the South, 1862–1870* (Nashville, 1941); Andrew E. Murray, *Presbyterians and the Negro: A History* (Philadelphia, 1966). Murray writes: "The greatest contribution which Presbyterians made to the newly-emancipated Negro was through their program of education" (p. 170). Their effort was second only to the Congregationalists, who were especially effective in this field.
19. There is a vast primary and secondary literature on the rise of liberal theology in America. See, e.g., Lloyd J. Averill, *American Theology in the Liberal Tradition* (Philadelphia, 1967); John W. Buckham, *Progressive Religious Thought in America* (Boston, 1919); Kenneth Cauthen, *The Impact of American Religious Liberalism* (New York, 1962); Harry Emerson Fosdick, *As I See Religion* (New York, 1932); Shailer Mathews, *The Faith of Modernism* (New York, 1924).
20. *Evolution and Religion* (Boston, [1886]), preface.
21. See, e.g., George H. Shriver, ed., *American Religious Heretics: Formal and Informal Trials* (Nashville, Tenn., 1966); Daniel D. Williams, *The Andover Liberals: A Study in American Theology* (New York, 1941).
22. *Our Country: Its Possible Future and Its Present Crisis* (New York, 1885), p. 30.
23. For example, see Thomas T. McAvoy, *A History of the Catholic Church in the United States* (Notre Dame, Ind., 1969), esp. chap. X, "An Era of Catholic Growth 1884–1895," and the reading list for that chapter.
24. "Immigation," *National Perils and Opportunities: The Discussions of the General Conference, held in Washington, D.C., ... 1887, under the Auspices and Direction of the Evangelical Alliance* (New York, 1887), p. 60.
25. *Minutes of the General Assembly of the Presbyterian Church in the United States of America*, 1876, pp. 58–59.
26. *Protestant Churches and Industrial America* (New York, 1949), II; see also Charles H. Hopkins, *The Rise of the Social Gospel in American Protestantism, 1865–1915* (New Haven, 1940), I.
27. Reprinted from the *North American Review*, 148 (1889), 653–

64, by Gail Kennedy, ed., *Democracy and the Gospel of Wealth* (Boston, 1949), along with other relevant primary and secondary materials, in particular Ralph H. Gabriel's penetrating analysis, "The Gospel of Wealth in the Gilded Age," *The Course of American Democratic Thought* (New York, 1940), pp. 143–60.

28. W. E. B. Du Bois, *Dusk of Dawn: An Essay Toward an Autobiography of a Race Concept* (New York, 1940), p. 18.
29. "Relation of the Church to the Capital and Labor Question," *National Perils and Opportunities*, p. 219.
30. Cf. Winthrop S. Hudson: "During the three decades from 1860 to 1890, the population of Detroit and Kansas City grew fourfold, Memphis and San Francisco fivefold, Cleveland sixfold, Chicago tenfold, Los Angeles twentyfold, and Minneapolis and Omaha fiftyfold and more. Even such previously major cities as New York, Philadelphia, and Baltimore more than doubled in population" (*Religion in America*, p. 293).
31. Samuel S. Nelles, president of Victoria College, Toronto, *Journal of the General Conference of the Methodist Episcopal Church*, 1884, p. 495.
32. *Our Country*, p. 129.
33. *The Church-Idea: An Essay Towards Unity* (3rd ed.; New York, 1884), pp. 128–29. On Huntington, see John F. Woolverton, "William Reed Huntington and Church Unity: The Historical and Theological Background of the Chicago-Lambeth Quadrilateral," unpub. Ph.D. thesis, Columbia University and Union Theological Seminary, 1963.
34. *Minutes of the General Assembly of the Presbyterian Church in the United States*, 1875, p. 49.
35. A. N. Littlejohn, *The Christian Ministry at the Close of the Nineteenth Century* (New York, 1884), p. 8.
36. Gaustad, *Historical Atlas of Religion in America*, p. 110.
37. Quotations from Simpson and Thompson are selected from an article by James E. Kirby, "Matthew Simpson and the Mission of America," *Church History*, XXXVI (1967), 302–3.
38. *Journal of the General Conference of the Methodist Episcopal Church*, 1884, p. 396.
39. *From Sacred to Profane America*, p. 162. On the revivals in the Confederate Army, which reached their climax in 1864, see Herman Norton, *Rebel Religion: The Story of the Confederate Chaplains* (St. Louis, 1961).

40. For example, cf. such works as Charles R. Erdman, *D. L. Moody: His Message for Today* (New York, 1928), William R. Moody and Richard K. Curtis, *They Called Him Mister Moody* (Garden City, 1962), with the analytic accounts of contemporary historians, e.g., McLoughlin, *Modern Revivalism,* and James F. Findlay, Jr., *Dwight L. Moody: American Evangelist, 1837–1899* (Chicago, 1969).
41. *The Great Tradition of the American Churches*, pp. 137–38.
42. Findlay, *Dwight L. Moody*, p. 186.
43. McLoughlin, *Modern Revivalism,* p. 294.
44. *The Life of the Mind in America: From the Revolution to the Civil War* (New York, 1965), p. 95.
45. *Proceedings of the Southern Baptist Convention*, 1872, p. 30.
46. As cited by Benjamin Quarles, *Black Abolitionists* (New York, 1969), p. 217.
47. *Proceedings of the Seventeenth General Conference of the United Brethren in Christ*, 1877, p. 6.
48. *Proceedings of the Nineteenth General Conference of the United Brethren in Christ*, 1885, p. 170. These two German bodies of Methodist theology and polity were to merge at last in 1946 as the Evangelical United Brethren Church, and to unite with the Methodist Church to form the United Methodist Church in 1968.
49. *Church, State, and the American Indians*, p. 156.
50. See *ibid*., pp. 123–68, for the whole story.
51. *Minutes of he National Council of the Congregational Churches in the United States*, 1871, p. 58.
52. *Journal of the General Conference of the Methodist Episcopal Church*, 1884, p. 335.
53. *Minutes of the General Assembly of the Presbyterian Church in the Confederate States of America*, 1862, p. 37. James W. Silver found that long after the war, Benjamin W. Jones believed that God withdrew from the South because of general and shameful violation of the Sabbath, and intemperance (*Confederate Morale and Church Propaganda*, p. 67).
54. *Minutes of the National Council of the Congregational Churches of the United States*, 1877, p. 27.
55. *Minutes of the General Assembly of the Presbyterian Church in the United States of America*, 1870, p. 131. The Presbyterians did more than pass resolutions; in 1876, for example, the assembly sent a special committee of thirteen from Brooklyn to Philadel-

phia to meet with the Commissioners of the Centennial Exposition then in progress to urge them to keep the centennial closed on the Sabbath. *Ibid.*, 1875, pp. 34–35.

56. *The Anglo-American Sabbath* (New York, [1863]), pp. 30–32, 50–51, 62–63.

57. George B. Bacon, *The Sabbath Question: Sermons Preached to the Valley Church, Orange, N.J.* (New York, 1868); Leonard W. and George B. Bacon, *The Sabbath Question: Sunday Observance and Sunday Laws* (New York, 1882), p. 65.

58. Francis P. Weisenburger, *Triumph of Faith: Contributions of the Church to American Life, 1865–1900* (Richmond, 1962), has an informative chapter on this matter, pp. 118–33.

59. *The Sabbath: What-Why-How, Day-Reasons-Mode* (New York, 1888), pp. 6–7. "Saturday-Sabbathism" refers to the seventh-day belief and practice of several small Protestant bodies which insisted that Saturday was the scriptural day for Sabbath rest. There was a large controversial literature on this subject; the major evangelical groups and most of the smaller ones insisted that the first day of the week, the Lord's day, the day of resurrection, was the proper Sabbath day in a Christian civilization.

60. *Minutes of the General Assembly of the Presbyterian Church in the United States of America*, 1875, p. 547.

61. *Ibid.*, p. 557.

62. *Minutes of the National Council of the Congregational Churches of the United States*, 1883, p. 22.

63. *Journal of the General Conference of the Methodist Episcopal Church*, 1884, pp. 391–92.

64. Spain, *At Ease in Zion*, p. 190.

65. "The Saloon," *National Perils and Opportunities*, pp. 139–40.

66. "Estrangement of the Masses from the Church," *ibid.*, pp. 106–7.

67. *Symbolic Crusade*, p. 71.

68. *Ibid.*, p. 78. On the later progressive connections of the movement and the shift to conservatism, see below, pp. 148–51.

69. *Minutes of the National Council of the Congregational Churches of the United States*, 1874, p. 122.

70. *Minutes of the General Assembly of the Presbyterian Church in the United States of America*, 1877, p. 589.

71. Eleanor Flexner, *Century of Struggle: The Woman's Rights Movement in the United States* (Cambridge, Mass., 1959). I have

not found much attention to this movement in the sources used for this study.

72. *The Puritan Ethic and Woman Suffrage* (New York, 1967), pp. 86–87.
73. For example, cf. Farish, *Circuit Rider Dismounts*, p. 325: "In general it may be said that the Methodist Episcopal Church, South, maintained traditional views with regard to the position of women in society." Spain, *At Ease in Zion*, p. 165: "Southern Baptists opposed the organized feminist movement and all other efforts to effect any significant change in the traditional role of woman in society."
74. See Weisenberger, *Triumph of Faith*, III, "The Faith of the Church as a Molder of Morality," pp. 67–159.
75. "Protestantism and the American Labor Movement: The Christian Spirit in the Gilded Age," *American Historical Review*, LXXII (1966–67), 101.

IV "THE RELIGION OF CIVILIZATION"

1. See E. Morris Fergusson, *Historic Chapters in Christian Education in America: A Brief History of the American Sunday School Movement, and the Rise of the Modern Church School* (New York, 1935), and the brief summaries in Robert W. Lynn, *Protestant Strategies in Education* (New York, 1964), pp. 22–26, and Hudson, *Religion in America*, pp. 234–36.
2. *Journal of the General Conference of the Methodist Episcopal Church, South*, 1870, p. 301. Nichols was employing the term "union" in a very general sense, as it was then often used. In twentieth-century ecumenical discussion "union" has come to refer primarily to specific organic union of churches; the more general word is "unity."
3. *Journal of the Proceedings of the Bishops, Clergy, and Laity of the Protestant Episcopal Church*, 1883, p. 469.
4. *Journal of the General Conference of the Methodist Episcopal Church, South* 1882, p. 75.
5. Philip Schaff and S. I. Prime, eds., *History, Essays, Orations, and Other Documents of the Sixth General Conference of the Evangelical Alliance . . . 1873* (New York, 1874), pp. 436–37.
6. See below, pp. 103–5.

7. "Necessity of Cooperation in Christian Work," *National Perils and Opportunities*, pp. 301–2.
8. *The Kingdom of Christ on Earth: Twelve Lectures Delivered before the Students of the Theological Seminary, Andover* (Andover, Mass., 1874), p. 2.
9. *Ibid.*, p. 87.
10. *Ibid.*, p. 100.
11. There was a long history leading up to that widespread opinion. See Tuveson, *Redeemer Nation*, esp. chapter 3, and above, pp. 33–35.
12. *Revivalism and Social Reform*, p. 236.
13. A. H. Lewis, *A Critical History of the Sabbath and the Sunday in the Church* (Alfred Centre, New York, 1886), pp. 495–96.
14. *Proceedings of the Nineteenth General Conference of the United Brethren in Christ*, 1885, p. 128. The Brethren hoped that the nation's moral problems would be settled in this way; in the same resolution they said: "We believe this nation should recognize the authority of our divine King, as over its authority, and the binding obligations of his law in the speedy settlement of such moral issues as temperance, the observance of the Sabbath, the integrity of the family, and the Bible in the schools; and that this authority and law should be given national recognition and legal force in the supreme law, the Constitution of the United States."
15. Quoted by Lewis French Stearns, *Henry Boynton Smith* (Boston, 1892), p. 158.
16. *Harvard Educational Review*, XXXVI (1966), 465. The citation is from the *Proceedings of State Teachers Association, 1884*, pp. 39–40. For an extended general discussion of these matters, see Robert Michaelsen, *Piety in the Public School: Trends and Issues in the Relationship between Religion and the Public School in the United States* (New York, 1970), esp. chaps. II–IV.
17. *Our Times: The United States, 1900–1925*, vol. II: *America Finding Herself* (New York, 1932), p. 85.
18. *Ibid.*, pp. 92–93.
19. On this and related matters, see the fine book by the late Thomas T. McAvoy, *A History of the Catholic Church in the United States*, pp. 236–37, 244–45.
20. "The City as a Peril," *National Perils and Opportunities*, p. 32. Dorchester's point was that the cities must not be surrendered to Catholic control.

21. *Minutes of the National Council of the Congregational Churches*, 1877, p. 24.
22. *Journal of the General Conference of the Methodist Episcopal Church*, 1872, p. 456.
23. *Ibid.*, 1880, p. 509.
24. *Minutes of the National Council of the Congregational Churches of the United States*, 1880, p. 177. Pascal was a French Catholic layman, brilliant mathematician and scientist of the seventeenth century, who wrote a biting satire on the Jesuits, *Provincial Letters*, in defending the Jansenists against them.
25. *The Kingdom of Christ on Earth*, p. 255. In his *Strangers in the Land: Patterns of American Nativism, 1860–1925* (New Brunswick, N.J., 1955), John Higham traces the background of Anglo-Saxonism and details its nativist outcomes.
26. See, e.g. Josiah Strong, *Our Country*, chap. xiii, "The Anglo-Saxon and the World's Future."
27. "Necessity of Cooperation in Christian Work," *National Perils and Opportunities*, p. 305.
28. "The Christian Resources of our Country," *ibid.*, p. 272.
29. *Ibid.*, pp. 333–334.
30. Quoted from *Proceedings of the Southern Baptist Convention*, 1890, p. viii, by Spain, *At East in Zion*, p. 125.
31. Issues of August 19, 1869, quoted by Spain, *ibid.*, p. 52.
32. Quoted from the *Southern Presbyterian*, XXIV (Aug. 8, 1889), p. 2, and from the *Proceedings of the Southern Baptist Convention*, 1890, p. 19, by Reimers, *White Protestantism and the Negro*, pp. 40–41.
33. *Sermons, Speeches and Letters on Slavery*, pp. 622–23, 626.
34. *White Protestantism and the Negro*, pp. 24, 55.
35. *Journal of the General Conference of the Methodist Episcopal Church*, 1880, p. 508.
36. "The State of the Country," *The A.M.E. Church Review*, VII (July 1890), 80.
37. T. Thomas Fortune, "The Afro-American League," *ibid.*, p. 3.
38. *Ibid.*, pp. 102–3.
39. *Negro Thought in America, 1880–1915: Racial Ideologies in the Age of Booker T. Washington* (Ann Arbor, 1963), pp. 24–25.
40. *The Kingdom of Christ on Earth*, p. 2.
41. *Gesta Christi: or A History of Humane Progress under Christianity* (New York, 1882), pp. vi–vii.

42. *Journal of the General Conference of the Methodist Episcopal Church*, 1876, p. 407.
43. *The Kingdom of Christ on Earth*, p. 175.
44. *National Perils and Opportunities*, p. 304.
45. *The Nation: The Foundations of Civil Order and Political Life in the United States* (New York, 1870), pp. 22, 414. See also his *Republic of God: An Institute of Theology* (Boston, 1881).
46. "National Ethos and the Church," *Theology Today*, XX (1963), 316.
47. *Ibid.*, p. 319. The generalization (which covers a longer time-span than does this chapter) is useful, but needs qualifying; the churches did exert an important Christian influence in national life, and were only in part nationalized—though the area of creative tension between church and culture was at times rather small.
48. *The Puritan Ethic and Woman Suffrage*, pp. 89.
49. *Journal of the General Conference of the Methodist Episcopal Church*, 1884, p. 494.
50. James Bryce, *The American Commonwealth* (2 vols.; New York 1910), II, 770.

V THE CHRISTIAN CONQUEST OF THE WORLD

1. *Christianity in the United States: From the First Settlement Down to the Present Age* (rev. ed.; New York, 1895), p. 699. The first edition appeared in 1888.
2. *Ibid.*, p. 788.
3. Church of the Holy Trinity v. United States, 143 U.S. 226 (1892), as quoted by Joseph Tussman, ed., *The Supreme Court on Church and State* (New York, 1962), p. 41.
4. *American Memoir* (Boston, 1947), p. 34.
5. *The Evidence of Christian Experience* (New York, 1890), p. 366.
6. Canby, speaking in general for his generation and with wider reference than to religion, could later say: "Our confidence was an illusion, but like most illusions it had many of the benefits of a fact" (*American Memoir*, p. 129).
7. S. Z. Batten, *The Christian State: The State, Democracy and Christianity* (Philadelphia, 1909), p. 307.

8. *A Study of Christian Missions* (New York, 1901), pp. 7, 30.
9. *Ecumenical Missionary Conference, New York, 1900: Report of the Ecumenical Conference on Foreign Missions, Held in Carnegie Hall and Neighboring Churches, April 21 to May 1* (2 vols.; New York, 1900), I, 11.
10. *The Evidence of Christian Experience*, p. 366.
11. *Ibid.*, p. 367.
12. *The New Era* (New York, 1893), p. 81.
13. *The Growth of the Kingdom of God* (New York, n.d. [*c.* 1897]), p. 307.
14. *Ibid.*, p. 316.
15. The story has been told by William A. Karraker, "The American Churches and the Spanish-American War," unpub. Ph.D. thesis, University of Chicago, 1940, and by John E. Smylie, "Protestant Clergymen and America's World Role, 1865–1900: A Study of Christianity, Nationality and International Relations," unpub. Th.D. thesis, Princeton Theological Seminary, 1959, chap. VII, pp. 389–94.
16. Ferdinand C. Iglehart, from the *New York Times*, March 28, 1898, p. 3, quoted by Smylie, *ibid.*, p. 415.
17. Smylie, *ibid.*, p. 419.
18. Quoted from the *New York Times*, April 25, 1898, by Smylie, *ibid.*, p. 449.
19. Quoted by Alan Geyer, *Piety and Politics: American Protestantism in the World Arena* (Richmond, 1963), p. 61.
20. In his *Twelve Against Empire: The Anti-Imperialists, 1898–1900*, (New York, 1968), Robert L. Beisner deals with "secular" anti-imperialists, and lists but does not discuss some of the leading clerical opponents of imperialism: Graham Taylor, Edward E. Hale, Henry C. Potter, Henry Van Dyke, Charles H. Parkhurst, Theodore L. Cuyler, and John Lancaster Spalding. Other anti-imperialist ministers were Leonard W. Bacon, Charles R. Brown, James M. Buckley, George D. Herron, William Reed Huntington, Charles E. Jefferson, and Robert Ellis Thompson. Cf. Smylie, "Protestant Clergymen and America's World Role," pp. 532–56.
21. Matthew S. Kaufman, in *Christian Advocate* (Sept. 14, 1898), p. 9, quoted by Kenneth M. MacKenzie, *The Robe and the Sword: The Methodist Church and the Rise of American Imperialism* (Washington, D.C., 1961), pp. 107–8.

22. *Expansion, Under New World-Conditions* (New York, 1900), pp. 280–81. The item in the *Outlook* appeared in the July 29, 1899, issue, p. 699.
23. *The Rights of Man: A Study in Twentieth Century Problems* (Boston, 1901), p. 274.
24. *Official Report of the Proceedings and Debates of the Twenty-Third General Conference of the United Brethren in Christ,* 1901, p. 24.
25. *Journal of the General Conference of the Methodist Episcopal Church,* 1900, pp. 511–13, 247. See below, pp. 141–42. On the many interchanges between Britain and America in the later nineteenth century that help to make all this explainable, see Winthrop S. Hudson, "How American is Religion in America?" in Jerald C. Brauer, ed., *Reinterpretation in American Church History,* esp. pp. 157–62.
26. Quoted from the issue of August 3, 1899, by Spain, *At Ease in Zion,* p. 126.
27. *Missionaries, Chinese, and Diplomats: The American Protestant Missionary Movement in China, 1890–1952* (Princeton, 1958), p. 56. See also Jerry Israel, " 'For God, for China and for Yale'—The Open Door in Action," *American Historical Review,* LXXV (1969–70), 796–807.
28. *The Journal of the Bishops, Clergy and Laity Assembled in General Convention,* 1901, p. 374.
29. R. Pierce Beaver, "Missionary Motivation through Three Centuries," in Brauer, ed., *Reinterpretation in American Church History,* p. 115.
30. See, e.g., Sherwood Eddy, *Pathfinders of the World Missionary Crusade* (New York, 1945); John R. Mott, *History of the Student Volunteer Movement for Foreign Missions* (Chicago, 1892), and *Five Decades and a Forward View* (New York, 1939), chap. 1; Robert P. Wilder, *The Student Volunteer Movement for Foreign Missions: Some Personal Reminiscences of Its Origin and Early History* (New York, 1935); and Clarence P. Shedd, *Two Centuries of Student Christian Movements: Their Origin and Intercollegiate Life* (New York, 1934), esp. chaps. xv–xxiii.
31. Robert P. Wilder, *The Great Commission* (London, n.d.), p. 20.
32. See W. Richey Hogg, *Ecumenical Foundations: A History of the International Missionary Council and Its Nineteenth-Century Background* (New York, 1952). On Mott, see Basil Mathews,

John R. Mott: World Citizen (New York, 1934), and Galen Fisher, *John R. Mott: Architect of Cooperation and Unity* (New York, 1952). Mott's role in the Y.M.C.A. is followed by Charles H. Hopkins, *History of the Y.M.C.A. in North America* (New York, 1951).

33. Ruth Rouse and Stephen C. Neill, eds., *A History of the Ecumenical Movement* (Philadelphia, 1954), p. 328.
34. On the relationship between millenarianism and fundamentalism, see Ernest R. Sandeen, *The Roots of Fundamentalism: British and American Millenarianism, 1800–1930* (Chicago, 1970), esp. chaps. 7 and 8. See below, pp. 194, 203.
35. *Pathfinders of the World Missionary Crusade*, pp. 259–60.
36. "Missionary Motivation through Three Centuries," in Brauer, ed., *Reinterpretation in American Church History*, pp. 131, 145.
37. *Christian Missions and Social Progress: A Sociological Study of Foreign Missions* (3 vols.; New York, 1897–1906), I, 31.
38. *Ecumenical Missionary Conference*, 1900, I, 10.
39. *Ibid.*, 9–10.
40. *Ibid.*, 39, 41.
41. *Ibid.*, 28.
42. *Ibid.*, 63.
43. *Ibid.*, 95.
44. Eddy, *Pathfinders of the World Missionary Crusade*, p. 104.
45. Quoted by Edward W. Capen, "Modern Principles of Foreign Missions," *The Annals of the American Academy of Political and Social Science*, XXX (Nov. 1907), 37.
46. *Missionaries, Chinese, and Diplomats*, pp. 3–4; cf. p. 76.
47. Beaver, "Missionary Motivation through Three Centuries," in Brauer, ed., *Reinterpretation in American Church History*, p. 115.
48. *The History and Program of the Laymen's Missionary Movement* (New York, n.d.), p. 11.
49. *Minutes of the General Assembly of the Presbyterian Church in the United States of America*, 1910, p. 282.
50. "Contributions of the S.V.M. to the Home Church," in *The Student Volunteer Movement after Twenty-five Years* (n.p., n.d. [1911]), pp. 46, 48, 53.
51. Shedd, *Two Centuries of Student Christian Movements*, p. 304.
52. "The United States" in Henry S. Leiper, ed., *Christianity Today: A Survey of the State of the Churches* (New York, 1947), p. 397.
53. *The Lively Experiment*, pp. 156–57.

54. *Missionaries, Chinese, and Diplomats*, p. ix.
55. "Missionary Motivation through Three Centuries," in Brauer, ed., *Reinterpretation in American Church History*, p. 139.
56. *Journal of the Proceedings of the Bishops, Clergy and Laity of the Protestant Episcopal Church*, 1898, p. 421.
57. *Ibid.*, 1901, p. 364.
58. *The Church and Society* (New York, 1912), pp. 4–5.
59. *Character and Opinion in the United States* (New York, 1920), pp. 14–15.
60. *Journal of the Proceedings of the Bishops, Clergy and Laity of the Protestant Episcopal Church*, 1898, p. 422.
61. *Journal of the General Conference of the Methodist Episcopal Church*, 1900, pp. 186–87.
62. *Modern Revivalism*, p. 310.
63. *The Nation and the Kingdom* (Boston, 1909), p. 16.
64. *A Study of Missions*, p. 193.
65. *Minutes of the General Assembly of the Presbyterian Church in the United States of America*, 1900, p. 173.
66. *Journal of the General Conference of the Methodist Episcopal Church*, 1900, pp. 63–64.
67. *Ibid.*, p. 77.
68. *Ibid.*, p. 75.
69. *Minutes of the General Assembly of the Presbyterian Church in the U.S.A.*, 1900, p. 30.
70. *The Journal of the Bishops, Clergy and Laity Assembled in General Convention*, 1901, pp. 373–74.
71. *The New Era*, p. 80. An earlier example of this plea can be found in a sermon by David H. Riddle, *Our Country for the Sake of the World: A Sermon in Behalf of the American Home Missionary Society . . .* (New York, 1851). I am indebted to Mr. Paul R. Meyer for calling this and other items to my attention.
72. *The Student Volunteer Movement after Twenty-five Years*, p. 24.
73. *Religion in Our Times* (New York, 1932), p. 156.
74. *Prohibition and the Progressive Movement, 1900–1920* (Cambridge, Mass., 1963), p. 135. Older studies of the prohibition movement in these years include Ernest H. Cherrington, *The Evolution of Prohibition in the United States of America* (Westerville, Ohio, 1920); D. Leigh Colvin, *Prohibition in the United States: A History of the Prohibition Party and of the Prohibition Movement* (New York, 1926); and Peter H. Odegard, *Pressure*

Politics: The Story of the Anti-Saloon League (New York, 1928).

75. *Journal of the General Conference of the Methodist Episcopal Church*, 1900, p. 72.
76. *Minutes of the General Assembly of the Presbyterian Church in the United States of America*, 1904, p. 188.
77. *Prohibition and the Progressive Movement*, p. 151.
78. *Symbolic Crusade*, p. 7.
79. As reported by Allen F. Davis, "Welfare, Reform and World War I," *American Quarterly*, XIX (1967), 529.
80. *The Twentieth Century Crusade* (New York, 1918), pp. 25, 56.
81. *The New Horizon of State and Church* (New York, 1918), p. 39.
82. *Preachers Present Arms* (New York, 1933).
83. "The Social Policy of the Federal Council of the Churches of Christ in America During World War I," unpub. Ph.D. thesis, Duke University, 1964, p. 2.
84. *Christian Principles Essential to a New World Order* (New York, 1919), p. 14.
85. *The Christian Crusade for World Democracy* (New York, 1918), p. 19.
86. *Christian Principles Essential to a New World Order*, p. 16.

VI NEW CHRISTIANITY AND OLD HOPES

1. For treatments of Christian social concern in earlier centuries, see, e.g., Gerhart B. Ladner, *The Idea of Reform: Its Impact on Christian Thoughts and Action in the Age of the Fathers* (Cambridge, Mass., 1959); Ray C. Petry, *Christian Eschatology and Social Thought: A Historical Essay on the Social Implications of Some Selected Aspects in Christian Eschatology to A.D. 1500* (New York, 1956); and John T. McNeill, *Christian Hope for World Society* (Chicago, 1937).
2. See, e.g., Peter d'A. Jones, *The Christian Socialist Revival, 1877–1914: Religion, Class, and Social Conscience in Late-Victorian England* (Princeton, 1968).
3. There is much information on conservative social Christianity in Aaron I. Abell, *The Urban Impact on American Protestantism, 1865–1900* (Cambridge, Mass., 1943).
4. See James Dombrowski, *The Early Days of Christian Socialism in America* (New York, 1936); Robert T. Handy, "Christianity

and Socialism in America, 1900–1920," *Church History*, XXI (1952), 39–54.

5. Henry F. May discussed in detail this typology of conservative, liberal and radical social Christianity in *Protestant Churches and Industrial America* (New York, 1949). Though he relied more on sociological than on theological considerations in his analysis, which was focused on nineteenth-century materials, the typology has proved to be very useful and has been widely accepted.
6. See Jacob Henry Dorn, *Washington Gladden: Prophet of the Social Gospel* (Columbus, Ohio, 1968).
7. Hopkins, *The Rise of the Social Gospel in American Protestantism*, pp. 113–115. The volume, *National Perils and Opportunities*, cited in the last chapter, was the report of the 1887 meeting sponsored by the alliance.
8. On Ely's social gospel views, see John R. Everett, *Religion in Economics: A Study of John Bates Clark, Richard T. Ely, Simon W. Patten* (New York, 1946). A considerable portion of Ely's *Social Aspects*, along with selections of other writings of his and of Gladden and Rauschenbusch, are reprinted in Robert T. Handy, ed., *The Social Gospel in America, 1870–1920: Gladden, Ely, Rauschenbusch* (New York, 1966), pp. 184–209. For a general treatment of Ely, see Benjamin G. Rader, *The Academic Mind and Reform: The Influence of Richard T. Ely in American Life* (Lexington, Ky., 1966).
9. After enjoying a wide hearing as the central figure in the "Kingdom movement" in the mid-1890's, Herron moved leftward to a radical Christian socialist position and finally moved out of the orbit of organized Christianity altogether. Robert T. Handy, "George D. Herron and the Kingdom Movement," *Church History*, XIX (1950), 97–115.
10. On the Brotherhood, see Frederick M. Hudson, " 'The Reign of the New Humantiy': A Study of the Background, History and Influence of the Brotherhood of the Kingdom," unpub. Ph.D. thesis, Columbia University and Union Theological Seminary, 1968. See also Dores R. Sharpe, *Walter Rauschenbusch* (New York, 1942).
11. *Working People and Their Employers* (Boston, 1876), p. 3.
12. "Is It Peace or War?" reprinted in *Applied Christianity: Moral Aspects of Social Questions* (8th ed.; Boston, 1894), p. 125, and in Handy, ed., *The Social Gospel in America*, p. 61.

13. Joseph W. Cochran, "The Church and the Working Man," *The Annals of the American Academy of Political and Social Science,* XXX (Nov. 1907), 21–22.
14. The book was published simultaneously on both sides of the Atlantic in 1866.
15. "The Church is Its Social Aspect," *Annals of the American Academy of Political and Social Science,* XXX (Nov. 1907), 6.
16. *Christianity and the Social Crisis* (New York, 1907), p. 185.
17. "The Church of the Future," in Lyman Abbott, *et al., The New Puritanism* (New York, 1897), p. 235.
18. *The Church and the Kingdom* (New York, 1894), p. 8.
19. *The Nation and the Kingdom,* p. 11.
20. *The New Era,* p. 240.
21. *A Theology for the Social Gospel* (New York, 1917), p. 139.
22. *Social Evangelism* (New York, 1915), pp. 26, 30.
23. Ross L. Finney, *Personal Religion and the Social Awakening* (Cincinnati, 1913), p. 33.
24. *Papers, Addresses and Discussions of the Twenty-Sixth Church Congress in the United Sattes,* 1908, p. 81.
25. Significantly, Sidney E. Mead subtitled one of his chapters on American Protestantism since the Civil War "From Denominationalism to Americanism" (*The Lively Experiment,* pp. 134–55).
26. *Christianizing the Social Order* (New York, 1912), p. 125.
27. *The Nation and the Kingdom,* pp. 7–8.
28. *Christianizing the Social Order,* pp. 144, 153.
29. *The Church and the Nation* (n.p., 1905), pp. 4, 10.
30. *The Social Law of Service* (New York, 1896), pp. 162–63, 173–74.
31. *The Christian State,* pp. 10, 31, 165, 253, 328, 425.
32. The social gospel was often vague on the practical steps to be taken in pursuit of its goals. In his helpful introduction to a manuscript Rauschenbusch wrote in his early career but which remained unpublished for seventy-five years, Max L. Stackhouse has explained that for Rauschenbusch "christianizing does not mean putting Christ into the Constitution, having Christian political parties, or having an established church. Rather, it means actualizing in the secular world by secular means patterns of justice and universality." Walter Rauschenbusch, *The Righteousness of the Kingdom,* ed. Stackhouse (Nashville, 1968), p. 37. This judgment does not give sufficient attention to the continu-

ing importance of the idea of voluntary Christianization and its achievement by the power of Christian public opinion. Rauschenbusch was more realistic and secularly oriented than many social Christians, but he also sought a specifically Christian civilization.

33. *The Church and Society*, p. 12.

34. *Southern White Protestantism in the Twentieth Century* (New York, 1964), pp. 42–43.

35. *Religion and the War* (New York, 1918), p. 129.

36. *Christian Principles Essential to a New World Order*, p. 10.

37. S. Earl Taylor and Halford E. Luccock, *The Christian Crusade for World Democracy*, p. 28.

38. *The New Era*, p. 314.

39. *The Christian League of Connecticut* (New York, 1883); *The Cosmopolis City Club* (New York, 1893).

40. From a resolution proposed to the General Conference; *Journal of the General Conference of the Methodist Episcopal Church*, 1900, p. 232.

41. The story of the formation of the Federal Council of Churches has been told a number of times, especially in books by Sanford, first corresponding secretary of the council, 1908–12, and by Charles S. Macfarland, general secretary, 1912–30. An informative, compact account appears in a work by Samuel McCrea Cavert, Macfarland's successor as general secretary, *The American Churches in the Ecumenical Movement, 1900–1968* (New York, 1968), chaps. 2, 3.

42. "Welcome to the Federal Council: Its Character, Purpose and Spirit Outlined," in Elias B. Sanford, ed., *Federal Council of the Churches of Christ in America: Report of the First Meeting . . .* (New York, 1909), pp. 323, 325.

43. Quoted by Creighton Lacy, *Frank Mason North: His Social and Ecumenical Mission* (Nashville, 1967), p. 125.

44. The full text of the report on "The Church and Modern Industry," including the "social creed," can be found in Elias B. Sanford, *Origin and History of the Federal Council of the Churches of Christ in America* (Hartford, 1916), pp. 493–503; see also Charles S. Macfarland, ed., *Christian Unity at Work: The Federal Council of the Churches of Christ in America in Quadrennial Session, 1912* (New York, 1913), pp. 176–77. The "inside story" of the social creed is told by Lacy, *Frank Mason North*, chap. 7. Apparently Harry F. Ward wrote the first draft; North guided it through the processes of adoption.

45. *Minutes of the General Assembly of the Presbyterian Church in the United States of America*, 1910, p. 285.
46. At least one of the early social gospel leaders found them too slow and ineffective. Though never repudiating his social gospel convictions, Ely became discouraged with Christian pluralism and the sectarian spirit, and turned his efforts into secular channels. He wrote: "There are now hundreds of various religious sects, and the unity of the various denominations seems remote, even with the best and most earnest efforts. One sort of unity of Christians, however, is found in the State. Men of all denominations act together in the administrative, legislative, and judicial branches of government for the establishment of righteousness. Let this unity be valued at its true worth, let it be cultivated and as much meaning be put into it as at any time the circumstances will admit!" (*The Social Law of Service*, p. 175). On the basis of this position, Ely turned his attention to the public sphere, and his role as a social prophet dropped into the background.
47. W. H. P. Faunce, *The Horizon of State and Church*, p. 94.
48. Kelly Miller, "Professional and Skilled Occupations," *The Annals of the American Academy of Political and Social Science*, XLIX (Sept. 1913), 14.
49. *Negro Thought in America, 1880–1915*, p. 23.
50. R. R. Wright, Jr., "The Negro in Unskilled Labor," *The Annals of the American Academy of Political and Social Science*, XLIX (Sept. 1913), 25.
51. *Minutes of the Twentieth Quadrennial Session of the General African Methodist Episcopal Zion Connection*, 1896, pp. 108, 109.
52. *Ibid.*, pp. 217, 222.
53. *Journal of the Twenty-second Quadrennial Session of the African Methodist Episcopal Church*, 1904, p. 74.
54. *Ibid.*, p. 65.
55. *Ibid.*, p. 96. The story of this painful shift in American history has been ably told by C. Vann Woodward, *The Strange Career of Jim Crow* (rev. ed.; New York, 1957).
56. *Journal of the Twenty-second Quadrennial Session of the African Methodist Episcopal Church*, 1904, pp. 172–73.
57. Cf. John M. Blum, *Woodrow Wilson and the Politics of Morality* (Boston, 1956), pp. 115–16: "In any case he [Wilson] permitted several of his cabinet to segregate, for the first time since the Civil War, whites and Negroes within executive departments.

Throughout the South the discharge or demotion of Negro federal employees attended the New Freedom. In response to liberal protests this in time was checked, but Wilson never openly took issue with the proponents of Jim Crow."

58. "Problems in Citizenship," *The Annals of the American Academy of Political and Social Science*, XLIX (Sept. 1913), 100.
59. The retreat of Congregationalists, Methodists, and Presbyterians in their southern institutions is discussed by Reimers, *White Protestantism and the Negro*, pp. 56–62, 137–39.
60. *Race: The History of an Idea in America* (Dallas, 1963), p. 177.
61. Washington Gladden Papers, Ohio Historical Society Manuscripts Collection. Used by permission.
62. Hudson, *Religion in America*, p. 321; cf. Dorothea R. Muller, "Josiah Strong and American Nationalism: A Reevaluation," *Journal of American History*, LIII (1966–67), 494–95.
63. *The New Era*, p. 350.
64. Woodward noted how seemingly different sounding phrases may not really be so different: "The professors called it 'the maintenance of Caucasion civilization' and the stump speakers called it 'white supremacy' " (*The Strange Career of Jim Crow*, p. 9).
65. *Expansion, Under New World-Conditions*, p. 41.
66. His views on race are discussed briefly, with bibliographical notes, by Reimers, *White Protestantism and the Negro*, pp. 53–54, and by Stackhouse in the introduction to *The Righteousness of the Kingdom*, p. 33.
67. Washington's views, controversial in his time and much more so since, are treated with penetration by August Meier, *Negro Thought in America, 1880–1915*.
68. *Journal of the Twenty-second Quadrennial Session of the General Conference of the African Methodist Episcopal Church*, 1904, p. 218.
69. *Journal of the Thirty-fifth Annual Session of the National Baptist Convention*, 1915, p. 235.
70. "The Relation of the South's Treatment of the Negro to Christianity," *African Methodist Episcopal Church Review*, XXXVI (Jan. 1920), 400–401.
71. *The History of the Negro Church*, p. 306.

VII THE SECOND DISESTABLISHMENT

1. *A Better World* (New York, 1920), pp. 90, 98–99. See John F. Piper, Jr., "The American Churches in World War I," *Journal of the American Academy of Religion*, XXXVIII (1970), 147–55.
2. *War and Peace: Presidential Messages, Addresses, and Public Papers (1917–1924)*, I, 551–52, Vol. V of Ray Stannard Baker and William E. Dodd, eds., *The Public Papers of Woodrow Wilson* (6 vols.; New York, 1927).
3. "From World War to World Brotherhood," *Federal Council Bulletin*, II (June 1919), 92.
4. "The Witness Bearing of the Church to the Nations," *ibid.*, p. 103.
5. *Ibid.*, II (Dec. 1919), 186.
6. The whole story of the Interchurch World Movement has been fully and competently told by Eldon G. Ernst, "The Interchurch World Movement of North America, 1919–1920," unpub. Ph.D. thesis, Yale University, 1968. Dr. Ernst kindly made a copy of the thesis available to me.
7. The denominational campaign experiences are summarized by Ernst, *ibid.*, pp. 102–14. See also John E. Lankford, "Protestant Stewardship and Benevolence, 1900–1941: A Study in Religious Philanthropy," unpub. Ph.D. thesis, University of Wisconsin, 1961, esp. pp. 190–256.
8. W. A. Brown, *The Church in America: A Study of the Present Condition and Future Prospects of American Protestantism* (New York, 1922), p. 119.
9. Ernst, "The Interchurch World Movement," p. 118 and Appendix I.
10. "Report of Special Committee on Survey-I," *Standard*, LXVI (June 14, 1919), 1054.
11. Ernst, "The Interchurch World Movement," p. 217.
12. "History of Interchurch World Movement" (2 vols.; typescript in the Union Theological Seminary Library, New York, n.d.), I, chap iii, p. 85.
13. Quoted by Virginius Dabney, *Dry Messiah: The Life of Bishop Cannon* (New York, 1949), p. 136.
14. *Federal Council Bulletin*, II (June 1919), 102.
15. *The Church in America*, p. 51.
16. *The American People and Foreign Policy* (New York, 1950), p. 43.

17. "What Happened to the Progressive Movement in the 1920's," *American Historical Review*, LXIV (1958–59), 833.
18. "The World Opportunity," in Burton St. John, ed., *North American Students and World Advance* (New York, 1920), pp. 17–19.
19. *Ibid.*, p. 196.
20. *A Better World*, p. 90. See above, p. 184.
21. Home Missions Council, *Annual Report*, 1919, p. 59.
22. Ernst, "The Interchurch World Movement," p. 329.
23. Some of the incompleted work of the movement was taken over by the Federal Council and the Home Missions Council, while a newly organized Institute of Social and Religious Research took over the bulk of the survey projects, completing some and undertaking others on its own. John R. Mott was chairman, and Galen M. Fisher, executive secretary. An anonymous donor, later known to be John D. Rockefeller, Jr., supplied the funds. See Cavert, *The American Churches in the Ecumenical Movement*, pp. 111–12.
24. This matter is discussed in full by Ernst, "The Interchurch World Movement," pp. 289–311, and in an article, "The Interchurch World Movement and the Great Steel Strike of 1919–1920," *Church History*, XXXIX (1970), 212–23; see also Walter W. Benjamin, "Bishop Francis J. McConnell and the Great Steel Strike of 1919–1929," in Stuart C. Henry, ed., *A Miscellany of American Christianity: Essays in Honor of H. Shelton Smith* (Durham, 1963), pp. 22–47.
25. Ernst, "The Interchurch World Movement," p. 374.
26. *A Better World*, p. v.
27. *Billy Sunday Was His Real Name* (Chicago, 1955), p. 260.
28. *The Church in America*, p. 80.
29. *The Church and Missions* (New York, 1926), pp. 83, 123, and *passim.*
30. Walter I. Clarke, "Christians, Save the Christian Sabbath!" *New Era Magazine*, III (March 1921), 155.
31. *The Crisis of the Churches* (New York, 1922), pp. 54, 112–13.
32. Hiram W. Evans, "The Klan's Fight for Americanism," *North American Review*, CCXXIII (March 1926), 52.
33. *The Confessions of a Puzzled Parson and Other Pleas for Reality* (New York, 1928), p. 14.

34. C. Luther Fry, *The U.S. Looks at its Churches* (New York, 1930), p. 76.
35. I have discussed this in greater detail in "The American Religious Depression, 1925–1935," *Church History*, XXIX (1960), 3–16; reprinted with the same title as a Facet Book, ed. Richard C. Wolf (Philadelphia, 1968).
36. Fennell P. Turner and Frank Knight Sanders, eds., *The Foreign Missions Conference of North America*, 1926 (New York, 1926), pp. 125–47.
37. Leslie B. Moss and Mable H. Brown, eds., *The Foreign Missions Conference of North America*, 1934 (New York, 1934), p. 148.
38. Moss, ed., *The Foreign Missions Conference of North America*, 1929 (New York, 1929), p. 152.
39. C. Luther Fry, "Changes in Religious Organizations," in *Recent Social Trends in the United States* (2 vols., New York, 1933), II, 1049.
40. William R. King, in the Home Missions Council, *Annual Report*, 1927, p. 80.
41. Hornell Hart, "Religion," *American Journal of Sociology*, XLVII (1941–42), 892; Fry, *Recent Social Trends*, II, 1055.
42. H. C. Weber, *Evangelism: A Graphic Survey* (New York, 1929), pp. 183–85.
43. "The Religious Breakdown of the Ministry," *Journal of Religion*, I (1921), 18–29.
44. *The Decline and Revival of the Social Gospel: Social and Political Liberalism in American Protestant Churches, 1920–1940* (Ithaca, N.Y., 1954), p. 77.
45. Halford E. Luccock, "Preaching in an Age of Disillusion," *Christian Century*, XLVII (July 30, 1930), 938.
46. "Religion and Science in American Philosophy," in *The Shaping of American Religion*, pp. 436–38.
47. William Pepperell Montague, *Belief Unbound: A Promethean Religion for the Modern World* (New Haven, 1930), p. 20.
48. *Does Civilization Need Religion?* (New York, 1927), p. 2.
49. See Stewart G. Cole, *The History of Fundamentalism* (New York, 1931); Norman E. Furniss, *The Fundamentalist Controversy, 1918–1931* (New Haven, 1954); and a useful source book edited by Willard B. Gatewood, Jr., *Controversy in the Twenties: Fundamentalism, Modernism, and Evolution* (Nashville, 1969).

For the struggle in Presbyterianism, see Lefferts A. Loetscher, *The Broadening Church: A Study of Theological Issues in the Presbyterian Church Since 1869* (Philadelphia, 1954). New perspectives on fundamentalism are presented by Ernest R. Sandeen, *The Roots of Fundamentalism: British and American Millenarianism, 1800–1930* (Chicago, 1970).

50. Ray Ginger, *Six Days or Forever? Tennessee v. John Thomas Scopes* (Boston, 1958).
51. For a less publicized evolution controversy, see Willard B. Gatewood, Jr., *Preachers, Pedadogues & Politicians: The Evolution Controversy in North Carolina, 1920–1927* (Chapel Hill, 1966).
52. "Recent Gains in Religion," in Kirby Page, ed., *Recent Gains in American Civilization* (New York, 1928), p. 240.
53. *A Catholic Runs for President: The Campaign of 1928* (New York, 1956), p. 168.
54. Quoted from a typed copy of *The American Issue*, "Ohio Edition (Sept. 21, 1928), p. 3., by Moore, *ibid.*, p. 187.
55. Quoted by Clarke A. Chambers, *Seedtime of Reform: American Social Service and Social Action, 1918–1933* (Minneapolis, 1963), p. 142.
56. *A Catholic Runs for President*, pp. 148, 195.
57. *Rum, Religion and Votes: 1928 Re-examined* (University Park, Pa., 1962), pp. vii, 50. Cf. also Robert M. Miller, *American Protestantism and Social Issues, 1919–1939* (Chapel Hill, 1958), chap. iv, "A Footnote to the Election of 1928."
58. Robert S. Lynd and Helen Merrell Lynd, *Middletown: A Study in Contemporary American Culture* (New York, 1929), p. 406.
59. *American Mercury*, IV (1925), 286; *Confessions of a Puzzled Parson*, p. 191.
60. William L. Sullivan, "Our Spiritual Destitution," *Atlantic Monthly*, 143 (Jan.-June 1929), 377–78.
61. *The Great Tradition of the American Churches*, p. 196.
62. Robert L. Lynd and Helen Merrell Lynd, *Middletown in Transition: A Study in Cultural Conflicts* (New York, 1937), p. 295.
63. *Research Memorandum on Religion in the Depression* (New York, 1937), p. 1.
64. "Why No Revival?" *Christian Century*, LII (Sept. 18, 1935), 1168–70.
65. *Middletown in Transition*, p. 311.
66. "Consensus in America: The Churches' Changing Role," *Journal*

of *the American Academy of Religion,* XXXVI (March 1968), 35–36.

67. *The Rights of Man in America, 1606–1861* (Columbia, Mo., 1960), pp. 314–15.
68. For example, see Cavert, *The American Churches in the Ecumenical Movement,* esp. chaps. 6–8, and Roswell P. Barnes, *Under Orders: The Churches and Public Affairs* (Garden City, N.Y., 1961).
69. For example, cf. Carter, *The Decline and Revival of the Social Gospel,* Miller, *American Protestantism and Social Issues,* and Donaly B. Meyer, *The Protestant Search for Political Realism, 1919–1941* (Berkeley, Cal., 1960).
70. There is a vast literature on so-called sect and cult movements; see, e.g., the books of Marcus Bach, especially *They Have Found a Faith* (Indianapolis, 1946), and *Report to Protestants* (Indianapolis, 1948); Charles S. Braden, *These Also Believe: A Study of Modern American Cults and Minority Religious Movements* (New York, 1949); Arthur H. Fauset, *Black Gods of the Metropolis: Negro Religious Cults of the Urban North* (Philadelphia, 1944); John T. Nichol, *Pentecostalism* (New York, 1966).
71. "Church, State and Community in Education," in Henry P. Van Dusen, *et al., Church and State in the Modern World* (New York, 1937), pp. 133–34.
72. *Second Chance for American Protestants* (New York, 1963), p. 34. "Placed Christianity" is that occupying specific ground, i.e., Christendom.
73. H. Richard Niebuhr, Wilhelm Pauck, Francis P. Miller, *The Church Against the World* (Chicago, 1935), p. 102.
74. *Ibid.,* pp. 123–24.
75. "Points of Tension between Church and State in America Today," in Van Dusen, *et al., Church and State in the Modern World,* pp. 191, 182.
76. *Protestant-Catholic-Jew: An Essay in American Religious Sociology* (Garden City, N.Y., 1955), pp. 139–40.
77. Protestantism remains the most highly pluralized of the major options, and it is difficult to deal with its many facets in one treatment. This study has focused almost wholly on the main line evangelical denominations of Anglo-American heritage. Little attention has been given to the Lutheran churches, for example, which have emerged into general prominence since

World War I, and have been engaged in a series of internal unions.

78. See, e.g., Jeffery K. Hadden, *The Gathering Storm in the Churches* (Garden City, N.Y., 1970).

79. In a perceptive analysis, *Education and Pluralism: Ideal and Reality* (Syracuse, N.Y., 1966), Thomas F. Green has observed that there are three main "ideal types" of religious pluralism, which he classifies as insular or segmented pluralism, half-way pluralism, and structural assimilation. In the first type, social relations of both the primary, face-to-face kind and the more formal and functional secondary kind are largely confined within a particular religious group. In "half-way pluralism" various religious groups interpenetrate at the secondary level of association but not at the primary. In the third type, integration takes place at both levels of association, and if completed would result in an open, secular society in which religious pluralism would dissolve into religious invisibility. Green believes that the long-range trend is toward the third type, though there are some survivals of the first and considerable continuations of the second.

80. A good short treatment is by Daniel D. Williams, *What Present-Day Theologians are Thinking* (rev. ed.; New York, 1959). A mid-century symposium which summarized the impact of the renaissance on the major theological disciplines was edited by Arnold S. Nash, *Protestant Thought in the Twentieth Century: Whence and Whither?* (New York, 1951). See also William E. Hordern, *The Case for a New Reformation Theology* (Philadelphia, 1959). A good introduction to Reinhold Niebuhr has been edited by Charles W. Kegley and Robert W. Bretall, *Reinhold Niebuhr: His Religious, Social, and Political Thought* (New York, 1956). On H. Richard Niebuhr, see Paul Ramsey, ed., *Faith and Ethics: The Theology of H. Richard Niebuhr* (New York, 1957), and Libertus A. Hoedemaker, *Faith in Total Life: Style and Direction of H. Richard Niebuhr's Theology* (Groningen, 1966).

81. *Does Civilization Need Religion?* p. 77.

82. Gordon D. Kaufman, "Theological Historicism as an Experiment in Thought," *Christian Century*, LXXXIII (March 2, 1966), 268.

83. *From Sacred to Profane America*, p. 11.

84. For example, the Consultation on Church Union. See below, p. 222.

85. *The Secular City: Secularization and Urbanization in Theological Perspective* (New York, 1965), pp. 105, 220.
86. *Religion in 20th Century America* (Cambridge, Mass., 1952), pp. 16–18, 206.
87. *The Surge of Piety in America: An Appraisal* (New York, 1958), p. 43.
88. *Protestant-Catholic-Jew*, pp. 95–96.
89. *The New Shape of American Religion* (New York, 1959).
90. *What Americans Believe, And How They Worship* (New York, 1952), pp. 13, 364, 371. In the revised edition of the book (1962), these statements are repeated; pp. 13, 476, 488.
91. *Requiem for a Lost Piety: The Contemporary Search for the Christian Life* (Philadelphia, 1966), p. 23.
92. The literature of American ecumenical history is vast; useful surveys with excellent bibliographical suggestions are by Samuel McCrea Cavert, *The American Churches in the Ecumenical Movement*, and *Church Cooperation and Unity in America, A Historical Review: 1900–1970* (New York, 1970). The Consultation of Church Union has published an annual *Digest* of its proceedings since 1962. On the impact of Pope John XXIII on Protestantism, see Eugene C. Bianchi, *John XXIII and American Protestants* (Washington, D.C., 1968).
93. See above, pp. 110–12, 170–74.
94. Markus Barth, "Pool of the Rich or Pilgrimage of Servants," in Robert McAfee Brown and David H. Scott, eds., *The Challenge to Reunion* (New York, 1963), p. 194.
95. "Ecumenism and Church Union," in John Macquarrie, ed., *Realistic Reflections on Church Union* (n.p., n.d.), p. 62.
96. *The Secular City*, p. 99.
97. J. Theodore Hefley, "Freedom Upheld: The Civil Liberties Stance of the *Christian Century* Between the Wars," *Church History*, XXXVII (1968), 189–90.
98. *The Church and Race Relations* (New York, 1946), p. 5.
99. Gerhard Lenski, *The Religious Factor: A Sociological Study of Religion's Impact on Politics, Economics, and Family Life* (Garden City, New York, 1961), p. 36.
100. Reimers, *White Protestantism and the Negro*, esp. chap. 6, "Church Unity and the Negro."
101. For example, cf. Robert W. Spike, *The Freedom Revolution and the Churches* (New York, 1965); Anna A. Hedgeman, *The Trumpet Sounds: A Memoir of Negro Leadership* (New York,

1964); Joseph C. Hough, Jr., *Black Power and White Protestants: A Christian Response to the New Negro Pluralism* (New York, 1968); James H. Cone, *Black Theology and Black Power* (New York, 1969), and *A Theology of Black Liberation* (Philadelphia, 1970).

102. *The Politics of God* (Boston, 1967), p. 126.
103. "The Religion of Black Power," in Donald R. Cutler, ed., *The Religious Situation: 1968* (Boston, 1968), p. 32.
104. *The Protestant Establishment: Aristocracy and Caste in America* (New York, 1964), pp. 4, 360.

Index